Reading and Variant in Petronius: Studies in the French Humanists and Their Manuscript Sources

Perhaps half of the *Satyrica* of Petronius, Nero's minister for taste, exists only in late, second-hand sources: sixteenth-century editions, manuscript apographs, and commentaries. All of this material has therefore been subject to scholarly mediation, deliberate or inadvertent, recorded and unrecorded. The result is a legacy of readings and variants, which may or may not be from actual manuscripts, that are inconsistent when they should agree, and agree when they should differ. This performance is paralleled in portions of the humanist editions founded on extant manuscripts as well; thus, once these manuscripts are identified, a quite detailed profile of manuscript use, misuse, and non-use may be drawn up and applied to the mediated content – in an effort to identify the missing manuscripts and secure readings of the best quality and pedigree (eliminating ghost-words, errors, emendations, and so on).

This book will be of use to classical scholars interested in textual tradition, to specialists in Petronius and the novel, and to historians of the Renaissance for its demonstration of how key figures in French humanism, to whom we owe much, acquired their material and created their editions. It evaluates their performance at a private, fundamental level and assesses the results for the Petronius text.

WADE RICHARDSON is a member of the Department of Classics, McGill University.

PHOENIX

Journal of the Classical Association of Canada
Revue de la Société canadienne des études classiques
Supplementary Volume XXXII
Tome supplémentaire XXXII

WADE RICHARDSON

Reading and Variant in Petronius: Studies in the French Humanists and Their Manuscript Sources

UNIVERSITY OF TORONTO PRESS

Toronto Buffalo London

© University of Toronto Press Incorporated 1993
Toronto Buffalo London
Printed in Canada
ISBN 0-8020-2866-7

Printed on acid-free paper

Canadian Cataloguing in Publication Data
Richardson, Wade, 1943–
Reading and variant in Petronius :
studies in the French humanists and their manuscript sources

(Phoenix. Supplementary volume ; 32 = Phoenix.
Tome supplémentaire, ISSN 0079-1784 ; 32)
Includes index.
ISBN 0-8020-2866-7

1. Petronius Arbiter – Criticism, Textual.
I. Title.   II. Series: Phoenix. Supplementary
volume (Toronto, Ont.) ; 32.

This book has been published with
the help of a grant from
the Canadian Federation for the Humanities,
using funds provided by the Social Sciences and
Humanities Research Council of Canada.

OPTIMIS PARENTIBUS

CONTENTS

PREFACE

Today's *Satyrica* is but a remnant of the comic novel usually attributed to Titus Petronius Niger, Nero's *elegantiae arbiter* in the pages of Tacitus. The archetype, which dates to near AD 800, presents roughly consecutive episodes late in the narrative. It is formed from the aggregate of three overlapping texts created in the same era by deliberate curtailments of varying kinds. Λ is the longest branch or hyparchetype, though one section of it plainly starts as an abridgment and then discontinues; the **Cena** is a complete transcription of this very section only; and **O** truncates the narrative and omits the **Cena** altogether.

The latter branches are communicated in extant manuscripts: the **Cena** in a unique text, **H**, copied in the Renaissance from a much earlier exemplar though not disseminated until after 1650 (thus unknown to the French humanists); and **O** in three medieval manuscripts, **BRP**, and fifteen Renaissance manuscripts (of which one produced the *editio princeps*) sired by a sibling of **P.** There is no witness to Λ, apart from some florilegia, that does not rest on the efforts of scholars, editors, commentators, and copyists in the sixteenth century.

The lines and text of the two branches based on the extant manuscripts are sufficiently established not to require a new treatment (though it has been necessary to broach again the connection of **B** and **P** with manuscripts used by the humanists), but the special challenge of Λ's readings, as recorded by about a score of French scholars working between 1560 and 1600, though often recognized, has not yet been fully met. It is here that the emphasis of several of the following studies will be found.

This was an altogether impressive age for classical scholarship, the flowering of the French Renaissance, and several of its acknowledged ornaments – Scaliger, Cujas, Turnèbe, Pierre Daniel, Pierre Pithou, de

Thou, Muret, men who attained eminence principally in other fields –
turned their minds and hands, often informally, to Petronius. What drew
their interest now was the new and remarkable text of this author that
came to light after the mid-century in two medieval manuscripts, **Benedictinus** and **Cuiacianus**, based on Λ. Professional curiosity may have
been piqued by the clear indication from these manuscripts that the
fragmentary *Satyrica* with which the scholars had been familiar from two
preceding editions was a clumsy foreshortening, undertaken mainly to
eliminate or tone down erotic content. There is some evidence that this
facet of the new material prompted hesitation over a proper scholarly
response, which may have affected not only the transmission history but
the survival of the manuscripts themselves.

For **Benedictinus** and **Cuiacianus** have perished, and with them has
gone the Λ witness free from humanist intervention. Recovery of Λ
readings might well have been secured by a full, faithful apograph or
manuscript collation. Though some were indeed made, they too are missing,
and we are left essentially with only the 'contaminated' products of
sixteenth-century scholarship – editions and commentaries. For these were
constructed by taking whichever was available of the two Λ-based manuscripts, **O** manuscripts (now sought out and used for the first time), and
florilegia, for collation against the familiar editions, usually both **c** and **s**.
The scholars did not always exercise good judgment; for instance, there
was excessive reliance on the early editions at the expense of the manuscripts, and they were quite unequal to the need to identify all the sources
clearly and to cite the readings and variants fully and consistently. Their
practices, especially insofar as they concern Λ-derived material, which
cannot be checked independently, have produced three tasks for this volume:
to determine sources, to evaluate scholarship, and to establish text.

ACKNOWLEDGMENTS

'The major problem in the study of the text [of Petronius] is to unravel the tangled skein of sixteenth-century work on this author ...' In the twenty years that have passed since I first read these words of B.L. Ullman and encountered K. Müller's *editio maior* I have slowly been gathering material and courage for this task, and for an edition which would follow it. The set of studies in this volume marks the result, to date. Their writing was commenced in 1988, during a sabbatical in Europe, and has continued up to the present, under the specific stimuli of Müller's third edition, the articles of M.D. Reeve and R.H. Rouse, and the ongoing multi-volume edition of C. Pellegrino. My debt to the above scholars will be clear, and all (except Ullman, naturally) have met my queries, in correspondence and in person, helpfully and in a sense of solidarity.

I should give an account here of the resources, both material and human, that were available to me during the gestation of this book. Apart from the recognized standards of published textual scholarship (and here I include, in addition to the above, the editions of F. Bücheler and the monograph of H. van Thiel), I was able to have at my elbow a microfilm typescript of the life task of E.T. Sage on the manuscript tradition of Petronius, envisaged in 1915 and worked on – not quite to completion – for the last twenty years of his life. The original sits in the Joseph Regenstein Library of the University of Chicago, unhappily shorn of the first third of the collation. It is of inconsistent merit, requiring a good editing, but with many kernels, duplicated in the largely independent work of Müller and van Thiel, of truth. Sage was assisted by an extraordinary stable of graduate students, whom, basically, he pointed in the direction of problems and set to collating. I have had full access to their results in the complete dissertations and theses on microfilm made for K.F.C. Rose, on loan from J.P. Sullivan, whose collaboration with Rose was cut off so sadly by Rose's death in 1967. An outline of the work of the Sage school may be found in collected abstracts in the *University of Pittsburgh Bulletin* 1925–38. I have thus had the advantage of seeing the results within the full contexts but have not used the collations, for two reasons: incompatible, outdated sigla that would require laborious translation, and a typical scholar's prejudice in favour of his own. These I was able to make on two fully-paid sabbaticals (1980–1, 1987–8)) from McGill University, assisted by handsome research grants from the Social Sciences and Humanities Research Council of Canada. I was able, a few years ago, to converse and correspond with several of these former pupils of Sage. J.P. Sullivan, with the dangerous generosity of de Mesmes, also gave me the use of some partial manuscript collations and rough notes made by K.F.C. Rose – a mark of his support. Again, I have not relied on the collations, and have employed the notes, well acknowledged, mainly for contrast. The death of Sullivan, as this goes to press, is a hard blow.

The interest and co-operation shown by the staff of the many libraries that I have visited, repeatedly, for consultation and services, have been unfailing, but I recall with especial warmth the trust and courtesy extended at Bern (Dr. von Steiger), Leiden (Dr. Obbema) Leuven (Dr. Koppens), Montpellier (Mme. Fontaine-Levent), Rosanbo (M. le Marquis), Troyes (Mme. Bibolet), and the Vatican (Fr. Boyle). I am grateful also to the libraries cited in the plate captions for permission to reproduce their copyrighted material. Two facilities in Paris have been a great boon: the Institut de Recherche et d'Histoire des Textes (Section Codicologie), for its unrivalled research staff and files, and the Institut de l'Histoire de Paris (M. Fleury, Mme. Auffray), for the provision of lodging. The manuscript owes much to the skill and judgment of George Ferzoco, who prepared the electronic versions. Also to be recorded with thanks are my copy editor, James Leahy, the readers consulted by the University of Toronto Press, and its editorial and production staff, Joan Bulger and Anne Forte in particular, all of whom tried to make this a more readable book. The final mention goes to Konrad Müller, whose editions have marked my way with scholarship, clarity, and trustworthiness, and who has extended every personal and professional courtesy. None of the foregoing implies that I have benefited from the named resources to the extent that I could, or enlists their approval now.

WORKS CITED

Aragosti, A. 1989. 'A proposito di una recente riedizione di Petronio.' *Orpheus* 10 150–61

Beck, C. 1863. *The Manuscripts of Petronius Arbiter.* (Cambridge, Mass.)

Bignami-Odier, J. 1973. *La Bibliothèque vaticane de Sixte IV à Pie XI: recherches sur l'histoire des collections de manuscrits.* (Vatican City)

Billanovich, G. 1956. 'Dall'antica Ravenna alle biblioteche umanistiche.' *Aevum* 30 319–53

Blok, F.F. 1974. *Contributions to the history of Isaac Vossius' library.* (Amsterdam)

BN. [Bibliothèque Nationale] 1744. *Catalogus codicum manuscriptorum bibliothecae regiae parisiensis.* VI, 3. (Paris)

– 1966. *Catalogue général des manuscripts latins.* V, 274–9. (Paris)

Boivin, J. 1715. *Petri Pithoei vita.* (Paris)

Bricquet, C.M. 1968. *Les Filigranes.* (Amsterdam)

Bücheler, F. 1862. *Petronii Saturae.* (Berlin)

Burman, P. 1743. *Titi Petronii Arbitri Satyricon Quae Supersunt.* (Amsterdam)

Callmer, C. 1977. *Königin Christina, Ihre Bibliothekare und Ihre Handschriften.* (Stockholm)

Chatelain, E. 1894–1900. *Paléographie des classiques latins.* t. 2. (Paris)

Clark, A.C. 1900. 'The Textual Criticism of Cicero's *Philippics.' Classical Review* 14 39–48

Courtney, E. 1991. *The Poems of Petronius.* (Atlanta)

Cujas, J. 1562. *Ad tres postremos libros Codicis Dn. Justiniani commentarii.* (Lyons)

Daniel, P. 1564. *Querolus.* (Paris)

de Job, C. 1881. *M.-A. Muret: un professeur français en Italie.* (Paris)

de Jonge, H.J. 1977. *The Auction Catalogue of the Library of J.J. Scaliger.* (Utrecht)

Delage, F. 1905. 'Marc-Antoine de Muret: un humaniste Limousin du XVIe s.'
   Bulletin de la Société archéologique et historique du Limousin. 147–80. (Limoges)
de la Mare, A.C. 1976. 'The Return of Petronius to Italy.' In J.J.G. Alexander
   and M.T. Gibson, eds., *Essays Presented to Richard William Hunt*. 220–54.
   (Oxford)
de Meyier, K.A. 1947. *Paul en Alexandre Petau en de Geschiedenis van hun Hand-*
   schriften. (Leiden)
– 1973. *Codices Vossiani Latini*. v. 1. (Leiden)
de Nolhac, P. 1883. 'La bibliothéque d'un humaniste du XVIe s.' *Mélanges d'ar-*
   chéologie et d'histoire de l'Ecole française de Rome. t. 3, 202–38. (Rome)
DNB. 1897. *Dictionary of National Biography*. 49. (London)
Dorez, L. 1899, 1928. *Catalogue de la Collection Dupuy*. 3 vols. (Paris)
Fremy, E. 1881. *Henri de Mesmes*. (Paris)
Fulmer, D. 1936. 'The Tornaesius Edition of Petronius.' *University of Pittsburgh*
   Bulletin 12 97–104
Fumaroli, M. 1980. *L'Age de l'Éloquence*. (Geneva)
Genevois, A.-M., Genest, J.-F., and Chalondon, A. 1987. *Bibliothèques de manu-*
   scrits médiévaux en France: relevé des inventaires du VIIIe au XVIIIe siècle. (Paris)
Gerlo, A., Nauwelaerts, M.A., and Vervliet, H.D.L. 1978. *Iusti Lipsi Epistolae*.
   v. 1. (Brussels)
Goldast, M. [G. Erhard] 1610. *T. Petronii Arbitri, Equitis Romani Satyricon, cum*
   Petroniorum Fragmentis. (Frankfurt)
Grafton, A. 1983. *Joseph Scaliger*. (Oxford)
Grosley, P.J. 1756. *Vie de Pierre Pithou*. 2 vols. (Paris)
Haag, E. and Haag, E. 1857. *La France Protestante*. (Paris)
Hagen, H. 1885. *Catalogus codicum Bernensium*. (Bern)
Hamacher, J. 1975. *Florilegium Gallicum: Prolegomena und Edition der Excerpta*
   von Petron bis Cicero. (Bern and Frankfurt)
HLF. 1868. *Histoire littéraire de la France*. t. 10. (Paris)
James, M.R., and Jenkins, C. 1939. *A Descriptive Catalogue of the Manuscripts in*
   the Library of Lambeth Palace. (Cambridge)
Keeley, D.R. 1970. *Foundations of Modern Historical Scholarship*. (New York)
Kinser, S. 1966. *The Works of J.-A. de Thou*. (The Hague)
Korn, M., and Reitzer, S. 1986. *Concordantia Petroniana*. (Hildesheim)
Lambin, D. 1567. *Q. Horatius Flaccus*. (Paris)
Lazeri, P. 1754, 1758. *Miscellanea ex MSS Libris Bibliothecae Collegii Romani*.
   (Rome)
Lodge, G. 1924. *Lexicon Plautinum*. (Leipzig)
Loewe. G. 1894. *Prodromus corporis glossariorum Latinorum*. (Leipzig)
Lotich, J.P. 1629. *T. Petronii Arbitri Satyricon*. (Frankfurt)
Martin, J. 1979. 'Uses of Tradition in Petronius and John of Salisbury.' *Viator*
   10 69–76

McClure, M. 1934. 'A Comparative Study of the Pithoeus Editions of Petronius.' *University of Pittsburgh Bulletin* 10 430

Michaud, J.F. 1843–65. *Biographie universelle, ancienne et moderne.* (Paris)

Müller, K. 1961. *Petronii Arbitri Satyricon.* (Munich)

Müller, K., and Ehlers, W. 1965. *Petronius Satyrica: Schelmengeschichten.*
(Munich)

– 1983. *Petronius Satyrica: Schelmenszenen.* (Munich)

Munk Olsen, B. 1985. *Catalogue des manuscrits classiques latins du IXe au XIIe
siècle.* v. 2. (Paris)

Muret, M.-A. 1562. *M. Tulli Cic. Philippicae et Scholiae ad Turnebum.* (Paris)

– 1581. *Tacitus Liber Secundus Annalium.* (Rome)

Nebbiai, D. 1985. *La Bibliothèque de L'Abbaye de Saint-Denis en France.* (Paris)

Omont, H. 1885. 'Catalogue des manuscrits de la Bibliothèque de Cujas.' In
Nouvelle Revue historique de droit français et étranger 9 233–7

– 1888. 'Inventaire des manuscrits de la Bibliothèque de Cujas (1590).' *Nouvelle
Revue historique de droit français et étranger* 12 3–12

– 1917. 'L'Edition du Satyricon de Pétrone par La Porte du Theil.' *Journal des
Savants* 15 513–20

Peiper, R. 1875. *Querolus.* (Leipzig)

Pellegrino, C. 1968. 'Su alcuni problemi della tradizione manoscritta del Satyricon.' *Rivista di cultura classica e medioevale* 10 72–85

– 1972. 'Il *Bellum Civile* nel Satyricon: possibilità di una nuova ricostruzione del
testo.' *Rivista di cultura classica e medioevale* 14 155–64

– 1975. *Petronio Arbitro Satyricon.* (Rome)

– 1986. *T. Petronio Arbitro, Satyricon: Introduzione, testo critico, commento, I: I
capitoli della retorica.* (Rome)

Pfeiffer, R. 1976. *History of Classical Scholarship.* (Oxford)

Pithou, P. 1565. *Adversariorum Subsecivorum Libri II.* (Paris)

Quesnel, J. 1679. *Catalogus Bibliothecae Thuanae.* (Paris)

Reeve, M.D., 1983. 'Petronius.' In L.D. Reynolds, ed., *Texts and Transmission: A
Survey of the Latin Classics.* 295–300. (Oxford)

Reeve, M.D., and Rouse, R.H. 1978. 'New Light on the Transmission of Donatus's *Commentum Terentii.' Viator* 9 235–49

Richardson, T.W. 1984. 'A New Petronius Manuscript: Indiana, Notre Dame 58
(I).' *Scriptorium* 38 89–100

– 1986. 'Pierre Dupuy, Petronius, and B.' *Revue d'Histoire des Textes* 16 319–24

Rini, A. 1937. *Petronius in Italy.* (New York)

Rose, K.F.C. 1967. Unpublished notes in the possession of J.P. Sullivan, Santa
Barbara, Ca.

Rose, V. 1893. *Die Handschriften-Verzeichnisse der Königlichen Bibliothek zu
Berlin.* b. 12, v. 1. (Berlin)

Rouse, R.H. 1976. 'The Florilegium Angelicum: its Origin, Content and Influence.' In J.J.G. Alexander and M.T. Gibson, eds., *Essays Presented to Richard William Hunt.* 66–114. (Oxford)

– 1979. 'Florilegia and Latin Classical Authors in Twelfth- and Thirteenth-Century Orléans.' *Viator* 10 131–60

– 1983. 'Cicero *De finibus.*' in L.D. Reynolds, ed., *Texts and Transmission: A Survey of the Latin Classics.* 112–5. (Oxford)

Ruysschaert, J. 1947. 'Le séjour de Juste Lipse à Rome (1568–1570).' *Bulletin de l'Institut historique belge de Rome* 24 139–92

– 1959. *Bibliothecae Apostolicae Vaticanae Codices Manuscripti: Codices Vaticani Latini, Codices 11414–11709.* (Vatican City)

Sage, E.T. 1916. 'Petronius, Poggio, and John of Salisbury.' *Classical Philology* 11 11–24

– 1936. *The Manuscripts of Petronius.* Unpublished MS in the Joseph Regenstein Library, University of Chicago

Sandys, J.E. 1958. *A History of Classical Scholarship.* v. 2. (Cambridge)

Scaliger, J. 1572. *Publii Virgilii Maronis Appendix.* (Lyons)

– 1609. *Catalogus librorum Bibliothecae illustr. viri Josephi Scaligeri.* (Leiden)

– 1668. in *Scaligeriana, sive ex ore Josephi Scaligeri, per F.F.P.P., secunda auctior et emendatior.* (Leiden)

Schmeling G., and Stuckey, J. 1975. *Bibliography of Petronius.* (Leiden)

Schmidt, P.L. 1974. *Die Überlieferung von Ciceros Schrift de Legibus in Mittelalter und Renaissance.* (Munich)

Stelling-Michaud, S. 1972. *Le Livre du Recteur de l'Académie de Genève (1559–1878).* v. 3. (Geneva)

Stolz, W. 1987. *Petrons Satyricon und François Nodot: Ein Beitrag zur Geschichte literarischer Fälschungen.* (Stuttgart)

Turnèbe, A. 1564–73. *Adversariorum Libri XXX.* (Paris)

Ullman, B.L. 1930a. 'Petronius in the Medieval Florilegia.' *Classical Philology* 25 11–21

– 1930b. 'The Text of Petronius in the Sixteenth Century.' *Classical Philology* 25 128–54

Usener, H. 1867. 'Eine Handschrift Peter Daniels.' *Rheinisches Museum* 22 413–21

van der Does, J. 1569. Letter to Falkenburg, in Goldast 1610, p. 16

– 1583, 1585. *Petronii Arbitri praecidaneorum libri tres.* (Leiden, Paris)

van Thiel, H. 1971. *Petron. Überlieferung und Rekonstruktion.* (Leiden)

Vidier, A 1965. *L'Historiographie à Saint-Benoît-sur-Loire.* (Paris)

Wehle, W. 1861. *Observationes Criticae in Petronium.* (Bonn)

White, L.A. 1933. 'The Early Editions of the Satyricon of Petronius.' *University of Pittsburgh Bulletin* 9 303–9

Wood, A. 1813–20. *Athenae Oxonienses*. New edition by P. Bliss, 4 vols. (London)

Wright, C.E. 1972. *Fontes Harleiani*. (London)

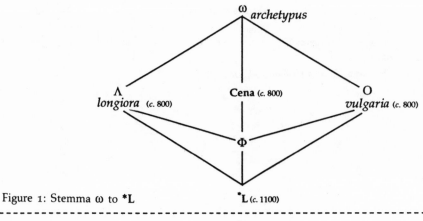

Figure 1: Stemma ω to *L

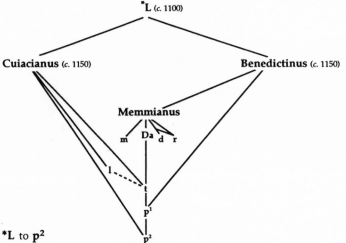

Figure 2a: Stemma *L to p²

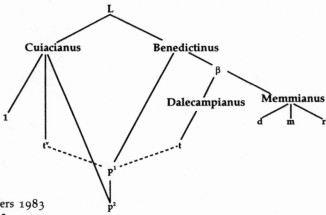

Figure 2b: Müller and Ehlers 1983
Stemma L to p²

SYMBOLS FOR MANUSCRIPTS AND EDITIONS

Ω	*Satyrica* archetype, consensus of Λ, **O**, and **Cena**
Λ	Hypothesized manuscript of 'longer excerpts,' written about 800 from the archetype, source of ***L** and φ
*L	Hypothesized manuscript, conflation of Λ, **O** and φ, parent of the lost manuscripts **Benedictinus** and **Cuiacianus**
l	Leiden, Universiteitsbibliotheek, **Scaligeranus 61**, edition in the hand of Scaliger, written around 1571, derived from manuscripts **Cuiacianus** and **P**, and from printed editions **c** and **s** of the **O** class
d	Bern, Stadt- und Universitätsbibliothek, **Bong.IV.665. (10)**, transcription in the hand of P. Daniel, written about 1564, of an excerpt (the *fragmentum veteris libri Cuiacii?*) from **Memmianus**, containing c. 1–15.4
Da	**Dalecampianus**, lost sixteenth-century manuscript transcribed from **Memmianus**, used only by de Tournes in constructing **t**
m	Città del Vaticano, Biblioteca Apostolica Vaticana, **Vaticanus Lat. 11428**, owned by Muret, handwritten edition, up to c. 80.9, made around 1565, conflating **Memmianus** with **s**

r

London, Lambeth Palace Library, **Lambethanus 693**, owned by Rogers, transcription of **Memmianus**, collated against a manuscript from φ, and, for c. 1–15.4, a *fragmentum veteris libri Cuiacii*, which is source or sibling of **d**

r^comm

Portion of **Lambethanus 693** (ff. 51–52v) which contains a transcription of the *Notae* of F. Daniel, written around 1570, which was first published from the original by Goldast 1610

r^m, r^c

In **Lambethanus 693** the marginalia and corrections, many in the hand of Rogers, which is shown most clearly in f. 41v (Plate 12)

t

Printed edition of de Tournes, Lyons 1575, derived mainly from **Dalecampianus** and **Cuiacianus** (the latter after c. 112.4), the first French editions of **O** (**c** and **s**), Scaliger 1572, and a manuscript from φ

t^v

From de Tournes' edition (**t**) the *variae lectiones ex collatione v.c.*, selected **Cuiacianus** variants unavailable for consideration for the text, extending to c. 112.4

p^1

First printed edition of Pithou, Paris 1577, derived mainly from the lost **Benedictinus**, **B** (**Autissiodurensis**), **P** (**Bituricus**), a φ manuscript, and **t**

p^2

Revised edition by Pithou of **p^1**, Paris 1587, employing the same sources, with the addition of **Cuiacianus**, called '*Thol.*' (**Tholosanus**)

p

Readings shared by the two editions of Pithou

p^1v, p^2v

In the two editions of Pithou the *varietas lectionum*, lists of lemmata together with rejected variants and manuscript attribution (**p^{2v'Thol.'}** = **Cuiacianus**)

p^v

Readings shared in the *varietas* of the editions of Pithou

Benedictinus

Lost manuscript, dating to about 1150, derived from *L, used by Pithou alone, from which **Memmianus** was copied

Cuiacianus   Lost manuscript, dating to about 1150, derived from ***L**, first owned by Cujas, used by F. Daniel, Scaliger, de Tournes and Pithou

Memmianus   Lost manuscript, copied in the sixteenth century from **Benedictinus**, cited by Turnèbe, source of **d Da m r**

Tholosanus   Manuscript so designated in **p²ᵛ** (as '*Thol.*'), which is the lost **Cuiacianus**

φ   Archetype, dating to about 1100, of florilegia culled from **Λ O Cena**

par   Paris, Bibliothèque Nationale, **Parisinus lat. 7647**, a florilegium MS of the 1200s annotated by P. Daniel.

O   Hypothesized manuscript, the consensus of **B R P**, reflecting the sum of the 'shorter' tradition, excerpted from Ω about 800

B   Bern, Bürgerbibliothek, **Bernensis 357** + Leiden, Universiteitsbibliotheek, **Vossianus Lat. Q. 30** ff. 58, 57 (c. 81–109 missing), ninth century, **O** class, known as *Autis.* or *Aut.* (**Autissiodurensis**) to Pithou, who alone used it extensively, though Dupuy cited readings from **Vossianus** only

R   Paris, Bibliothèque Nationale, **Parisinus lat. 6842 D**, twelfth century, **O** class, not known to the French scholars of the sixteenth century

P   Paris, Bibliothèque Nationale, **Parisinus lat. 8049**, twelfth century, **O** class, used by Scaliger and Pithou for their editions, wherein cited as *Bit.*, *Brit.*, *Bitur.*, *Biturig.*, i.e. **Bituricus**

a   The *editio princeps* of the **O**-based text [Milan 1482], unknown to the sixteenth-century French scholars

b   Reprinting of **a**, with changes, Venice 1499, unknown to the sixteenth-century French scholars

c   The *editio Chalderiana*, second reprinting of **a**, with further
                   changes, Paris 1520, widely used by the scholars in their first
                   acquaintance with Petronius

s   The *editio Sambuci*, Antwerp 1565, influential final edition of
                   O class only, founded on **c** but corrected on a better manu-
                   script, Wien, Österreichische Nationalbibliothek, **Vindobo-
                   nensis 3198**

Cena   Lost manuscript, possibly the **codex Coloniensis** seen by
                   Poggio, ninth century, transcription of c. 26.7–78 from Ω

H   Paris, Bibliothèque Nationale, **Parisinus lat. 7989**, the part
                   containing a separate transcription of c. 26.7–78, i.e. the *Cena
                   Trimalchionis*, from the lost **codex Coloniensis** or exemplar,
                   made in 1423

THE PLATES

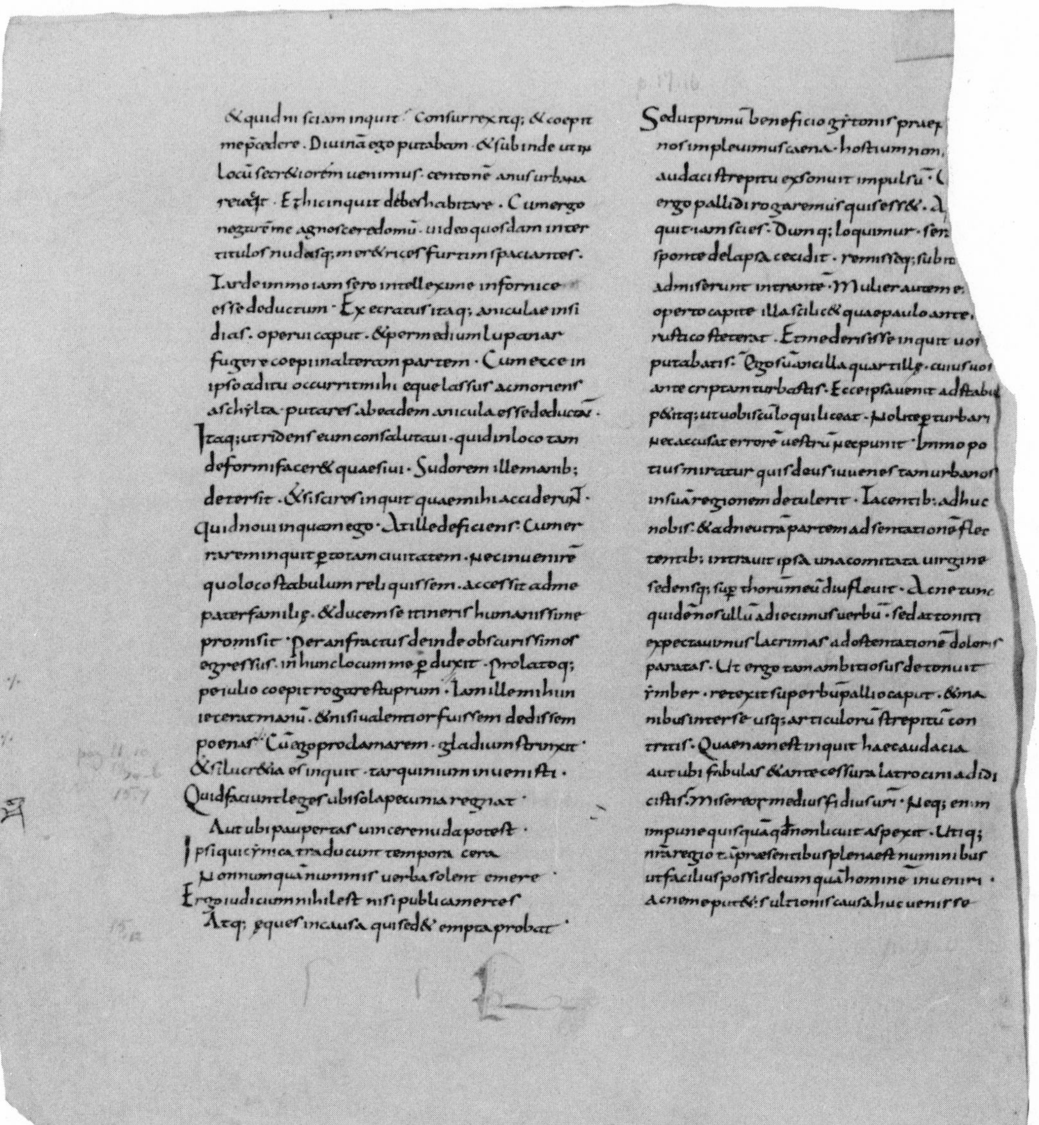

Plate 1. Leiden, Universiteitsbibliotheek, **Vossianus Lat. Q. 30**, f. 58v, 240 × 225 mm (170 × 170 mm), *s.* ix, = **B**, c. 7.1–17.6. Illustrates how at 16.3 *sacrum* may be missing (second column, end of tenth line) through damage to the leaf (Chs. 3, 8). [By permission]

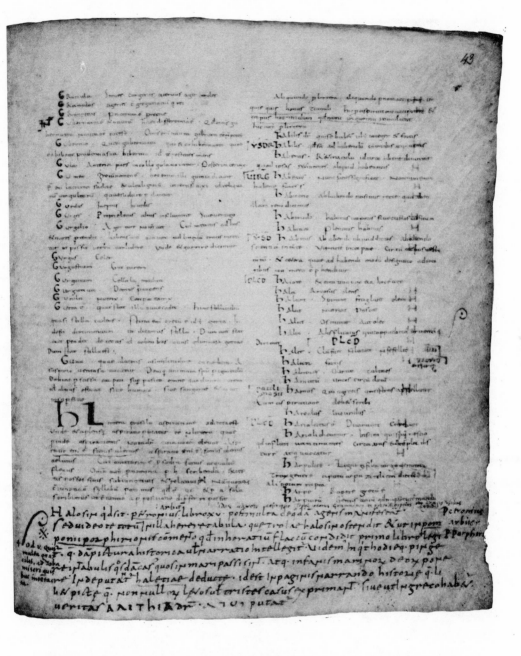

Plate 2. London, British Library, **Harleianus 2735**, f. 43, 220 x 190 mm (155 x 145 mm), *s.* ix. Glossary owned by P. Daniel, with marginalia in ninth-century hand (below), assigning the Sack of Troy (c. 89) to Book 15: *'Halosin quid sit, Petronius Arbiter libro XV ...'* (Ch. 4). [By permission of the British Library]

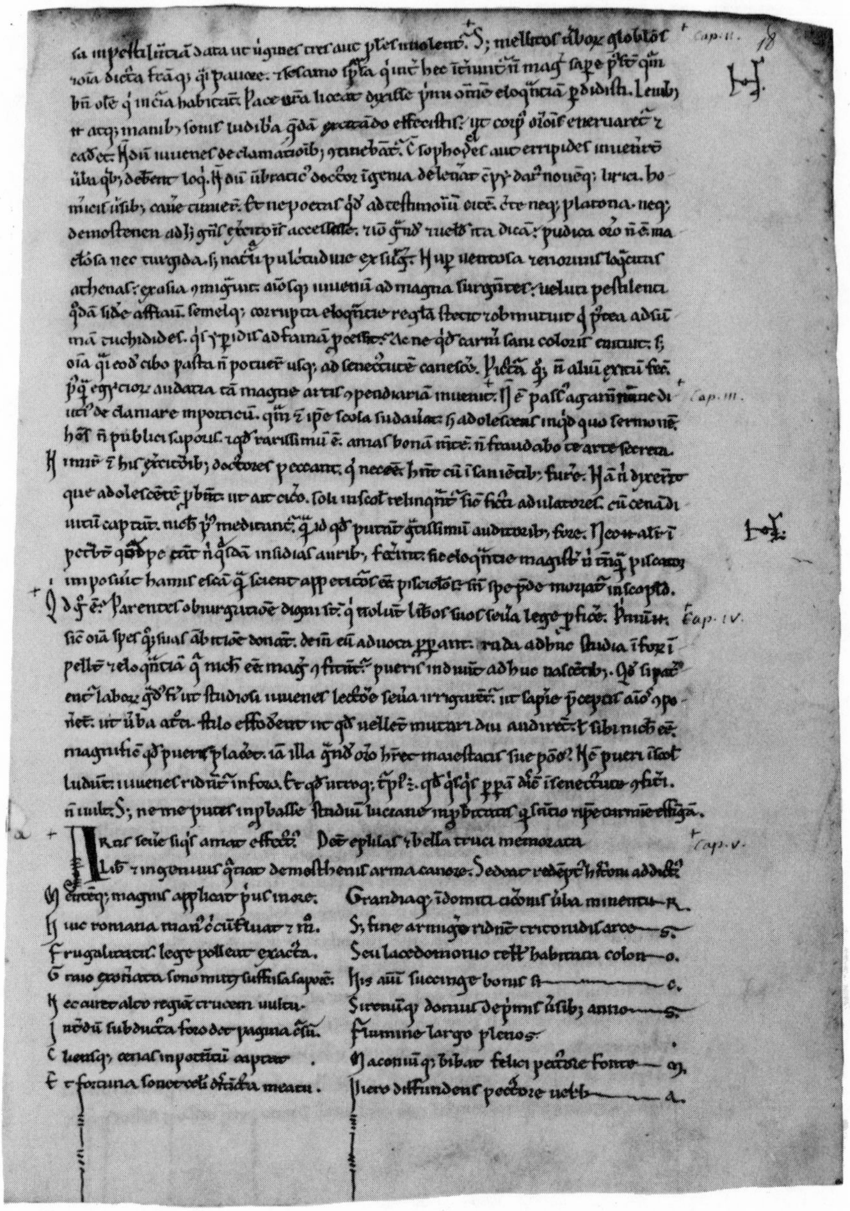

Plate 3. Paris, Bibliothèque Nationale, **Parisinus lat. 8049**, f. 18, 270 × 190 mm (230 × 140 mm), s. xii, = **P**, c. 1.3–5.1.22. Illustrates how palaeographic and textual difficulties could have led to discrepancies between **P** and the readings cited for **Bituricus** (Ch. 3). [Phot. Bibl. Nat. Paris]

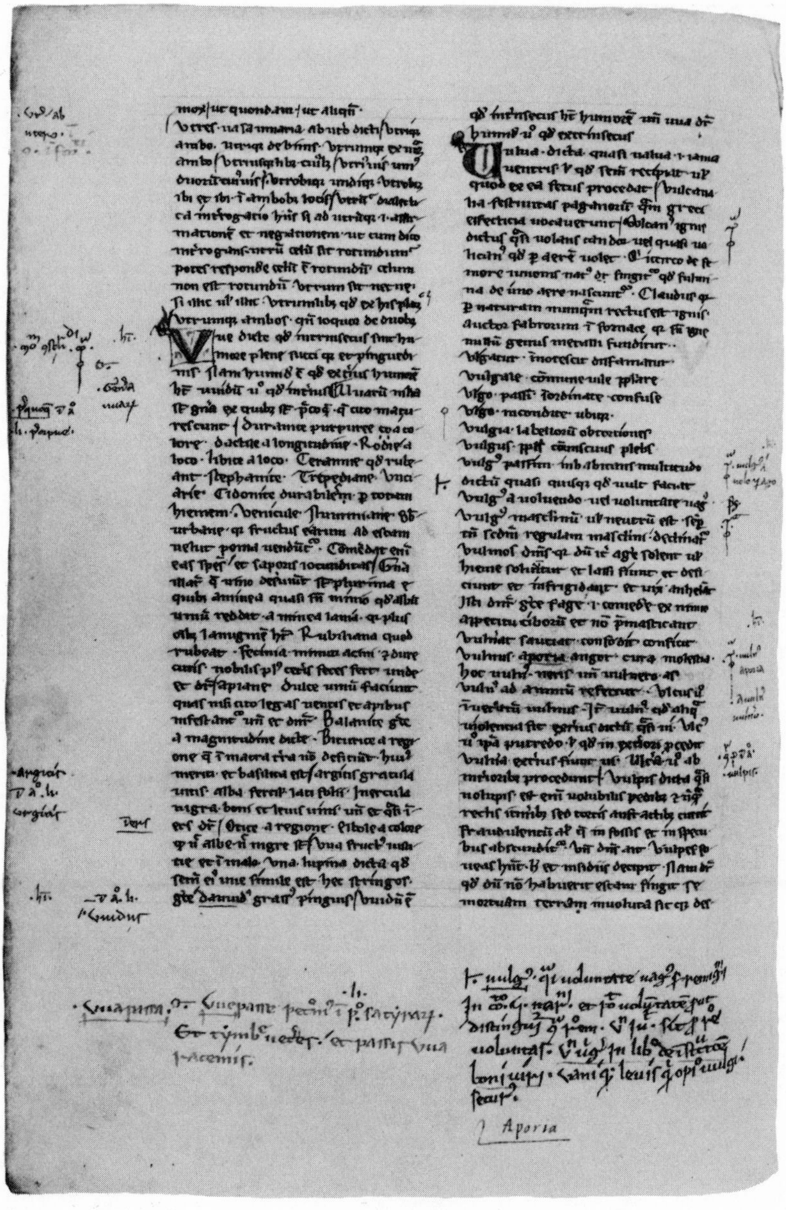

Plate 4. Bern, Bürgerbibliothek, **Bernensis 276**, f. 256v, 270 x 185 mm (185 x 125 mm), *s.* xiii. Glossary owned by P. Daniel, with marginalia (below, left column) assigning c. 135.8.14 *et thymbrae veteres et passis uva racemis* to 'Petronius in libro primo satyrarum' (Ch. 4). [By permission]

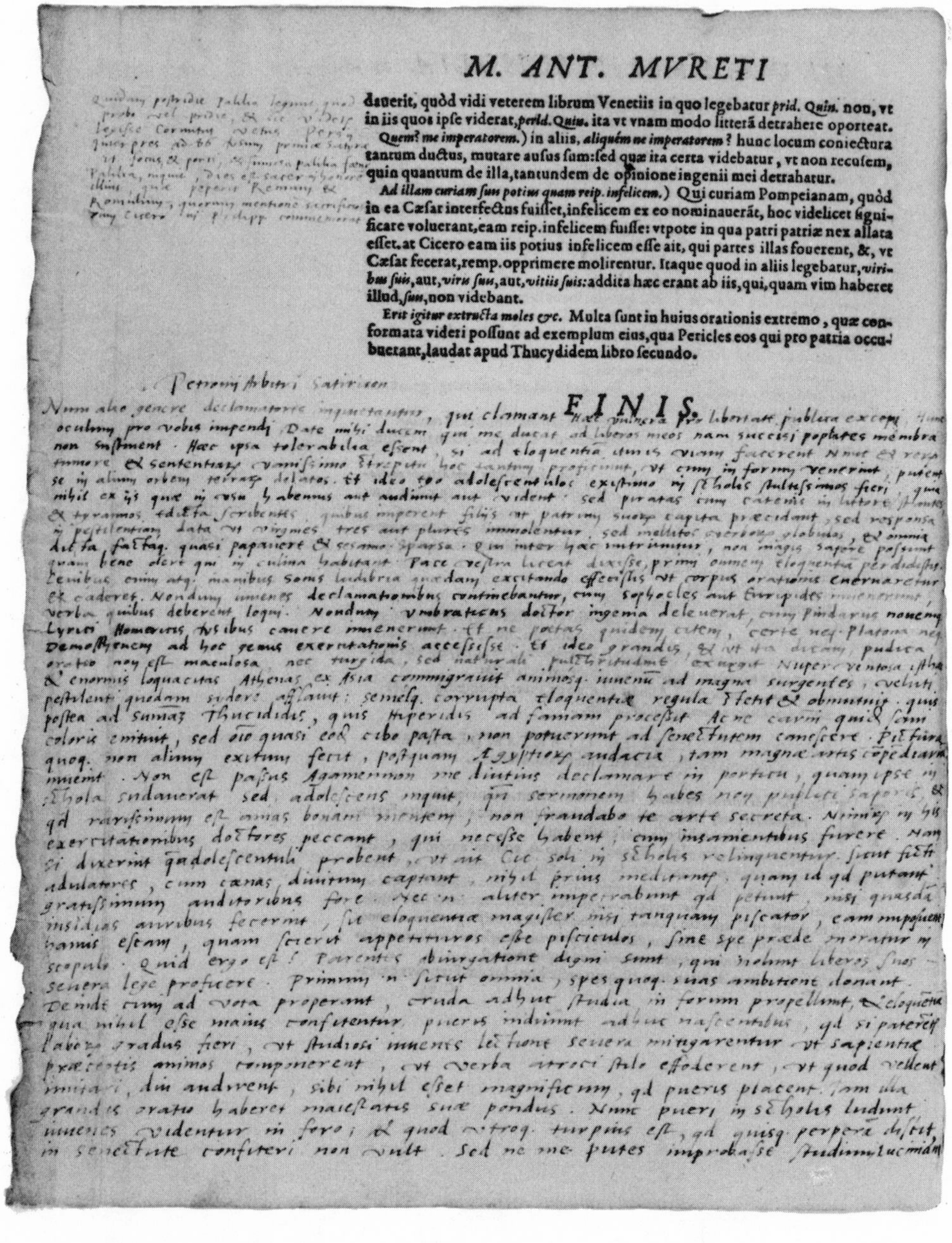

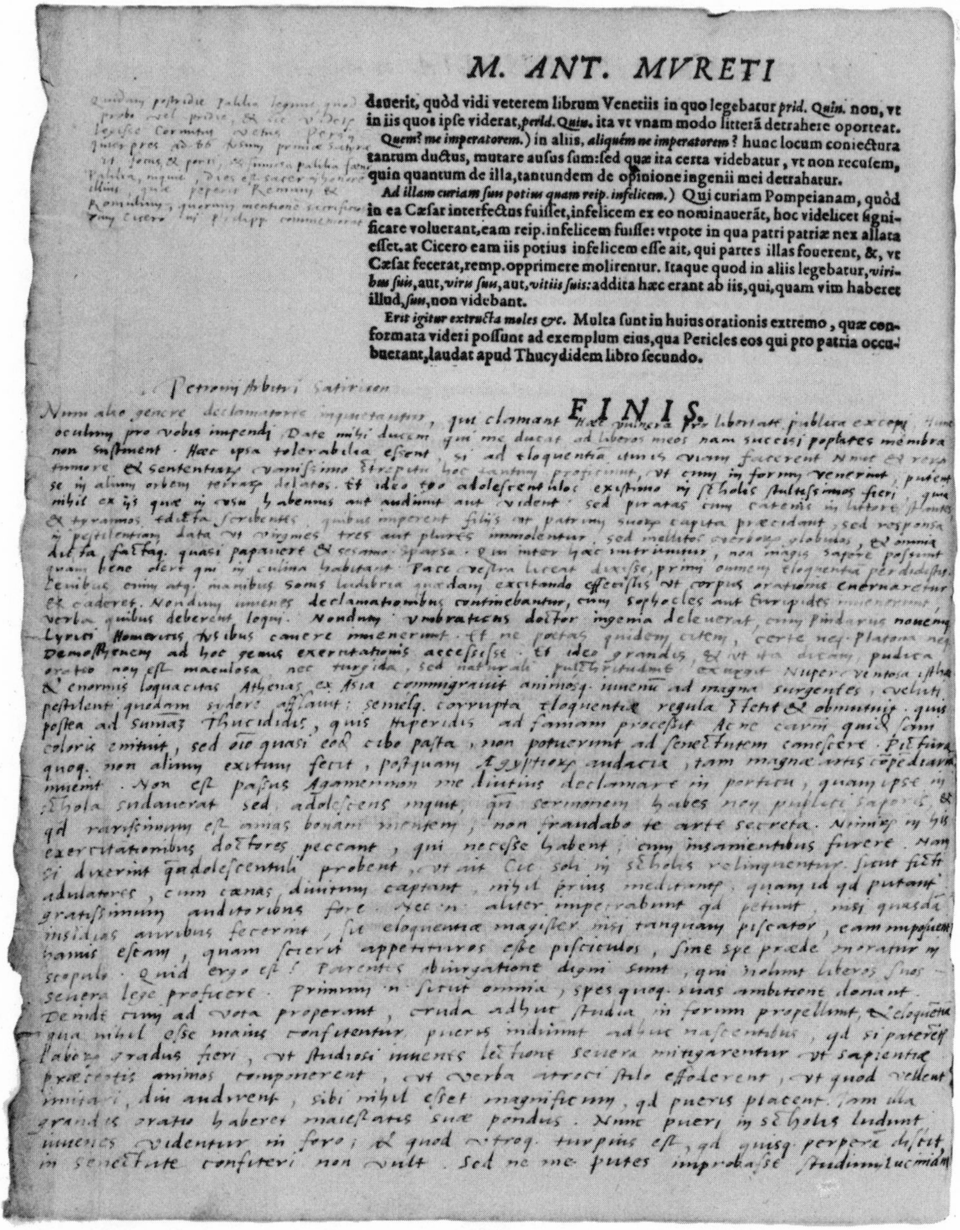

M. ANT. MVRETI

dauerit, quòd vidi veterem librum Venetiis in quo legebatur *prid. Quin.* non, vt in iis quos ipse viderat, *perid. Quin.* ita vt vnam modo litterã detrahere oporteat.

Quem? me imperatorem.) in aliis, *aliquém ne imperatorem?* hunc locum coniectura tantum ductus, mutare ausus sum: sed quæ ita certa videbatur, vt non recusem, quin quantum de illa, tantundem de opinione ingenii mei detrahatur.

Ad illam curiam sua potius quam reip. infelicem.) Qui curiam Pompeianam, quòd in ea Cæsar interfectus fuisset, infelicem ex eo nominauerãt, hoc videlicet significare voluerant, eam reip. infelicem fuisse: vtpote in qua patri patriæ nex allata esset. at Cicero eam iis potius infelicem esse ait, qui partes illas fouerent, &, vt Cæsar fecerat, remp. opprimere molirentur. Itaque quod in aliis legebatur, *viribus suis*, aut, *viris suis*, aut, *vitiis suis:* addita hæc erant ab iis, qui, quam vim haberet illud, *suis*, non videbant.

Erit igitur extructa moles &c. Multa sunt in huius orationis extremo, quæ conformata videri possunt ad exemplum eius, qua Pericles eos qui pro patria occubuerant, laudat apud Thucydidem libro secundo.

FINIS.

Petronij Arbitri Satiricon

Num alio genere declamatores inquietantur, qui clamant Hæc vulnera pro libertate publica excepi, hunc oculum pro vobis impendi. Date mihi ducem qui me ducat ad liberos meos nam succisi poplites membra non sustinent. Hæc ipsa tolerabilia essent, si ad eloquentiã ituris viam facerent Nunc et rerum tumore & sententiarum vanissimo strepitu hoc tantum proficiunt, vt cum in forum venerint, putent se in alium orbem terrarum delatos. Et ideo ego adolescentulos existimo in scholis stultissimos fieri, quia nihil ex iis que in vsu habemus aut audiunt aut vident, sed piratas cum catenis in littore stantes & tyrannos edicta scribentes, quibus imperent filiis vt patrum suorum capita præcidant, sed responsa in pestilentiam data vt virgines tres aut plures immolentur, sed mellitos verborum globulos, & omnia dicta, factaq. quasi papauere & sesamo sparsa. Qui inter hæc nutriuntur, non magis sapere possunt quam bene olere qui in culina habitant. Pace vestra liceat dixisse, primi omnem eloquentiã perdidistis. Lenibus enim atq. inanibus sonis ludibria quedam excitando effecistis vt corpus orationis eneruaretur et caderet. Nondum iuuenes declamationibus continebantur, cum Sophocles aut Euripides inuenerunt verba quibus deberent loqui. Nondum vmbraticus doctor ingenia deleuerat, cum Pindarus nouemq. Lyrici Homericis versibus canere timuerunt. Et ne poetas quidem citem, certe neq. Platona neq. Demosthenem ad hoc genus exercitationis accessisse. Et ideo grandis, & vt ita dicam, pudica oratio non est maculosa nec turgida, sed naturali pulchritudine exurgit. Nuper ventosa ista & enormis loquacitas Athenas ex Asia commigrauit animosq. iuuenũ ad magna surgentes, veluti pestilenti quodam sydere afflauit: semelq. corrupta eloquentiæ regula stetit & obmutuit. quis postea ad summam Thucididis, quis Hyperidis ad famam processit. Ac ne carmen quid sani coloris emituit, sed oĩa quasi eod. cibo pasta, non potuerunt ad senectutem canescere. Pictura quoq. non alium exitum fecit, postquam Ægyptiorum audacia, tam magnæ artis cõpendiaria inuenit. Non est passus Agamemnon me diutius declamare in porticu, quam ipse in schola sudauerat sed adolescens inquit, qui sermonem habes non publici saporis, & qd rarissimum est amas bonam mentem, non fraudabo te arte secreta. Nimirum in his exercitationibus doctores peccant, qui necesse habent, cum insanientibus furere. Nam si dixerint q̃ adolescentuli probent, vt ait Cic. soli in scholis relinquentur. sicut ficti adulatores, cum cœnas diuitum captant, nihil prius meditantur, quam id qd putant gratissimum auditoribus fore. Nec n. aliter impetrabunt qd petunt, nisi quasdã insidias auribus fecerint, sic eloquentiæ magister nisi tanquam piscator, eam imposuerit hamis escam, quam scierit appetituros esse pisciculos, sine spe prædæ morantur in scopulo. Quid ergo est? Parentes obiurgatione digni sunt, qui nolunt liberos suos seuera lege proficere. Primum n. sicut omnia, spes quoq. suas ambitioni donant. Deinde cum ad vota properant, cruda adhuc studia in forum propellunt, & eloquentiã qua nihil esse maius confitentur, pueris induunt adhuc nascentibus, qd si paterentur laborum gradus fieri, vt studiosi iuuenes lectione seuera irrigarentur vt sapientiæ præceptis animos componerent, vt verba atroci stilo effoderent, vt quod vellent imitari, diu audirent, sibi nihil esset magnificum, qd pueris placent. Iam illa grandis oratio haberet maiestatis suæ pondus. Nunc pueri in scholis ludunt iuuenes videntur in foro; & quod vtroq. turpius est, qd quisq. perperã discit, in senectute confiteri non vult. Sed ne me putes improbasse studium lucinianum

Plate 5. Bern, Stadt- und Universitätsbibliothek, **Bong. IV.665 (10)**, f. 11v, 225 × 175 mm (220 × 165 mm), *c.* 1564, = **d**, c. 1–4.5, in the hand of P. Daniel (Ch. 5). [By permission]

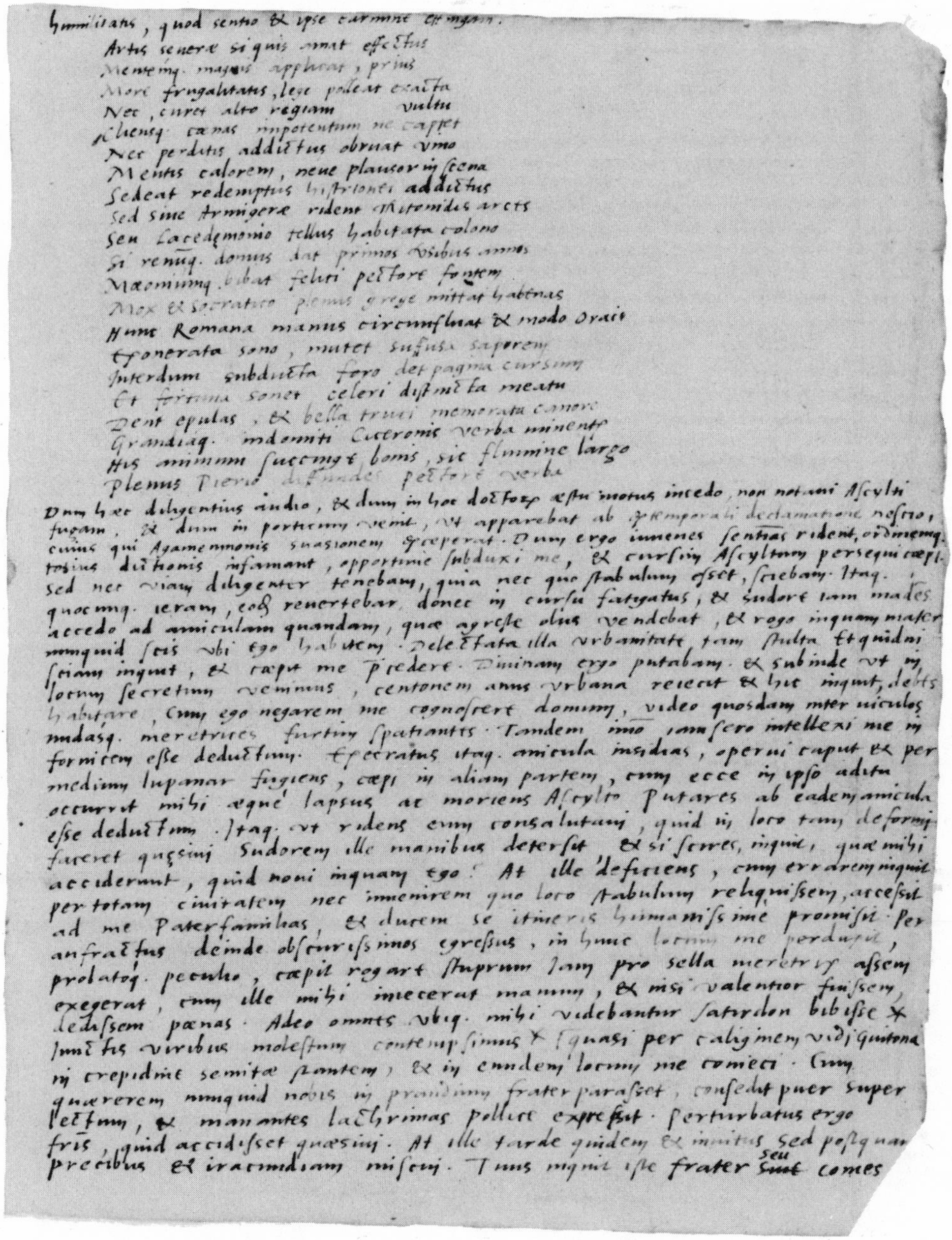
humilitatis, quod sentio et ipse carmine effingam.
Artis severae si quis amat effectus
Mentemque magnis applicat, prius
More frugalitatis lege polleat exacta
Nec, curet alto regiam vultu
Cliensque cenas impotentum ne captet
Nec perditis addictus obruat vino
Mentis calorem, neve plausor in scena
Sedeat redemptus histrioni addictus
Sed sive armigerae rident Tritonidis arces
Seu Lacedemonio tellus habitata colono
Sirenumque domus dat primos versibus annos
Maeoniumque bibat felici pectore fontem
Mox et Socratico plenus grege mittat habenas
Hinc Romana manus circumfluat et modo Graio
Exonerata sono, mutet suffusa saporem
Interdum subducta foro det pagina cursum
Et fortuna sonet celeri distincta meatu
Dent epulas, et bella truci memorata canore
Grandiaque indomiti Ciceronis verba minentur
His animum succinge bonis, sic flumine largo
Plenus Pierio defundes pectore verba

Dum haec diligentius audio, et dum in hoc doctorum aestu motus incedo, non notavi Ascylti fugam, et dum in porticum venit, ut apparebat ab extemporali declamatione nostro, cuius qui Agamemnonis suasionem exceperat. Dum ergo iuvenes sententias rident, ordinemque totius dictionis infamant, opportune subduxi me, et cursim Ascyltum persequi coepi. Sed nec viam diligenter tenebam, quia nec quo stabulum esset, sciebam. Itaque quocumque ieram, eodem revertebar, donec in cursu fatigatus, et sudore iam madens accedo ad aniculam quandam, quae agreste olus vendebat, et rogo inquam mater numquid scis ubi ego habitem? Delectata illa urbanitate tam stulta et quidni sciam inquit, et coepit me praecedere. Divinam ergo putabam. et subinde ut in locum secretum venimus, centonem anus urbana reiecit et hic inquit, debes habitare. Cum ego negarem me cognoscere domum, video quosdam inter titulos nudasque meretrices furtim spatiantes. Tandem imo iam sero intellexi me in fornicem esse deductum. Execratus itaque aniculae insidias, operui caput et per medium lupanar fugiens, coepi in aliam partem, cum ecce in ipso aditu occurrit mihi aeque lapsus at moriens Ascyltos. Putares ab eadem anicula esse deductum. Itaque ut ridens eum consalutavi, quid in loco tam deformi faceret quaesivi. Sudorem ille manibus detersit et si scires, inquit, quae mihi acciderunt. Quid novi inquam ego? At ille deficiens, cum errarem inquit per totam civitatem nec invenirem quo loco stabulum reliquissem, accessit ad me Paterfamilias, et ducem se itineris humanissime promisit. Per anfractus deinde obscurissimos egressus, in hunc locum me perduxit, prolatoque peculio, coepit rogare stuprum. Iam pro cella meretrix assem exegerat, cum ille mihi iniecerat manum, et nisi valentior fuissem, dedissem poenas. Adeo omnes ubique mihi videbantur satyrion bibisse. Iunctis viribus molestum contempsimus. Quasi per caliginem vidi Gitona in crepidine semitae stantem, et in eundem locum me conieci. Cum quaererem numquid nobis in prandium frater parasset, consedit puer super lectum, et manantes lachrimas pollice expressit. Perturbatus ergo fris, quid accidisset quaesivi. At ille tarde quidem et invitus sed postquam precibus et iracundiam miscui. Tuus inquit iste frater ~~sunt~~ seu comes

Plate 6. Bern, Stadt- und Universitätsbibliothek, **Bong. IV.665 (10)**, f. 12, 225 x 175 mm (220 x 165 mm), *c.* 1564, = **d**, c. 4.5–9.4, in the hand of P. Daniel (Ch. 5). [By permission]

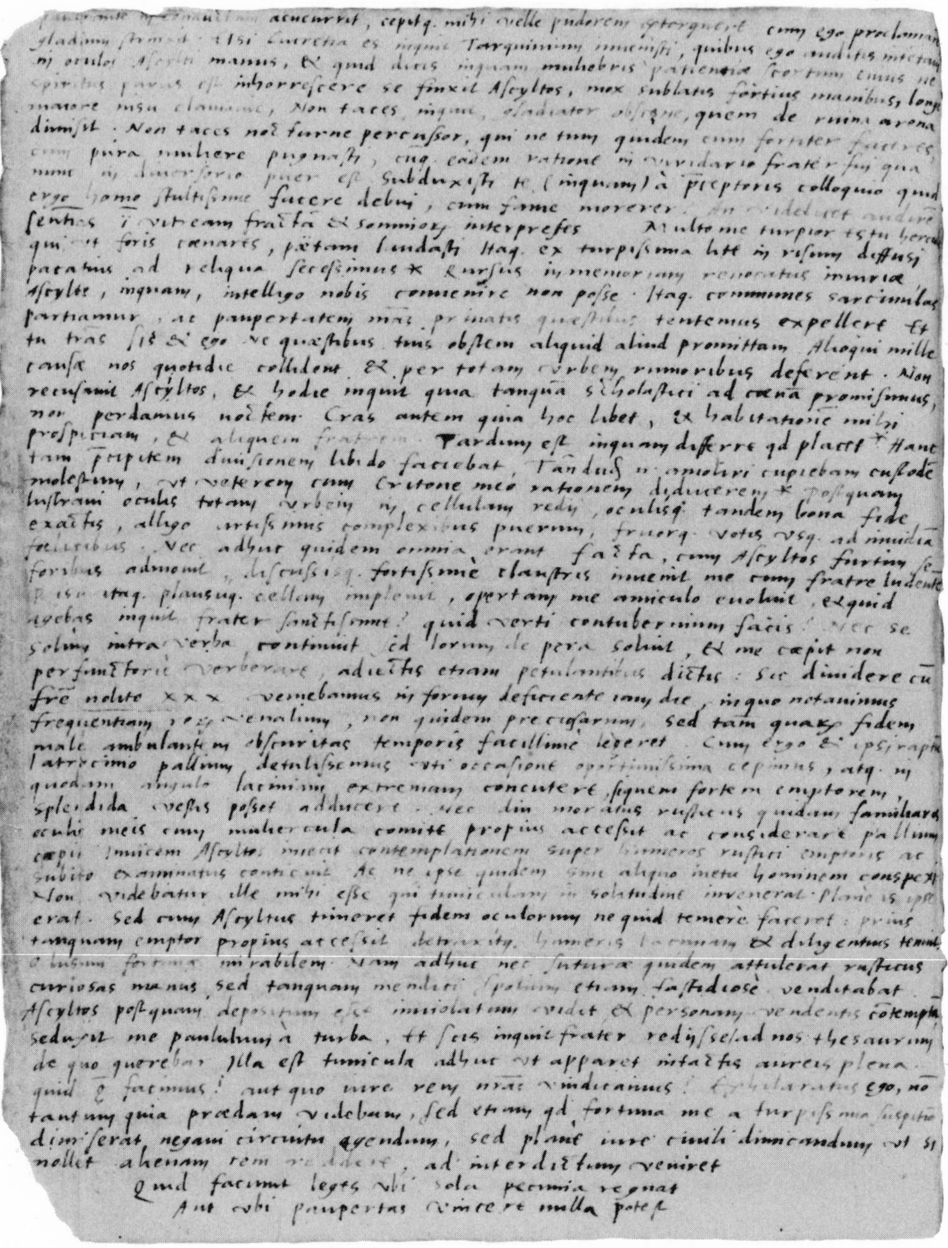
acucurrit, cepitq. mihi velle pudorem extorquere. cum ego proclamarem
gladium strinxit. Si Lucretia es inquit Tarquinium invenisti, quibus ego auditis intentavi
in oculos Ascylti manus, & quid dicis inquam muliebris patientiae scortum cuius ne
spiritus purus est. inhorrescere se finxit Ascyltos, mox sublatis fortius manibus, longe
maiore nisu clamavit, Non taces, inquit, gladiator obscene, quem de ruina arena
dimisit. Non taces nocturne percussor, qui ne tum quidem cum fortiter faceres,
cum pura muliere pugnasti, cuius eadem ratione in viridario frater fui qua
nunc in diversorio puer est. Subduxisti te (inquam) a praeceptoris colloquio. quid
ergo homo stultissime facere debui, cum fame morerer? An videlicet audirem
sententias, id est vitrea fracta & somniorum interpretes. Multo me turpior es tu hercule
qui ut foris cenares, poetam laudasti. Itaq. ex turpissima lite in risum diffusi
pacatius ad reliqua secessimus * Rursus in memoriam revocatus iniuriae
Ascylte, inquam, intelligo nobis convenire non posse. Itaq. communes sarcinulas
partiamur, ac paupertatem nostram privatis quaestibus tentemus expellere. Et
tu litteras scis & ego. ne quaestibus tuis obstem aliquid aliud promittam. Alioqui mille
causae nos quotidie collident & per totam urbem rumoribus deferent. Non
recusavit Ascyltos, & hodie inquit quia tanquam scholastici ad cenam promisimus,
non perdamus noctem. Cras autem quia hoc libet, & habitationem mihi
prospiciam, & aliquem fratrem. Tardum est inquam differre quod placet. Hanc
tam praecipitem divisionem libido faciebat. Iamdudum enim amoliri cupiebam custodem
molestum, ut veterem cum Gitone meo rationem deducerem * postquam
lustravi oculis totam urbem, in cellulam redii, osculisq. tandem bona fide
exactis, alligo artissimis complexibus puerum, fruorq. votis usq. ad invidiam
felicibus. Nec adhuc quidem omnia erant facta, cum Ascyltos furtim se
foribus admovit, discussisq. fortissime claustris invenit me cum fratre ludentem.
Risu itaq. plausuq. cellam implevit, opertum me amiculo evolvit, & quid
agebas inquit frater sanctissime? quid verti contubernium facis? Nec se
solum intra verba continuit sed lorum de pera solvit, & me coepit non
perfunctorie verberare, adiectis etiam petulantibus dictis: Sic dividere cum
fratre nolito xxx veniebamus in forum deficiente iam die, in quo notavimus
frequentiam rerum venalium, non quidem pretiosarum, sed tamen quarum fidem
male ambulantem obscuritas temporis facillime tegeret. Cum ergo & ipsi raptum
latrocinio pallium detulissemus, uti occasione opportunissima coepimus, atq. in
quodam angulo laciniam extremam concutere, siquem forte emptorem
splendida vestis posset adducere. Nec diu moratus rusticus quidam familiaris
oculis meis cum muliercula comite propius accessit ac considerare pallium
coepit. Invicem Ascyltos iniecit contemplationem super umeros rustici emptoris ac
subito exanimatus conticuit. Ac ne ipse quidem sine aliquo motu hominem conspexi.
Nam videbatur ille mihi esse qui tuniculam in solitudine invenerat. Plane is ipse
erat. Sed cum Ascyltus timeret fidem oculorum ne quid temere faceret, prius
tanquam emptor propius accessit detraxitq. umeris laciniam & diligentius temptavit
O lusum fortunae mirabilem. Nam adhuc nec suturae quidem attulerat rusticus
curiosas manus, sed tanquam mendici spolium etiam fastidiose venditabat.
Ascyltos postquam depositum esse inviolatum vidit & personam vendentis contemptam
seduxit me paululum a turba, & scis inquit frater rediisse ad nos thesaurum
de quo querebar. Illa est tunicula adhuc ut apparet intactis aureis plena.
quid ergo facimus? aut quo iure rem nostram vindicamus? Exhilaratus ego, non
tantum quia praedam videbam, sed etiam quod fortuna me a turpissima suspitione
dimiserat, negavi circuitu agendum, sed plane iure civili dimicandum, ut si
nollet alienam rem reddere, ad interdictum veniret

Quid faciunt leges ubi sola pecunia regnat
Aut ubi paupertas vincere nulla potest

Plate 7. Bern, Stadt- und Universitätsbibliothek, **Bong. IV.665 (10)**, f. 12v, 225 x 175 mm (220 x 165 mm), *c.* 1564, = **d**, c. 9.4–14.2.2, in the hand of P. Daniel (Ch. 5). [By permission]

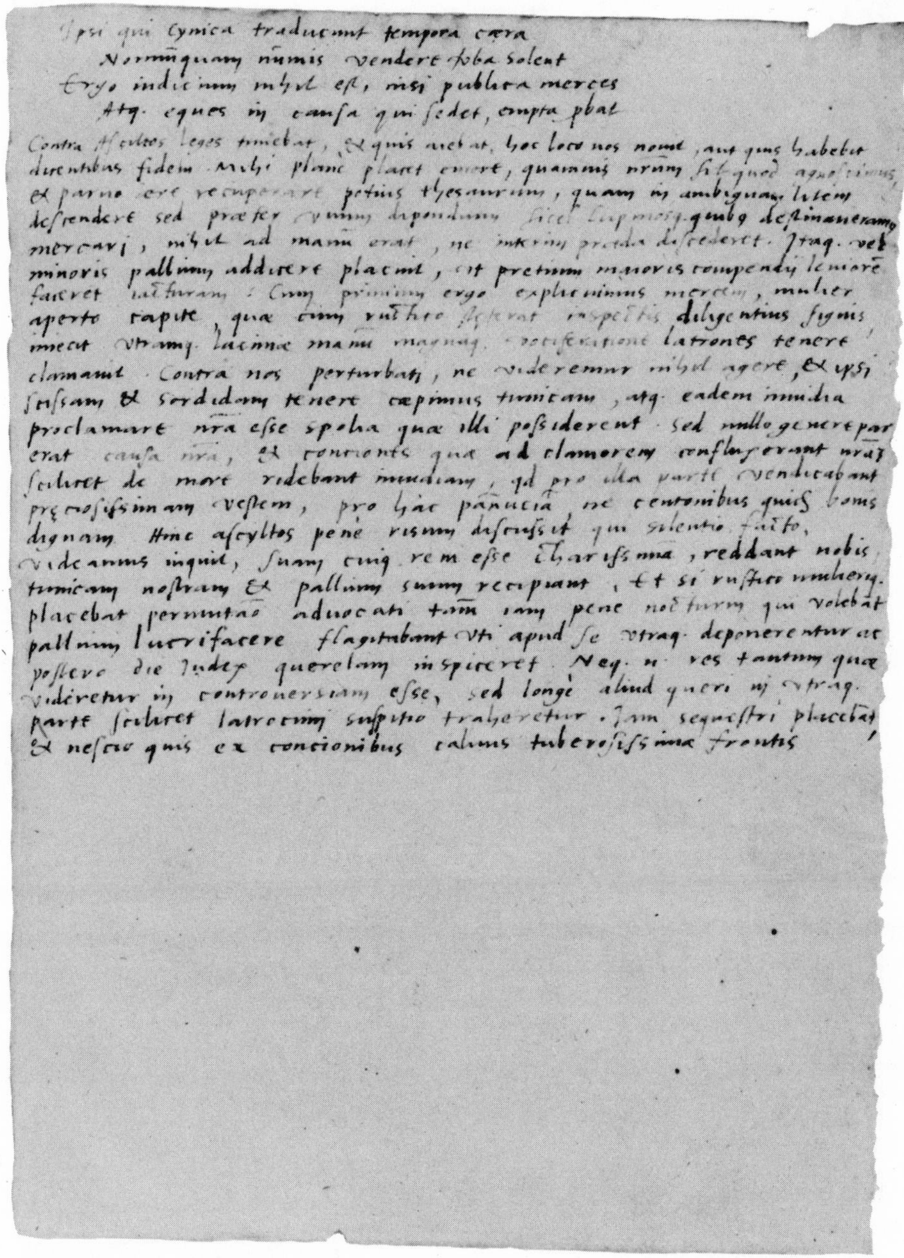

Ipsi qui Cynica traducunt tempora cena
   Nonnumquam nummis vendere verba solent
Ergo iudicium nihil est, nisi publica merces
   Atque eques in causa qui sedet, empta probat.

Contra Ascyltos leges timebat, & quis aiebat, hoc loco nos novit, aut quis habebit
dicentibus fidem mihi plane placet emere, quamvis nostrum sit quod agnoscimus,
et parvo aere recuperare potius thesaurum, quam in ambiguam litem
descendere sed praeter unum dipondium licet lupinos quibus destinaveramus
mercari, nihil ad manum erat, ne interim praeda discederet. Itaque vel
minoris pallium addicere placuit, ut pretium maioris compendii leviore
faceret iacturam. Cum primum ergo explicuimus mercem, mulier
operto capite, quae cum rustico steterat, inspectis diligentius signis
iniecit utramque laciniae manu magnaque vociferatione latrones tenere
clamavit. Contra nos perturbati, ne videremur nihil agere, & ipsi
scissam & sordidam tenere coepimus tunicam, atque eadem invidia
proclamare nostra esse spolia quae illi possiderent. Sed nullo genere par
erat causa nostra, & cociones qui ad clamorem confluxerant nostram
scilicet de more ridebant invidiam, quod pro illa parte vindicabant
pretiosissimam vestem, pro hac pannucia, ne centonibus quidem bonis
dignam. Hinc Ascyltos pene risum discussit qui silentio facto,
videamus inquit, suam cuique rem esse charissimam, reddant nobis
tunicam nostram & pallium suum recipiant, et si rustico mulierique
placebat permutatio aduocati tamen iam pene nocturni qui volebant
pallium lucrifacere flagitabant uti apud se utraque deponerentur ac
postero die iudex querelam inspiceret. Neque n. res tantum quae
viderentur in controversiam esse, sed longe aliud quaeri in utraque
parte scilicet latrocinii suspicio traheretur. Iam sequestri placebat
& nescio quis ex concionibus calvus tuberosissima frontis

Plate 8. Bern, Stadt- und Universitätsbibliothek, **Bong. IV. 665 (10)**, f. 13, 225 × 175 mm (220 × 165 mm), *c.* 1564, = **d**, *c.* 14.2.2–15.4, in the hand of P. Daniel (Ch. 5). [By permission]

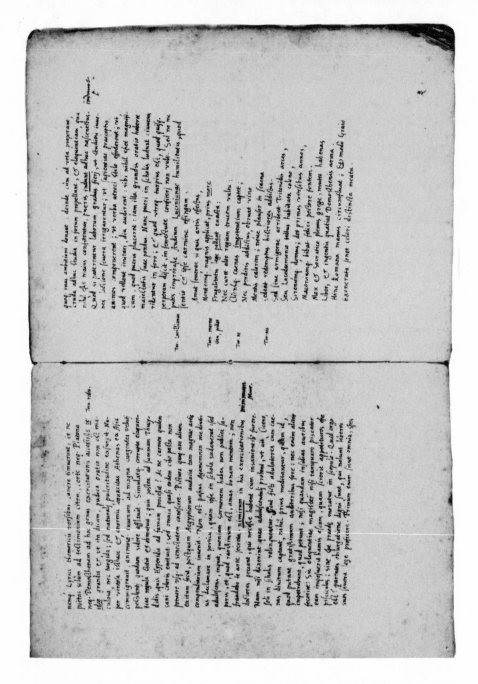

Plate 9. Città del Vaticano, Biblioteca Apostolica Vaticana, **Vaticanus Lat. 11428**, ff. 1v–2, 215 × 170 mm (140 × 110 mm), *c.* 1565, = **m**, c. 2.4–5.1.18. Illustrates scribe's hand as not that of Muret, who however has supplied the marginalia, including a conjecture assigned to himself, a correction (*induunt*; note the 'd' and cf. with Plate 10), and readings of Turnèbe. Note also omission of two lines after *exonerata* (last verse) by haplography *sono/sonet* (Ch. 1). [By permission]

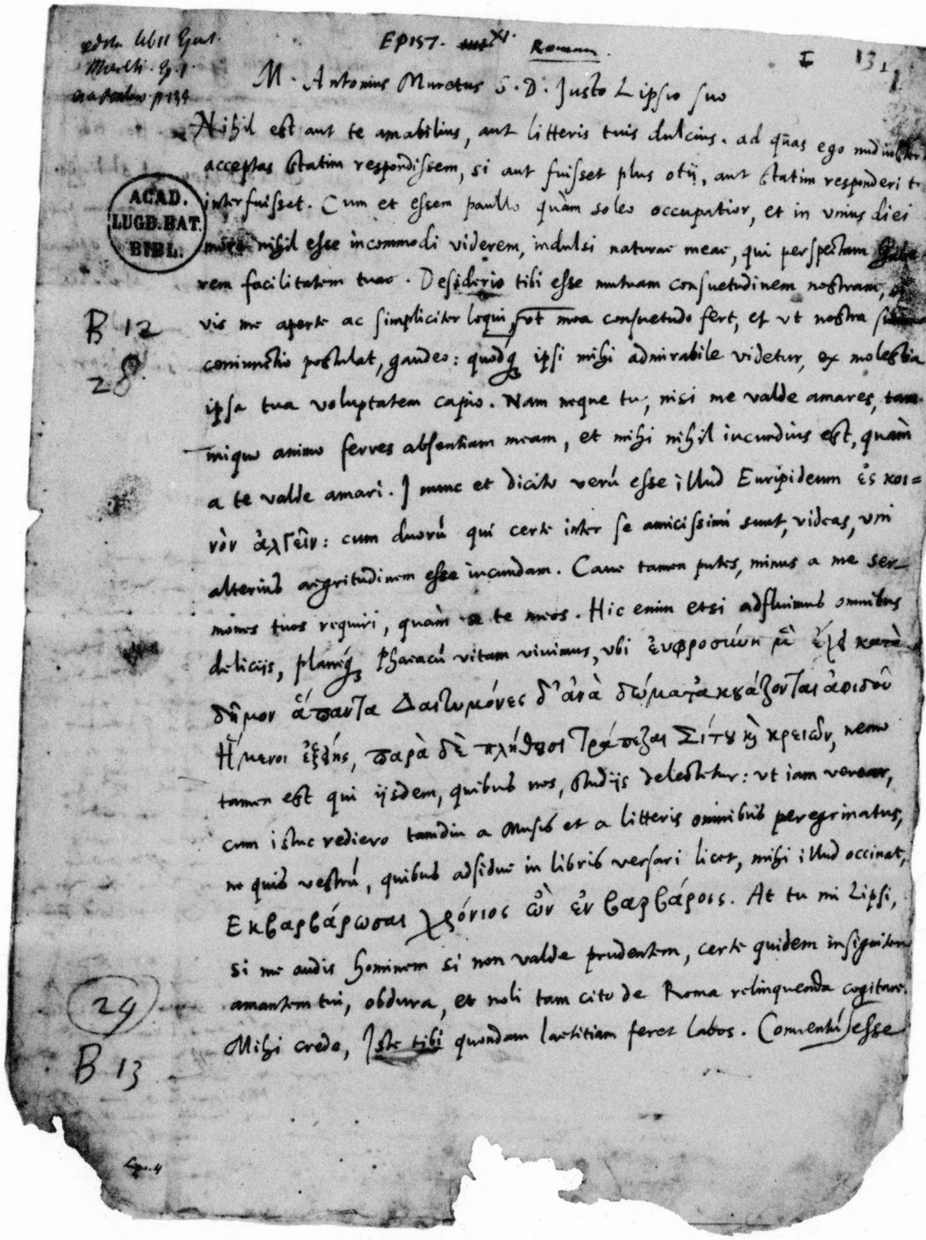

EPIST. ... Romam

M. Antonius Muretus S. D. Iusto Lipsio suo

Nihil est aut te amabilius, aut litteris tuis dulcius. ad quas ego multo ... acceptas statim respondissem, si aut fuisset plus otii, aut statim respondere interfuisset. Cum et essem paullo quam soleo occupatior, et in unius diei mora nihil esse incommodi viderem, indulsi naturae meae, qui perspectam habe... rem facilitatem tuae. Desiderio tibi esse mutuam consuetudinem nostram, vis me aperte ac simpliciter loqui, ut mea consuetudo fert, et ut nostra ... coniunctio postulat, gaudeo: quodque ipsi mihi admirabile videtur, ex molestia ipsa tua voluptatem capio. Nam neque tu, nisi me valde amares, tam magno animo ferres absentiam meam, et mihi nihil iucundius est, quam a te valde amari. I nunc et dicito verum esse illud Euripideum ἴς κοινὸν ἀλγεῖν: cum duorum qui certe inter se amicissimi sunt, videas, unius alterius aegritudinem esse iucundam. Cave tamen putes, minus a me ... mores tuos requiri, quam a te meos. Hic enim etsi adfluimus omnibus deliciis, planeque Phaeacum vitam vivimus, ubi εὐφροσύνη μὲν ἔχῃ κατὰ δῆμον ἅπαντα Δαιτυμόνες δ' ἀνὰ δώματ' ἀκουάζωνται ἀοιδοῦ ἥμενοι ἑξείης, παρὰ δὲ πλήθωσι τράπεζαι σίτου καὶ κρειῶν, nemo tamen est qui iisdem, quibus nos, studiis delectetur: ut iam verear, cum istuc rediero tamdiu a Musis et a litteris omnibus peregrinatus, ne quis vestrum, quibus adsidue in libris versari licet, mihi illud occinat, Ἐκβαρβάρωσαι χρόνιος ὢν ἐν βαρβάροις. At tu mi Lipsi, si me audis hominem si non valde prudentem, certe quidem insigniter amantem tui, obdura, et noli tam cito de Roma relinquenda cogitare. Mihi crede, Iste tibi quondam laetitiam feret labor. Commenti esse

Plate 10. Leiden, Universiteitsbibliotheek, **Lips. 4. Muretus**, f. 1, 275 x 205 mm (215 x 155 mm), 1569. The hand of Muret in a letter to Lips in Rome (Ch. 1). [By permission]

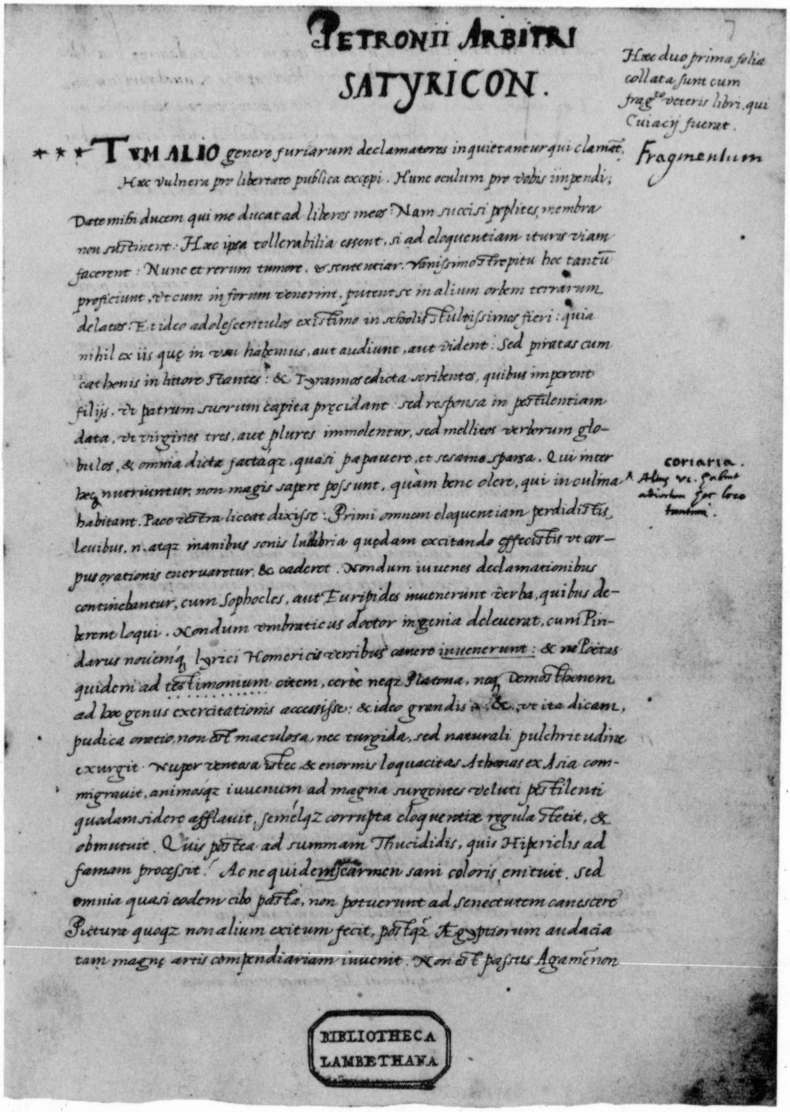

Plate 11. London, Lambeth Palace Library, **Lambethanus 693**, f. 7, 295 × 210 mm (215 × 155 mm), *c.* 1570, = **r**, c. 1–3.1. At beginning, top, marginal reference by scribe, not Rogers, to collation of the exemplar against a MS fragment earlier owned by Cujas; but Rogers supplies a variant: '*Alius v.c.* [probably a florilegium] *habet adverbium hoc loco* tantum' (Chs. 5, 7). [By permission of His Grace the Archbishop of Canterbury and the Trustees of Lambeth Palace Library]

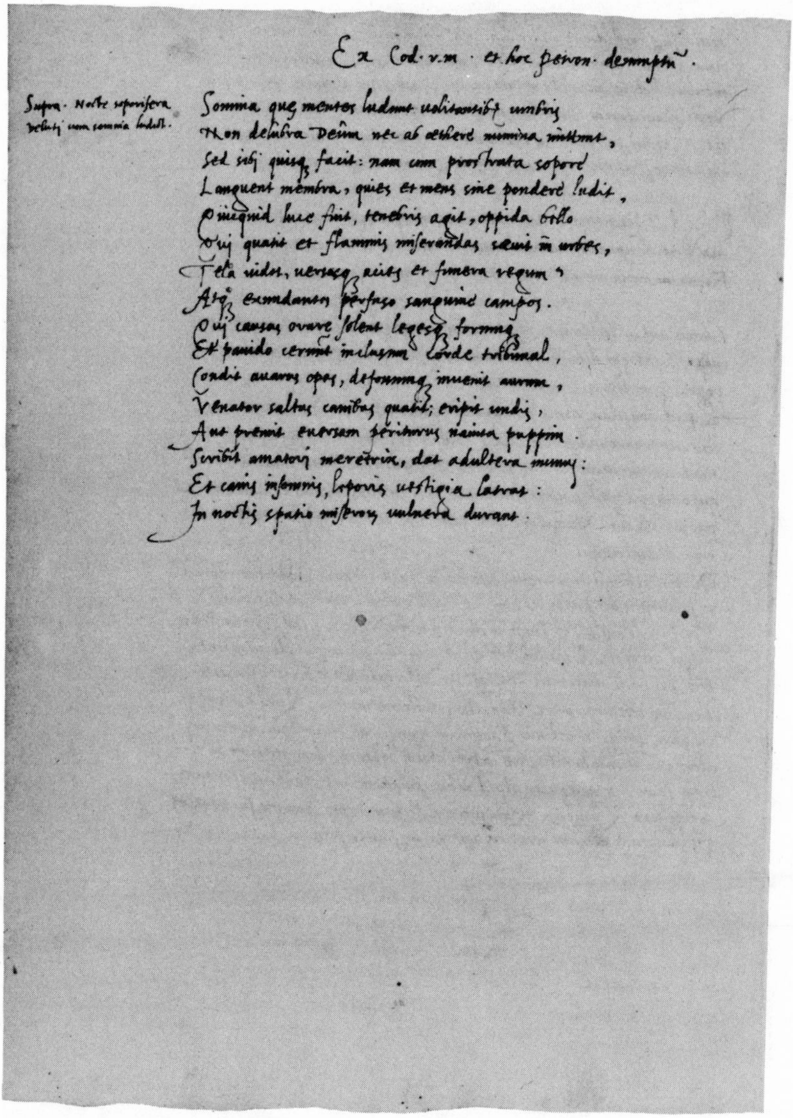

Ex Cod. v.m. et hoc Petron. desumptũ.

Supra. Nocte soporifera veluti cum somnia ludũt.

Somnia quę mentes ludunt volitantib; umbris
Non delubra Deûm nec ab aethere numina mittunt,
Sed sibi quisq; facit: nam cum prostrata sopore
Languent membra, quies et mens sine pondere ludit,
Quicquid luce fuit, tenebris agit, oppida bello
Qui quatit et flammis miserandas saevit in urbes,
Tela videt, versasq; acies et funera regum,
Atq; exundantes perfuso sanguine campos.
Qui causas orare solent legesq; forumq;
Et pavido cernunt inclusum corde tribunal,
Condit avarus opes, defossumq; invenit aurum,
Venator saltus canibus quatit; eripit undis,
Aut premit eversam periturus navita puppim.
Scribit amatori meretrix, dat adultera munus:
Et canis in somnis leporis vestigia latrat:
In noctis spatio miserorum vulnera durant.

Plate 12. London, Lambeth Palace Library, **Lambethanus 693**, f. 41v, 295 x 210 mm (215 x 155 mm), *c.* 1570, = **r**, Frg. XXX. Probable hand of Rogers copying this poem from a source close to Scaliger (divergences from the MS, Leiden, Universiteitsbibliotheek, **Vossianus Lat. F. 111**, in accord with Scaliger 1572; Chs. 1, 5, 7). [By permission of His Grace the Archbishop of Canterbury and the Trustees of Lambeth Palace Library]

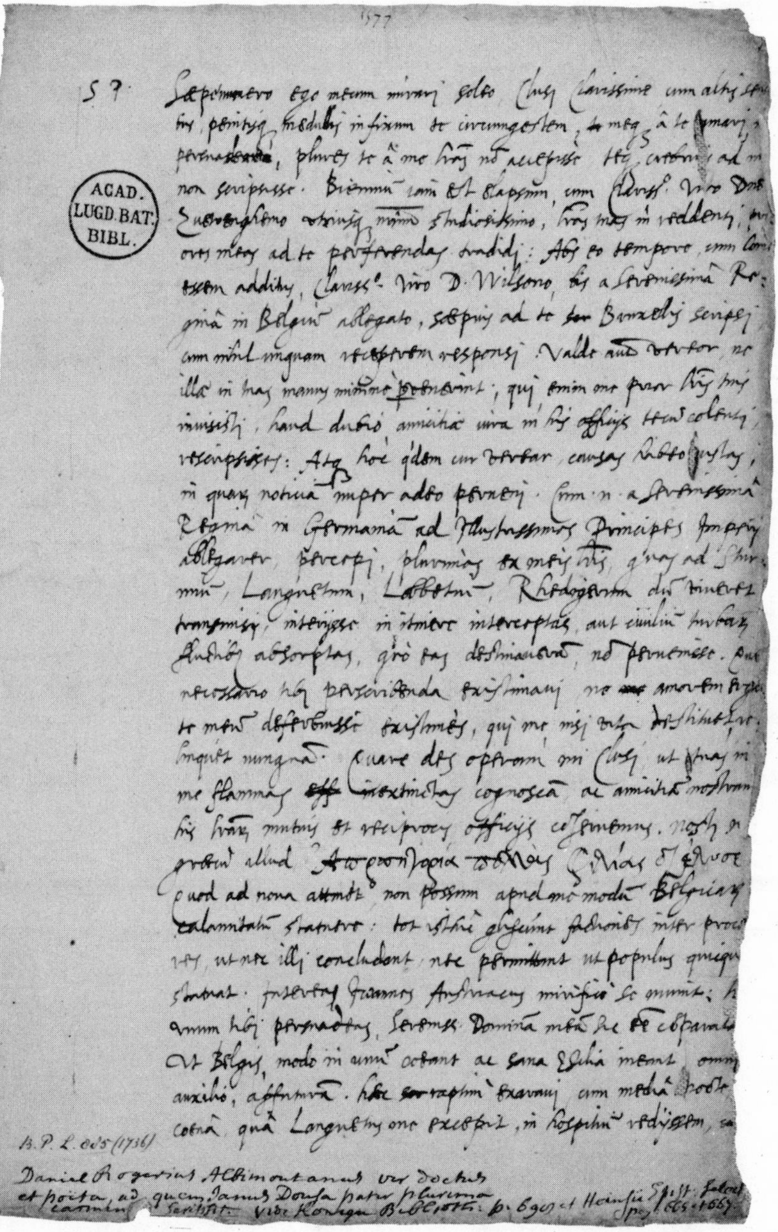

Plate 14. Leiden, Universiteitsbibliotheek, **BPL 885 Daniel Rogerius**, f. 1, 320 ×
200 mm (275 × 150 mm), 1577. The hand of Rogers; cf. with Plate 12 (Ch. 5).
[By permission]

adiectis etiam petulantibus verbis, sic diuidere cum
fratre nolito. *   *   veniebamus in forum deficiente
iam die, in quo notauimus frequentiam rerum uenaliū,
non quidem preciosarum: sed tamen quarum fidem
malo ambulantem obscuritas temporis male tegeret.
Cum ergo et ipsi raptum latrocinio pallium detulissemus,
uti occasione opportunissima cepimus, atq; in quodam
angulo laciniam extremam concutere, si quem forte
emtorem splendor uestis posset adducere. Nec diu
moratus rusticus quidam familiaris oculis tuis cum
muliercula comite propius accessit. ac diligentius
considerare pallium cepit. Inuicem Ascyltos iniecit
contemplationem super humeros rustici emtoris. ac
subito exanimatus conticuit. ac nec sine ipse quidem
sine aliquo metu hominem conspexi. Nam mihi
videbatur ille mihi esse, qui tuniculam in solitudine
inuenerat. Plane is ipse erat. Sed cum Ascyltos
timeret fidem oculorum, ne quid temere faceret, prius,
tanq; emtor propius accessit, detraxitq; humeris
laciniam, et diligentius tenuit. o lusum Fortunae
mirabilem. Nam adhuc nec futura quidem attulerat
rusticus curiosas manus. Sed tanq; mendici spolium
etiam fastidiose uenditabat. Ascytos postq; depositum
esse inuiolatum uidit, et personam uendentis contemtam,
seduxit me paululum a turba: et, scis, inquit, frater,
rediisse ad nos thesaurum, de quo querebar? illa est
tunicula adhuc, ut apparet, intactis aureis plena. quid
ergo facimus? aut quo iure rem nostram uindicamus?
  *   *   * exhilaratus ego non tantum, quia praeda
videbam, sed etiam quod fortuna mea a turpissima
suspitione dimiserat; negaui circuitu agendum: sed
plane iure ciuili dimicandum: ut, si nollet alienam rem
dño reddere, ad interdictum ueniret.

DESVNT·

facillime

M.

teneris. mis

cuius

fortuna, scelera

1. sub tui

DESVNT·

Plate 15. Leiden, Universiteitsbibliotheek, **Scaligeranus 61**, f. 6v, 180 × 135 mm
(160 × 100 mm), c. 1571, = **1**, c. 11.4–14.1. The hand of Scaliger, showing
marginal conjectures and asterisks (Ch. 6). [By permission]

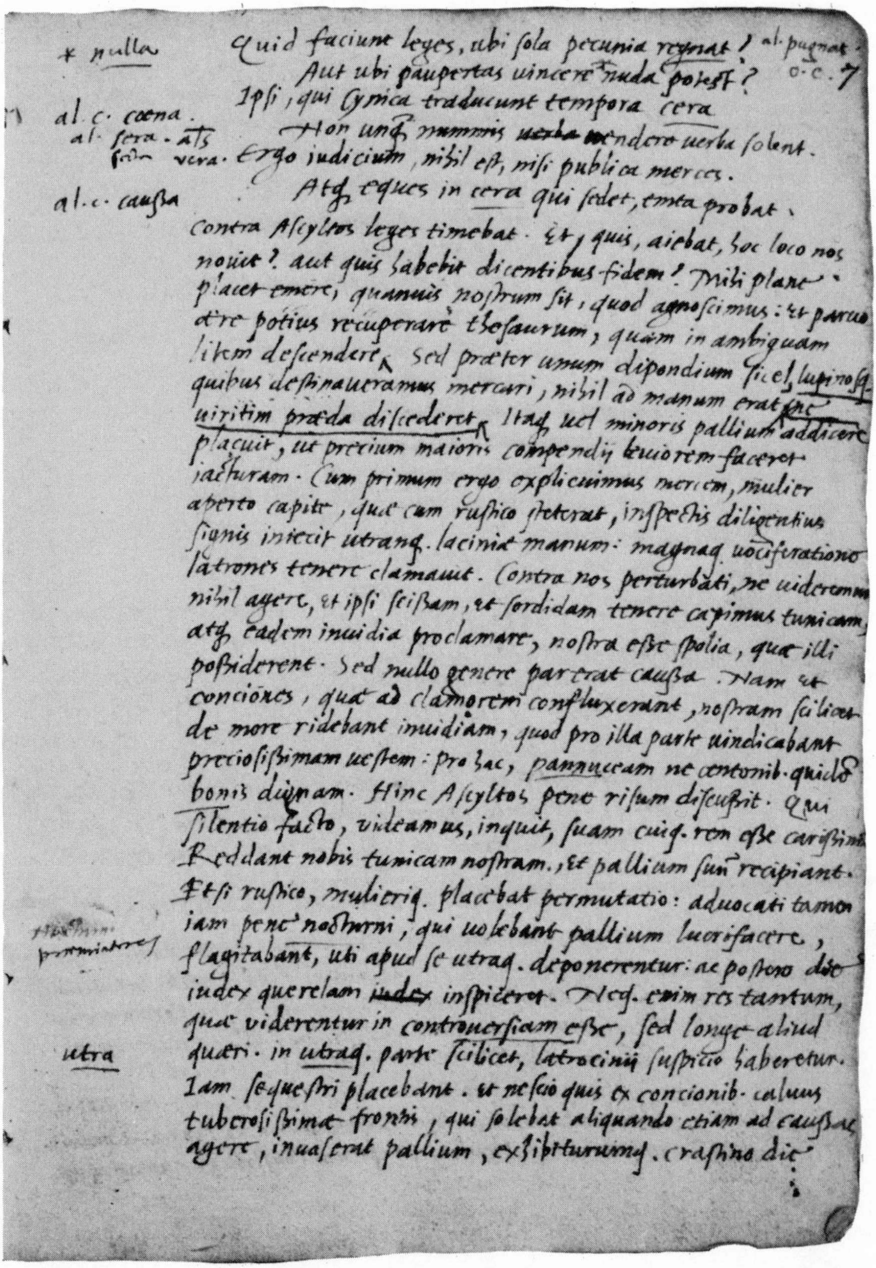

Quid faciunt leges, ubi sola pecunia regnat?   al. pugnat.
Aut ubi paupertas uincere nulla potest?   o.c. 7

al. c. coena.
al. sera. ats
fecit vera.

Ipsi, qui Cynica traducunt tempora coena
Non unquam nummis uerba uendere uerba solent.
Ergo iudicium, nihil est, nisi publica merces.

al. c. caussa

Atque eques in cera qui sedet, empta probat.
Contra Ascyltos leges timebat. Et, quis, aiebat, hoc loco nos
nouit? aut quis habebit dicentibus fidem? Mihi plane
placet emere, quamuis nostrum sit, quod agnoscimus: et paruo
aere potius recuperare thesaurum, quam in ambiguam
litem descendere, sed praeter unum dipondium sicel, lupinosq
quibus destinaueramus mercari, nihil ad manum erat ne
uiritim praeda discederet. Itaq, uel minoris pallium addicere
placuit, ut precium maioris compendij breuiorem faceret
iacturam. Cum primum ergo expliciimus mercem, mulier
aperto capite, quae cum rustico steterat, inspectis diligentius
signis iniecit utranq. laciniae manum: magnaq uociferatione
latrones tenere clamauit. Contra nos perturbati, ne uideremur
nihil agere, et ipsi scissam, et sordidam tenere coepimus tunicam,
atq eadem inuidia proclamare, nostra esse spolia, quae illi
possiderent. Sed nullo genere par erat caussa. Nam et
conciones, quae ad clamorem confluxerant, nostram scilicet
de more ridebant inuidiam, quod pro illa parte uindicabant
preciosissimam uestem: pro hac, pannuceam ne centonib. quidé
bonis dignam. Hinc Ascyltos pene risum discussit. Qui
silentio facto, uideamus, inquit, suam cuiq. rem esse carissim
Reddant nobis tunicam nostram, et pallium suum recipiant.
Etsi rustico, mulieriq. placebat permutatio: aduocati tamen
iam pene nocturni, qui uolebant pallium lucrifacere,
flagitabant, uti apud se utraq. deponerentur: ac postero die
iudex querelam index inspiceret. Neq. enim res tantum,
quae uiderentur in controuersiam esse, sed longe aliud
quaeri. in utraq. parte scilicet, latrocinij suspitio haberetur.
Iam sequestri placebant. et nescio quis ex concionib. caluus
tuberosissima fronti, qui solebat aliquando etiam ad caussae
agere, inuaserat pallium, exhibiturumq. crastino die

Plate 16. Leiden, Universiteitsbibliotheek, **Scaligeranus 61**, f. 7, 180 × 135 mm
(170 × 100 mm), c. 1571, = l, c. 14.2.1–15.4. The hand of Scaliger, showing
marginal conjectures and methods of MS attribution. (Ch. 6). [By permission]

Reading and Variant in Petronius

INTRODUCTION

The entry on Petronius by M.D. Reeve offers both a starting point and a useful focus for this new set of investigations, and the projected multi-volume *Satyrica* edition of C. Pellegrino, of which the first volume has appeared, is a further stimulus.[1] Among the merits of Reeve's article are crisp decisions on the controversies and a delineation of the most promising areas for further progress. Yet there is a tension between soundness and brevity, and want of data makes the positions taken difficult to evaluate – this on controversies that have swirled back and forth for a century and more.[2]

Pellegrino's intended contribution, promising to extend well into this decade, is of a different order, for, in providing a new consideration of the textual history, and what looks like the fullest apparatus possible, he bids fair to replace Bücheler.[3] Here too much will remain at issue, even as Pellegrino himself reinterprets the evidence used by K. Müller and other predecessors and develops his own.

For as we reassemble and re-evaluate the foundations of our modern Petronius text we are confronted by one problem of peculiar and overriding difficulty: the need to select readings not from manuscripts but from sixteenth-century, i.e. secondary, sources – usually editions. Some of these sources have been given the status of manuscripts, while others may cite a manuscript for their reading or a variant; but the fact remains that second-hand citation is a far cry from the verifiable medieval manuscript, and by modern standards these are edition prototypes. Silent scholarly interventions, printing errors, poor citation practices, and inconsistencies all have to be weighed before we can be sure that it is transmitted readings in rival or even identical sources that we are comparing.

This volume assumes the task of evaluating, afresh and in far more detail than previous editors have granted themselves, the performance of the sixteenth-century French humanists and the source puzzles that they have left in their editions and commentaries. My perspective has been both codicological (in the sense of tracing aspects of a manuscript's physical history) and palaeographic, and I think the complementary approach has produced results; but I concern myself only with the evidence found in the material under review: that part (the major part) of the text and apparatus which I should be seeking to improve and rationalize is not concerned with the rich subsequent history of conjectural emendation on many of the points of detail, since it is medieval sources and not the archetype which one intends to re-create, although one hopes that they are usually the same. Further, conjectural readings, even if successful, have little part to play in settling the relation of the *L sources, an important task of this set of studies. I have thus sought to establish the best manuscript authority for the text from that group which has been called the L class, with the clearest view possible in the apparatus of affiliations and rejected variants.

[margin note: autograph]

The volume is thus intended as a prolegomenon to a critical edition using these data and principles. I foresee an apparatus less bulky in its use of symbols than that of Müller and now Pellegrino, since one must be emboldened to forsake the largely duplicating evidence of occurrence in this and that sixteenth-century source – as irrelevant to tradition – for only the originating source. This requires a careful review of the chronology of the sources and of the lines of borrowing, which I now address. In return for this 'streamlining' I should offer a larger number of readings and variants for consideration. The evidence has, in most of the following studies, been from the sixteenth century and long available. One can hope for discovery, still, of a medieval manuscript used by these scholars, but in the mean time such evidence, new conclusions, and the advances made in linked traditions and fields are the best basis for the Petronius text.[4]

Another consequence of the difficulty of the tradition has been the tendency to force the pace of knowledge with speculation and inference. The road to Petronius is paved with confident speculation (and there will be some fresh stones here), and even the reasoning of so great a scholar in the field as Ullman has had to be abandoned more than once, as he himself predicted that it would.[5] There are many examples, as we shall see, of scholars borrowing the faulty arguments of predecessors and building upon them. Hence the need for treating earlier conclusions, usually based on selected data interpreted in a single way, with caution and reassessing their basis.

The subject of this volume, then, though not treated exhaustively, is the use and misuse by sixteenth-century editors and scholars of their Petronius manuscript sources. My selection of the material in the individual chapters was guided by my own interest in bringing to bear new codicological and text-historical researches upon many of the textual controversies that haunt modern editions, generating new pedigrees for some readings while showing reasons for disinheriting others. I include below a chapter-by-chapter summary of content and conclusions.

Chapter 1 recounts the historical considerations in uniting **m** with its first owner, Muret, then describes, dates, and associates the text in relation to its L-class siblings and **s**. As appropriate for the first chapter, there is introductory information on the recovery of this tradition as a whole, and a justification for renaming it the *L class. I commence the debates on the number of *L-class manuscripts, on the **Dalecampianus/Cuiacianus** mix in **t** and on the reliability of the **t** readings as a **Benedictinus** indicator, showing **m**'s role, and contrasting these with **t**^{v} and the **Cuiacianus** branch. I conclude that **Dalecampianus** is a sibling of **m** (not a great-uncle).

Chapter 2 continues with a central problem: the sources of de Tournes' edition and the reliability of the depiction of them, using the information supplied in the preface of **t**. I offer further remarks on calculating the number of available manuscripts, centering on the attestations of **Memmianus**, before reviewing the Pithou citations in the margin of **t**. Conclusion (at variance with Pellegrino): conjectures of Pithou supplied on the eve of that scholar's first edition. I treat the meaning of citation conventions like *v.c.* and *al.* (exclusivity, specificity) and review the special problem of the *v.c.* citations in the margins of **t**'s account of the *Bellum Civile*, with their indications of a disturbed order (conclusion at variance with Pellegrino), and possible association with **Cuiacianus.**

Chapter 3 addresses the three specific sources named by Pierre Pithou for his two editions, *Aut.*, *Bit.*, and *Thol.*, and their relation to extant and non-extant manuscripts; and the now-familiar generic citations like *vet.* and *al.* I conclude (against Pellegrino) that *Aut.* is assuredly **B** and (against Müller) that *Bit.* is **P**, on the basis of new codicological findings which support the evidence of palaeography and contemporary scholarly practice and ability. I list the differences in the **p**^{1} and **p**^{2} *varietates* for clues to consistency in citation practice. Conclusion: the same manuscript may be cited in different ways; terms like *vet.* and *al.* may couch **Tholosanus** or **Autissiodurensis** readings, and, a fortiori, will not apply exclusively to any one manuscript. Ullman's equation of **Tholosanus** with **Cuiacianus** (readings of which are overwhelmingly scorned by Pithou) is supported, despite some contrary evidence in Scaliger's **l**, which may be reconciled by the important notion that Scaliger had access to **t** readings (if not to the actual edition) of the **Benedictinus** group for his handwritten edition.

Chapter 4 presents the Petronius citations in the margins of **Bernensis**

276, a glossary manuscript once owned by Pierre Daniel, and equates this manuscript with one used by Daniel for the same citations in his Petronius commentary and designated the *Glossarium S. Dionysii*. This points to the Abbey of St. Denis as the manuscript's prior possessor. Evidence for use in the same commentary of another glossary manuscript, **Harleianus 2735**, is reviewed. The data supplied by the marginalia of **Bernensis 276** is too skimpy for an exact match with the tradition; however, it points to more than one source being used: an **O**-style manuscript and a lexical collection. Use of an ***L** or **Cena** manuscript, or Λ, is not likely.

Chapter 5 presents the complete photographed text, with a transcript and appraisal, of **d**, an ***L** manuscript of only the initial 15 chapters of the *Satyrica*, personally copied by Pierre Daniel into the back of a contemporary edition of Cicero by Muret. **d** is a largely faithful, unedited rendition of **Memmianus**, and an example of that rush of scholarly activity on Petronius in the 1560s. The relation of **d** to a manuscript, formerly belonging to Cujas, used in the same period by the scribe of **r** for collation, is strong: **d** is probably a copy (possibly a sibling), thus reflecting **Memmianus** at one remove.

Chapter 6 demonstrates the ability of a second, older copy of the *Notae* of François Daniel – that written into **r** after the text in about 1570 (the first known published by Goldast in 1610) – to generate textual information and knowledge of current scholarly practices and limitations; this from direct comparison of independent palaeographic efforts of two contemporary scholars (with implications for the reliability of **r**) and consideration of the role of the misprint in conveying false manuscript information. Collation of the two texts provides a reliable basis for examining the varied sources used by Daniel for his *Notae*. An acceptable minimum would be **c**, **P**, and **Cuiacianus.**

Chapter 7 is a description of **r**. Discussed are: sources and character; the scribe (not Rogers); the main margin user (Rogers, not van der Does); relation to r^m, r^{comm} and the *fragmentum veteris libri Cuiacii*; and role in assisting with the stemma of the so-called **L** texts. I conclude (against Müller) that the text of **r** may not be 'contaminated' and that its peculiarities are due, rather, to the copying defects of a mediocre scholar.

Chapter 8 shows that Pierre Dupuy collated his copy of p^2 against a *v.c.* which is almost certainly the Leiden fragment of **B.** Evidence points to this occurring in about 1604. The dismemberment to which this attests, I argue, may have everything to do with the death of its owner, Pierre Daniel, in the same year, and a division among the heirs.

It may be remarked that Scaliger and **l** still do not obtain their due. It is true that I do not offer a complete collation of **1** (along with a dissection of all of **Scaligeranus 61**), the only thorough way to start, for it would unbalance a prolegomenon. The indexes will confirm Scaliger's presence and role as a leading player in this textual history, and there are some new points on him to be made.

Marc-Antoine Muret and **m**

The significant part that **Vaticanus Lat. 11428** (= **m**), a sixteenth-century paper manuscript, plays in the all-important reconstruction of the so-called **L** manuscript readings, was demonstrated in Müller 1961, though a good deal remained to be found out. The existence of **m** and its stemmatic allegiance had in fact been known somewhat earlier, for it seems to have been turned up shortly after 1930 by Ullman, who passed notes and a collation of it on to Sage. Sage and his pupil Dorothy Fulmer believed that it was the source indicated in the preface of de Tournes' edition (= **t**) under the name of *Fragmenta*. This inference was accepted recently by Rose 1967; if true, it would join **Dalecampianus** as a second **Benedictinus** descendant for the production of the text of **t**.[6]

In 1937 Rini gave the first published account, and some 20 years later it was in a new volume of the *Codices Vaticani Latini*.[7] Müller 1961 then took it up, and established that it, together with manuscripts **d** and **r**, was copied from the non-extant **Codex Memmianus**, up to then known to the editors mainly from the *Adversaria* of Adrien Turnèbe, published in 1564. Müller could also demonstrate that **m** was unfortunately not a pure copy, for its readings in passages shared by the **O** class were a conflation of **LO** sources, with the latter provided from the Sámboki edition (= **s**) of 1565.[8]

Yet some questions pertinent to a proper evaluation of **m** remain. Where did the manuscript come from? Who wrote it? Why does it terminate at c. 80.9 with only about one-quarter of the **L** text transcribed? What affiliations would a fuller collation of **m** reveal? Was **m** known to the French editors? Finally, what role is **m** able to play in revealing the true character of its predecessors, the **Memmianus** and the **Benedictinus**, and hence the so-called **L** class?

m resides presently among the more than 50 Vatican **Latini** manuscripts between **11415** and **11604** that were once the property of the Franco-Italian humanist Marc-Antoine Muret, scholar and educator, born in France but residing in Italy from 1554 until his death in 1585. The manuscripts were acquired in 1912 '*dono Pio X*' as the most prized remnant of the Muret collection that had been willed to the Collegio Romano, the Jesuit university, by Muret's nephew and heir in the late sixteenth century.[9] The library of Muret was rich also in printed books, of which many had passed into the Vatican perhaps rather earlier, in the 1870s, when the Collegio Romano lost its charter in the drive to secularize. Others are to be found today in the Biblioteca Nazionale Centrale Vittorio Emanuele II, Rome.

The library awaits the bibliographer's reconstruction.[10] No catalogue dating to Muret's lifetime is known, though in **Lat. 11562** we do possess a catalogue '*Bibliothecae Mureti*' of printed books first drawn up shortly after his death and added to steadily by subsequent hands until about 1720. It is thus an enigmatic source for determining the holdings of Muret. Ruysschaert's 1959 comparison of the original core list with a number of titles to be found in the Vatican today leads him to state that some were never owned by Muret but came from other quarters, while other works added to the list in the eighteenth century indeed belonged to Muret. His inference is that the designation '*ex bibliotheca Mureti*' was applied to a collection in the Collegio Romano assembled in honour of Muret.[11]

No list of the manuscripts owned by Muret – which he did not sign – has been found. The collection pieced together by Ruysschaert seems a respectable remnant, though no doubt there were others that have gone. Thus in **m** we have one of the fortunate survivors; Ruysschaert has no hesitation in making Muret a former possessor on the basis not of the designation '*catal[ogo] inscr[iptus] ex Bibl[iotheca] Mureti*' at the top of folio 1, but of a few marginal notations deemed by him to be in Muret's hand.[12]

The date of the manuscript may be approached in two ways. Its readings, as noted, are on occasion shared by **s** alone (see below), which conveniently sets the date of writing to 1565 or thereafter; and it contains marginalia in the hand of the scribe taken from the *Adversaria* of Turnèbe, which appeared in 1564. Thus, though we cannot fix the precise year (any between 1565 and 1585 would in fact be possible), there is an effective double *terminus post quem*, and likelihood decreases with distance from that date.[13]

Confronted by the obvious superiority of the **L** texts, it is hard for us today to appreciate the influence of **s** and the advantage it presented as a collating copy over an actual manuscript such as the **Memmianus**, despite the latter's inclusion of brand-new material from the **L** class. But both in **m** and in **l**, the handwritten edition of Scaliger, we see not infrequently, to our indignation, a genuine medieval reading displaced by one that we know today to come from a very inferior Renaissance archetype, or perhaps even from a conjecture.[14]

Yet in order to understand the sixteenth-century editors and their texts better we must be fair and realistic. The French scholars of the day, apparently unaware of the two earliest Italian editions, **a** and **b**, had been brought up on the Paris edition of 1520, **c**. By the rapidly improving standards of the time this was an unimpressive edition. We know it as a reproduction of the earlier ones with corrections and new mistakes, and of course handicapped by the poor quality of the Renaissance manuscript source, which ironically was the worst of the 15 such manuscripts known today.[15] The humanist editors could regard **s** as a great improvement. Not only was there some new text, brought about by the use of a better Renaissance manuscript approaching a 'complete' **O** version, but Sámboki's listing of his sources and use of the margins made it modern and 'raisonné.'

Yet from our perspective the text is obsolescent. Although no edition expanded by the inclusion of exclusive **L** material was to appear for another 10 years, citations from these sources (as, again, we now know) had been leaking out in the works of Cujas, Turnèbe, and Lambin, since 1561, and we are already looking ahead.[16] It may be that the subject matter of the new material from the **L** manuscripts, presenting a not altogether welcome added dimension to the scholar's acquaintance with Petronius, was responsible for the 15-year delay before publication of the full edition.

It was de Tournes who took the plunge in 1575 with **t**, yet inhibitions two years later were still strong enough to cause Pierre Pithou to preserve official anonymity as editor of his first edition (= **p¹**), with a result so confusing to posterity (if not to his contemporaries) that his compendious biographer Grosley was unaware of a Pithou Petronius edition before the second one of 1587 (= **p²**).[17] Of course no difficulties of this sort could attend the publication of **s**, and so it held on to its primacy in the brief period from 1565 to 1575, with familiar consequences for the text of Petronius. For it should not escape us that it was exactly during this decade that, in all probability, were composed both **m** (post-1565) and **l** (around 1571). An exception to the use of **s** at this time is **Lambethanus 693** (= **r**): evidently the scribe intended, in the main, not an edition but a close rendering of his exemplar.[18]

We should start with a test of the influence of **s** on **m**. In the portions of **m** which offer text communicated by the **O** class, the source for **m**'s readings, we remember, could be both **c** and **s**, and there are, as we would expect, many readings shared by these editions but differing from other sources. Naturally these have no value for determining **s** influence. However, other readings shared by **s** and **m** appear in no other source and some seem quite definitive. In these cases the scribe seems either to have 'corrected' his **L** manuscript on **s**, or else his eye remained too long on **s** as he constructed his text:

UNIQUE ms AGREEMENTS IN ERROR

1.3   *papavere et sesamo*] *papavere et sampsucho* **ms**
6.1   *Ascylti*] *Ascyltae* **ms**
6.2   *Ascylton*] *Ascyltan* **ms**
8.3   *per anfractus*] <u>*om.*</u> **ms**
17.9   *faciatis*] *referatis* **ms**
18.6.4 *abire*] *obire* **ms**

The above is sufficient to demonstrate the role of **s** in the composition of **m** and set a date of 1565 or later. We arrive at the same *terminus post quem* via marginalia in **m** in the scribe's hand assigned to Turnèbe (see Plate 9). Some appear, similarly acknowledged in **t**^{margine}.

INFLUENCE OF TURNÈBE'S Adversaria

4.5   *Lucilianae*] *Lucinianae* **Memmianus m**: *Lucillianae 'Tur.'* **m**^{margine}
5.1.2   *mores*] *more* **m**: *morem 'Turn.'* **m**^{margine}: *merae*
5.1.3   *poliat*] *polleat* **m**: *pellat 'idem.'* **m**^{margine}
5.1.5   *impotentium*] <u>*sic*</u> **m**: *ne potentium 'Tur.'* **m**^{margine}
5.1.8   *histrionis*] *histriones* **m**: *histrionis 'Tur.'* **m**^{margine}
21.2   *ballaenaciam*] *balenatiam* **m**: *balenatam 'Tur.'* **m**^{margine}: *Kalenatiam* **m**^c

These variants appear to be emendations by Turnèbe of the manuscript before him, **Memmianus**. One concludes that **m** was made probably in the late 1560s and almost certainly in France (see below). Muret's ownership (cf. Ruysschaert) and use are evinced by the following corrections:

THE HAND OF MURET

4.2   *induunt*] *indunt* **m**: *induunt* **m**^{margine}
22.6   *Tricliniarches*] *Tricliniarchis* **m**: *Tricliniarches* **m**^{margine}
80.6   *deliberavit*] *liberavit* **m**: *deliberavit* **m**^{margine}

While these appear to be obvious corrections to scribal inaccuracies needing to boast no attribution, a further intervention by a hand other than the scribe's, at 3.2 *nimium: minimum 'Mur.'*, carries an evident reference to its source, Muret (see Plate 9). This is the hand of Muret the scholar staking a claim more formally to an interesting emendation.

During the late 1560s Muret was no longer in France, having left under a cloud in 1554 for what was to prove permanent domicile in Italy. However, he did return to his native country for most of the years 1561 to 1563 in the diplomatic entourage of Cardinal Ippolito d'Este, his Roman patron and protector. Muret spent much of his time in those extremely significant years for Petronian scholarship haunting Paris bookshops and libraries, patching up old academic quarrels, and renewing an especial friendship with Turnèbe.[19]

These years are of course too early for the composition of **m**, yet it would be unlikely that the two scholars did not discuss the new Petronius manuscript of de Mesmes and the current Petronius activities of acquaintances like Cujas and Pierre Daniel. It was even physically possible, then, for Muret to have acquired a transcript of the **Memmianus** (as, evidently, Daniel had for the production of **d**), which could have formed the basis for the writing of **m** a couple of years later. The paper, as we have seen, was manufactured in France, but there is no way of telling whether it was imported into Italy blank or copied in France in 1565 or so and then brought south.

Whatever the case, **m** is to my mind quite definitely not in Muret's own hand, of which we have many good specimens in a variety of sources and locations: original drafts of later-published speeches and correspondence (**Vaticanus Lat. 11591, 11593**), original correspondence in collections in Rome and elsewhere, and a host of annotations in printed editions of Latin authors, either his own or belonging to him.[20] Of particular interest in the Petronian connection are the annotations in what looks to be Muret's own copy of a **c**, very likely the book listed in the catalogue, **Vaticanus Lat. 11562** f. 66. These are in a bewildering variety of pens and styles, and no doubt moods, presenting an untidy picture, and could quite easily give the impression of being in different hands. I think, rather, that they are Muret's over the years, from the scribblings of the schoolboy to the settled reflections of the mature scholar.[21]

There is surprisingly little other hard evidence to tie Muret to Petronius. It seems that this prolific, tireless speechifier on behalf of the classical curriculum held no special brief for our author in his expanded guise. I have not found anything in print of Muret even acknowledging the *Satyrica*'s existence. Thus **c** and **m** give the concrete sum of Muret's proveable association. One may speculate on the extent to which his troubles as a young man, given their particular nature in charges of debauchery and homosexuality, prompted a lifetime of circumspection, an eschewing of any formal connection with Petronius which could be taken by his enemies for advocacy. We know that Pierre Pithou had to satisfy public opinion with a sort of disclaimer on the new **L** material and an intention to keep it under lock and key.[22]

One must, however, account for the mention in the *Notae* of Pierre Daniel, printed in Goldast 1610, of Muret's possession of an old Petronius manuscript from which he was said to be preparing an exhaustive edition.[23] Apparently Mentel suggested that this was the Trogir fragment (= **Parisinus lat. 7989, AH**);[24] but if there is anything behind the rumour, it might relate to a garbling of Muret's connection with **Memmianus**, or possibly even to his possession of **m**. Another possibility is that Petronius was confused with a different author. There is certainly no trace of a Petronius edition by Muret and no further mention of a Petronius manuscript or connection, to my knowledge; but such was Muret's prestige as a scholar that Goldast, and de Juges and Burman after him in their reprints, had no scruple in trumpeting 'unpublished' *Mureti Annotationes* in his *Index Interpretum* to the 1610 edition. One seeks in vain for this promise, finding in possible fulfilment only a few citations of '*Muret*' in the *Symbolae Georgii Erhardi* attached to glosses of words that may have come from Petronius.[25]

Thus we return to **m** and Muret's copy of **c** for evidence of Muret's scholarly connection with Petronius, an unofficial one, but not before taking stock of an interesting association with a future giant of Petronian scholarship. Joseph Scaliger, an admirer of Muret's latinity and almost brother to him, as Muret says, because of the filial light in which Jules-César viewed him, saw much of Muret while on a visit to Rome in 1565–6.[26] Again, the time-frame is a perfect fit, and while I have no direct evidence of it yet among the correspondence of either Muret or Scaliger one might consider that the two Latinists discussed Petronius; indeed, it is now possible for Scaliger to have brought **m** from Paris with him.[27] The meeting was not in all respects a success. Scaliger took an impertinent view of Muret's *embonpoint*, and Muret later was to let down some of the younger man's self-esteem with a good jape.[28]

To return to the manuscript and its stemmatic context: **m** is one of four surviving manuscripts which, together with the contemporary printed editions **t** and **p**, carry at least some of the Petronius text known as **L**, the long excerpts – virtually everything except a complete *Cena Trimalchionis*.[29] L is not so much a manuscript class as a designation for the content and sum of these texts, most of which are formed on a mix of readings from **O** and φ sources, as well as from 'longer' manuscripts containing additional material. As we have seen, **m** used one of the latter, **Memmianus**, plus readings from **s**, to construct its text. Clearly, such sources make a determination of the readings of longer manuscripts very difficult where the two traditions overlap. However, we are assured of good **O** readings from the survival of manuscripts of this tradition of sufficient age and worth.

The longer tradition derives from non-extant manuscripts, whose number has been estimated, from direct attribution in the humanist editors, external evidence and stemmatic extrapolation, at between three and five.[30] The very name for this manuscript class, as I have noted, causes difficulty. The usual symbol of **L** reverts to Bücheler, who is found employing the same letter to refer to Scaliger's **l**. For, as mentioned above, it was in **l** and in the printed editions **t** and **p** that Bücheler found the *summa excerptorum* of this 'class,' and he gave a position of pre-eminence to Scaliger's text in accord with its manuscript character. But, in the more than a century since, it has been established not only that '**L**' is a conflation of **O** sources and a longer manuscript by the sixteenth-century editors, but that the latter had itself been infiltrated by **O** readings earlier, in the medieval period. Therefore no pure, single-class view of common passages is furnished by '**L**,' and surely we must cease using it with two or even three conflicting meanings: to designate one, or two, medieval archetypes and the sixteenth-century texts which combine these with sources from **O** and φ.

One may still refer with some validity to an **L** context, but not to an **L** manuscript. In order to distinguish the readings truly carried in the non-**O** tradition, whether or not they be also in the **O** class, their manuscript class must be given a different symbol, and from this point on I propose to use *L to refer to this source. These readings are to be determined from sifting the sixteenth-century evidence and **B** (= **Bernensis 357** + **Vossianus Lat. Q. 30**), though I readily admit that contamination between *L and a coeval **O** manuscript might make this a vain prospect on occasion.

The advantage of this new symbol is that it can denote the legitimate medieval manuscript class interspersed throughout the *Satyrica* whether sharing contexts with the other classes (such as **O** and **H**) or not. If the contexts are not shared we have the unobstructed view, whereas in the other cases the actual *L readings may be revealed only intermittently, either when they are cited with differentiated readings in known *L manuscripts like **Cuiacianus**, or by a process of elimination: after the readings of the other classes have been checked and accounted for. Beyond the *L class is a shadowy core of longer tradition uncontaminated by the comparison of **O** class readings mentioned above. This purest representative of the original longer excerpt of the archetype reverting to Carolingian times shall be called Λ.[31]

In the mean time the undisguised text of *L is available where there is no coverage in other classes. Here the editors, including the scribe of **m**, were at least limited to one class, though not necessarily to one manuscript. What we see in it is a portion which is at times the most disturbed and lacunose of the *Satyrica*, suffering not only from accidental damage and deliberate abridgment, but also, apparently, from the not very successful attempt at reconstruction which is the *L archetype. Any sixteenth-century recombination of the manuscript branches available would alter the appearance of the medieval *L text in only minor ways, in my opinion. My reason is the slight difference between a largely faithful *L manuscript such as **r** (see Chapter 7) and the multi-sourced, edited editions such as **l**, **t**, and **p**.

Müller 1961 founded the *L-class archetype (and here I adapt to my symbol) on two medieval manuscripts, **Cuiacianus** and **Benedictinus**. He postulates the copying of the latter to produce β, and two copies of β – **Dalecampianus** and **Memmianus** – all in the sixteenth century (see his latest stemma, Figure 2b). None of the above survives, but it is from **Memmianus** that **m** descends directly. My review of the kinds of disagreement in the sixteenth-century sources convinces me that β may and perhaps should be eliminated. The chief reason for its presence is variance in **t** from the **Memmianus**-aligned manuscripts that may be explained in other ways.[32]

Behind all the debate over age, number and affiliation of the *L-class manuscripts is our concern with the relative reliability of **Benedictinus** and **Cuiacianus**, and their joint testimony against **O**, for the production of a modern text. It has been assumed that there is not much to choose between the two, though now Pellegrino has mounted an effort to show that they were of very differing worth.[33]

The familiar evidence concerns not **m** but **t**, but I should like to review it here for its general value. The editor of **t** commenced his work with a single *L manuscript, identified by Goldast as belonging to Jacques Dalechamps (= **Da**), but he received another after the first 67 pages or so had already gone to the printer. This second manuscript, for whose identity we are again indebted to Goldast, belonged to Jacques Cujas; and we know that it too was *L-class because **t** in a *varietas lectionum* quotes readings from it that appear in the *L passages alone. These variants conclude after page 67, since from that point on the editor chooses between two manuscripts for his *L reading and does not list the rejected alternatives, except possibly when he refers to a '*v.c.*' in the margin. These notations actually had commenced long before page 67 but in *LO passages only, and may refer here with equal likelihood to an *L or to an **O** manuscript.

It is thus the editor-printer de Tournes who provides us in the first 67 pages of his edition with a good opportunity to compare **Cuiacianus** (t^v) with the **Dalecampianus** (= approximate **Benedictinus**) readings of his text (t) and decide which may be the better branch of the *L tradition. **m** too plays a role in approaching **Benedictinus**, via **Memmianus**. On the whole, therefore, one expects a high degree of agreement in the **dmrt** readings (for the **Benedictinus**) where the separative traits of **Cuiacianus** have been identified (principally in the *variae lectiones* of t, in l, and in p^2, especially in p^{2v} s.v. '*Thol.*').[34]

Since **m** ceases at c. 80.9 and the **Cuiacianus** variants in t^v go to c. 112, it is possible to test for potential **Benedictinus-Memmianus** readings in the entire text of **m** in the exclusive *L passages. Of the 81 **Cuiacianus** variants cited by the editor of t for contrast with his readings from a variety of sources, 20 qualify by virtue of their exclusive *L context as readings putatively of **Dalecampianus**, though potential for error and emendation by the editor produces uncertainty. I have included the bracketed examples, below, in order to exhibit a few individualities, both in t and in **m**, and to show how at times these may confuse the stemmatic picture. Reading of Müller and Ehlers 1983 is underlined:

THE READINGS OF t^v AGAINST t IN THE *L CONTEXT, WITH
AGREEMENTS

9.4   *aucucurrit* t: <u>*accucurrit*</u> t^v**mlp^1**

9.10   <u>*inquam*</u> **tmp^1**: *inquit* t^v**l**

10.4   *quaestionibus* t: <u>*quaestibus*</u> t^v**lmp^1**

[10.4   *conemur* t: <u>*temptemus*</u> **mlp^1**]

12.2   *splendida* **tmp^1**: <u>*splendor*</u> t^v**l**

12.3   *considerare* **tm**, **dr^c**: <u>*diligentius considerare*</u> t^v**lp^1**,**r**

12.5   <u>*motu*</u> t: *metu* t^v**mlp^1**

13.1   <u>*suturae*</u> **tmp^1**: *furtive* t^v: *futurae* **l^{margine}** (see Plate 15)

[13.3   *igitur* **tp^1**: <u>*ergo*</u> **ml**]

[13.4   <u>*ego*</u> **tlp^1**: *ergo* **m**]

13.4   *quia non tantum* **tm**: <u>*non tantum quia*</u> t^v**lp^1**,**d**

13.4   *rem reddere* **tmp^1**: *rem* <u>*domino*</u> *reddere* t^v**lm**

20.3   *periculosum alienis interesse secretis* **tmp^1**: *p.* <u>*esse*</u> *a.* <u>*intervenire*</u> t

21.1   *huic* t: <u>*hinc*</u> t^v**mlp^1**

[21.6   <u>*inundamur*</u> **tp^1**: *inundabamur* **mr**: *mundamur* **l**]

23.2   *carmen* t: <u>*carmina*</u> t^v**mlp^1**

24.2   <u>*intellexeras*</u> **tmp^1**: *intelligis* t^v**l**

24.3   <u>*meo*</u> **tmlp^1**: *modo* t^v

27.6   <u>*illa*</u> **tm**: *ille* t^v**lp^1**

18   Reading and Variant in Petronius

[33.5   *sunt* **tlp**^{1}: *sint* **m**]
[33.8   *pinguissimam* **ltp**^{1}: *pinguissima* **m**]
33.8   *piperatio* **t**: *piperato* **t**^{v}**ml**
[35.3   *ac rienes* **ltp**^{1}: *ac riones* **m**]
35.3   *lericulam* **t**: *stericulam* **t**^{v}**lp**^{1}: *tericulam* **m**
36.3   *int culis quarum* **t**: *interculis garum* **t**^{v}**ml**: *utriculis* **p**^{1}
79.8.5   *ego* **lmp**^{1}: *ego sum* **t**^{v}**l**
79.9   *indormitavit* **t**: *indormivit* **t**^{v}**mlp**^{1}

Out of the 20 citations, 12 show **tm** differences against **Cuiacianus** (**t**^{v}). We may presume the basic reason for this to be **Cuiacianus**: **Benedictinus** divergence, for which both **t** (**Dalecampianus**) and **m** (**Memmianus**) would thus appear to be credible witnesses. Reinforcing this view is the fact that of these **tm** readings, eight, or two-thirds, agree with **Benedictinus**-derived **p**^{1}, showing that they carry the actual readings of **Benedictinus**; the other four, in differing, must evince errors (at 12.3, 13.4, 27.6, 35.3) that entered at **Memmianus** (Müller would say β; see Chapter 7 for more detail on these readings). In another eight instances, however, **m** is found to have the reading of **Cuiacianus**, parting company with **t** and seemingly contradicting the equation, to yield **t**: **t**^{v}**m**. The reliability of **t** as an *L source and of a part of Müller's stemma depends to some extent on the proper evaluation of this phenomenon. One possible reason is independent transmissional error in **t**'s source, **Dalecampianus**; another is a change or misreading in **t** itself, since the readings are wrong in all cases except one. In fact, most of the differences are consistent with a divergent palaeographic interpretation of an exemplar (9.4 *aucucurrit: accucurrit*, 21.1 *huic: hinc*, etc.). As indicated, it is hard to establish whether these entered **Dalecampianus** (for we have no other witness to its readings) or are due to de Tournes' misreading his manuscript.

Another explanation in these instances for superior readings in **m** might be scribal correction or emendation – so successful that the readings have been brought into line with the actual tradition on numerous occasions. This I would tend to discount, for there are in fact many more **t**: **m** disagreements, necessitating for this explanation an emending operation of very considerable scope together with a high degree of success, and **m** does not show other signs of individuality. We should note that Müller and Ehlers 1983 adopts 12 readings from **Cuiacianus** sources and six from witnesses to **Benedictinus**, the two remaining being emendations. Thus here at least **Cuiacianus** has the edge in *bonitas*.

In our quest to evaluate the comparative reliability of the two major **Benedictinus** sources (**Dalecampianus** and **Memmianus**) we are obliged to list **t**: **m** divergences, again in areas where we may be fully confident that the influence of an **O** manuscript or text has not intervened:

READINGS OF **m** AGAINST **t** IN THE *L CONTEXT, WITH
AGREEMENTS

27.2   *paterfamilias* **t**: _paterfamiliae_ **mlp¹**

27.2   *sparsiva* **t**: *sparcina* **m**: *sparsina* **lp¹**: _prasina_

27.2   *eam amplius* **tlp¹**: *etiam amplius* **mr**: _amplius eam_

30.3   _bilychnis_ **tlp¹**: *bilignis* **m**: ισως *bilychnis* **m**ᵐᵃʳᵍⁱⁿᵉ

31.2   _gratia_ **tlp¹**: *gratiam* **ml**

31.3   _nivatam_ **tlp¹**: *innatam* **m**

31.8   _novo more_ **tlp¹**: *novo morae* **m** [?]

31.9   _Corinthius_ **tlp¹**: *Corinthus* **m**

31.11   *trimatula* **t**: *turnatula* **m**: *tumatula* **l**: _tomacula_ **l**ᵐᵃʳᵍⁱⁿᵉ**p¹**

32.2   *pallio enim* **tlp¹**: _om._ *enim* **m**

32.2   *incluserat* **tlp¹**: *inclusus erat* **m**: _excluserat_

32.3   _stellis ferruminatum_ **tlp¹**: *stelferruminatum* **m**ᶜ

33.1   *absentius* **t**: *diutius absens* **mt**ᵐᵃʳᵍⁱⁿᵉ: *diutius absentius* **l**: *absentivus* **p¹**:
        diutius absentivus

33.1   _negavi_ **t**: *negavit* **mr**

33.2   _notavique_ **tlp¹s** ισως *notaviq.* _sic_ _s._ [s?] **m**ᵐᵃʳᵍⁱⁿᵉ: *natamque* **m**

33.3   *testarum* **t**: *testorum* **mlp¹**: _textorum_

33.5   *sunt* **tlp¹**: _sint_ **m**

33.8   _pinguissimam_ **tlp¹**: *pinguissima* **m**

33.8   *vitelio* **t**: _vitello_ **m**: *vitellio* **lp¹**

34.5   _obiter_ **tl**: *obit* **m**: *obīt* **p¹**

34.5   *ei praedissum* **t**: *per discessum* **t**ᵐᵃʳᵍⁱⁿᵉ: *p̄di sum* **m**: *p̄dissimi* **lp¹**:
        perditissimi **l**ᵐᵃʳᵍⁱⁿᵉ

35.3   *ac* _rienes_ **tlp¹**: *acriones* **m**

35.4   *lericulam* **t**: *tericulam* **m**: *stericulam* **lp¹**: _steriliculam_

35.7   _rus_ **tlp¹**: *in ius* **m**

36.1   _abstulerunt_ **tlp¹**: *abstulerant* **m**

36.3   *Marsias* **t**: *martias* **m**: _Marsyas_ **lp¹**

36.3   *int culis quarum* **t**: *interculis* _garum_ **ml**: _utriculis_ _garum_ **p¹**

37.1   _fabulas_ **tlp¹**: *tabulas* **m**

37.4   _noluisses_ **tlp¹**: *voluisses* **m**

Here we see evidence primarily of copying and not transmissional individualities in **m**. On the basis of our present knowledge there is really no other reason why **t** and **m** readings should differ substantially, since their texts depend on a **Benedictinus**-group manuscript. If differences do revert to a manuscript (and not to capricious change) they show a copying difference in **Dalecampianus** from the parent **Memmianus**, as I would posit. Yet a distinction such as at 35.3 rests on misreading part of a single letter; and so with others.

Our view of **m** would have to change substantially were it to be identified with the *Fragmenta* referred to in the preface of **t**. We have seen above that there are many **tm** differences, for various reasons: **Dalecampianus**: **Memmianus** division, unique readings in **m**, emendations and even misprints in **t**, etc. On the other hand certain unique affinities might reveal a relationship that could only point to the dependence of the one source on the other. The best evidence is adduced by the following readings:[35]

UNIQUE tm READINGS

15.8	*calumniantium* **tm**
21.5	*iamque* **tm**: *utcumque* **t**^{margine}**lp**
23.5	*sudantes* **tm**: *sudantis* **t**^{margine}
33.1	*diutius absens* **t**^{margine}**m**
33.1	*permittetis* **tm**: *permittitis* **lp**
34.5	*obit ei p̄di sum* **mr**: *obiter ei praedissum* **t**
36.3	*interculis* **m**, *int culis* **t**
55.6.15	*aequum est enim ducem* **t**, *aequum est .e. ducem* **m**

In addition, after 22.5 *coeperunt*, 28.1 *accipere*, and 36.8 *imperat* **t** prints asterisks, with the marginal caution that these were not in a *v.c.*[36] They are in the *L context only, at points where **t** is presumed to have had direct access to a single long manuscript, **Dalecampianus**; thus the inference is that the asterisks were not in it but were supplied from some other *L source. The only other qualifying manuscript source available to E.T. Sage containing asterisks was **m**. But they occur in **r** also, **m**'s sister manuscript. This demonstrates that they were in **Memmianus**, and entered into that source perhaps as conjectures, since they exist at these points nowhere else. Though this does not preclude **t** using **m**, it does add another possibility: **t** derived this information indirectly, either from a marginal variant in **Dalecampianus** or from a **Memmianus** reading communicated to the editor. This perhaps strengthens my case for **Dalecampianus** being a direct copy of **Memmianus**, hence a sibling of **m**, **d**, and **r**.

There are two more instances of **t** signalling the absence of asterisks in *L contexts: after 98.1 *tangebat* and 115.20 *mittit*. Obviously these did not come from **m** since that manuscript breaks off at 80.9, and this points to one of the other explanations for all of them.[37]

The evidence of asterisk use from all the ***L**-derived sources in the above five instances is not very conclusive: in the first three instances they are in **mrt** but not in **p¹p²l** (except for 22.5 **p²**). Their occurrence does not imply a **Benedictinus: Cuiacianus** division, but does seem to show that they were at least not in the latter, and **p²** could have obtained the exception from a printed text such as **t**.[38] The final two uses above are even harder to interpret; in the former, 98.1, an asterisk occurs in all sources except **lr**, indicating presence in **Benedictinus**, absence in **Cuiacianus**; while after 115.20 *mittit* two to four asterisks occur in every ***L**-derived source, so it is puzzling that **t** should signal their absence elsewhere. If this is reliable they can only have been dropped from or emended out of his ***L** manuscript source, **Dalecampianus**, at this point. The interim judgment on a **tm** connection on the basis of the asterisks must be *non liquet*.[39]

However, the half-dozen other associations cited above do show interesting features. To make much of 33.1 *diutius absens* **mt^margine**, occurring as it does in a crux in both **H** and ***L**, may not be sound, but the evidence is there: the reading of **lMemmianusrp** (**p** = *absentiuus*) is *diutius absentius*; **t** also has *absentius* but omits *diutius*, either through its own error or initiative or because it was not in the text of **Dalecampianus**.[40] **t^margine** proposes it in the margin, thus supplying the reading found in **m**. Whence came it into **t^margine**? **m** is certainly a possibility, but if so, **t** is not following **m** in the next line, where **t** prints *negavi* (*negant* **mr**). The marginal note *diutius absens* in **t** to me has the flavour of a gloss on *absentius*. The reading with marginalia could have been imported wholesale from **Dalecampianus**, with resemblance to **m** a coincidence. 33.1 *permittetis* is the reading of **Memmianus**, as **mr** show. If it be correct, the error in **Cuiacianus-Benedictinus** was thus made good. In 34.5 it is again **Memmianus** that supplies the **mr** reading *obit*, which is also **Benedictinus** (*'vetus Pithoei'*). *Obiter* in **t** must be a successful correction in **t** or **Dalecampianus**, since **t** did not yet have access to the **Cuiacianus** reading. The *p̄di sum: praedissum* similarity denotes possibly some local corruption in **t** and may be dismissed. In the final similarity cited, at 55.6.15 *.n. ducem* is again the **Memmianus** reading, thus the *enim ducem* of **t** is probably not due to borrowing from **m** but to differing adaptation of a common source.

I believe that the sum of the above evidence is not sufficient to deduce a unique **tm** connection. The appearance, particularly, of a number of the shared readings in **r** also tips the balance in favour of a common transmission. Admittedly, *diutius absens* is hard to account for, but one must wonder why, if **m** was available to **t** as the *Fragmentum* referred to in the listing of sources in the preface, it was not used more often.[41] I daresay that Sage, if he had seen **r**, would not have held on to the possibility. On this point Rose was simply influenced by Sage. We may conclude that the lack of

comprehensive internal evidence for a direct **tm** link is consistent with the
the external picture. The details of paper, script, ownership, and final
domicile of **m** point away from any use by de Tournes, and **m** seems to
have remained unknown except to a private circle during the sixteenth
century, and was not cited.

To be dealt with finally is the reason for **m**'s termination in mid-word
at c. 80.9.1: *nomen amicitiae sic, quate*[*nus*] ...: *si quate* **m**, yielding only a
quarter of the *L text.[42] One ready explanation is that **m**'s exemplar ended
at this point. However, **m**'s demonstrable closest ancestor, **Memmianus**,
does not seem to have been foreshortened, to judge from the other
descendant, **r**, and from the citations of it by Turnèbe; thus a curtailed
intermediary would have to be postulated. If we reject this, we must infer
that the scribe of **m** simply stopped doing the job, although the text
continued, through a constraint of time or some other occupation. This
explanation is supported by one small detail: he commenced a new page
(14v) for the single half-line of verse remaining; had he seen his exemplar
ending here he would likelier have put this half-line at the bottom of f. 14,
a page with plenty of room for it since it carries only 26 lines as against
the copying norm of 28 for continuous prose. One compares f. 6 of the
manuscript, running for 25 lines of prose before going without a line break
into the first two lines of the poem at c. 18.6 *contemni turpe est* ... The
scribe's commitment to a new page for the end of the poem implies the
presence of text in his exemplar beyond the break-off point.

If this is correct, we can only assume that **m**'s conclusion here is due to
the accidental physical separation of it from its source; time ran out and
the manuscript was delivered to its possessor, quite possibly Muret, in a
partial but evidently acceptable state. One wonders when this eventuality
is best fitted into the chronological data advanced above for date of
composition and Muret's movements. We have seen that it was post-1565,
or possibly dating to that year. It is likely, I repeat in summarizing, to
have been made in France, and then to have been brought to Italy for
Muret. Muret himself had returned from a visit to France two years earlier
and was never to go back. Could it have been copied in haste, and only
partially, to enable its inclusion in the Scaliger entourage setting out for
Rome in that very year? Both the dates and the interests of the two scholars
make this possible, though internal evidence is lacking. For example, if
Scaliger knew of this manuscript, one might consider it reasonable to turn
up traces in his own handwritten text **l**, whose composition was inspired
by seeing **Cuiacianus** in about 1571. It is of course equally likely that an
ignotus delivered the manuscript to Muret in Italy.

SUMMARY OF FINDINGS AND CONCLUSIONS

1 The text of **m** was constructed by taking the 1565 edition of Petronius (**s**) and expanding it with the new material which the scribe found in an *L manuscript, which was probably **Memmianus.** The scribe was aware of another source of **Memmianus** readings from Turnèbe, but seems only to have used that scholar's emendations, and sparingly. The copyist was not the owner, Muret.

2 Muret owned **m** and a copy of **c**, but cannot be associated strongly in formal scholarship on Petronius.

3 Use of **m** by other sixteenth-century scholars, and published evidence of a specific **m** exemplar, is very doubtful.

4 **m** is of some use in clarifying the readings of the **Benedictinus** through comparison with **t**. For **m** used **Memmianus** and **t** used **Dalecampianus**, both being **Benedictinus**-derived manuscripts. Comparison with actual **Benedictinus** readings derived from **p¹** tests the copying reliability of **t** and **m**, and the enhanced knowledge of **Benedictinus** yields a more informed decision when we are obliged to choose between readings which differ from **Cuiacianus. m** is thus useful for clarifying the distinction between transmitted readings and individualities in many of our so-called L-texts. **m** thus plays a role in testing Müller's stemma, especially on the role and interpretation of **tm** agreements and differences.

5 **m** does not seem to be a source for **t**, or vice-versa. The *L sources for both 'editions' may thus be kept distinct and are as above described. For some reason **m** discontinues with only about one-quarter of an *L text transcribed. This was probably not because of a defective exemplar. Despite excessive reliance on **s**, and hence not very useful for recovering *L readings in the *LO contexts, **m** elsewhere provides an *L text of good quality, with not many individual errors, and holding its own against **drptl**, the other exponents, some of whom combined **Benedictinus** and **Cuiacianus** knowledge and hence obscure the relative value of these two manuscripts. There may be some successful correction in **m**, but a superior text is usually due to deterioration in siblings.

6 **Dalecampianus**, the most important *L source for **t**, is copied from **Memmianus** and is hence a sibling of **m**, **d**, and **r**. The *L witness in **t** is inferior to and less reliable than **dmrDa**.

2

Jean de Tournes and **t**

The editorial practices of the scholars of the sixteenth century, producing the editions upon which we rely so heavily for our Petronius text today, are by no means fully understood. The cause of particular difficulty is the latitude they gave themselves in the use of their manuscript sources. The editors placed themselves under no obligation to cite variants on every occasion of occurrence, and when they cited their alleged origins they were inclined to be vague, in the convention of the day.[43] Furthermore, though no doubt very good Latinists, these scholars were not necessarily infallible palaeographers. Finally, we must always be on the look-out for typographical error in the editions themselves. It is not surprising, therefore, that contradictory results sometimes attend the attempts today to identify the manuscript sources of these variants, construct their relations, and make our selections from their readings for the modern text.

Despite these problems, the modern editors since Bücheler, and largely thanks to him, have been in broad agreement on most of the evidence, and on the correlation of the ascriptions with the actual manuscript sources, some of them now lost, used by de Tournes and Pithou for their printed editions, and by Scaliger for his handwritten edition (respectively, **t**, **p¹** and **p²**, and **l**). However, a new interpretation of some of the ascriptions, giving rise both to different conclusions on the use of sources by de Tournes and to a new view of the relative quality of the ***L** manuscripts, makes it necessary to examine the variants with their ascriptions more fully than has yet been done.[44]

We may at least be agreed that the sixteenth-century editors used a mix of manuscripts from three of the four classes identified today (the exception being **Cena**), either directly or through the printed representatives of that class. We may also agree that an important difficulty is created by the fact that the manuscripts of the longest class, which I am calling ***L**, do not survive; thus independent, autoptic confirmation of their readings, and verification of the editions' reliability in citing them, are usually impossible.

It was Bücheler who first reviewed the evidence for the number, character, and identity of these manuscripts, though he stopped short of investigating their interrelations.[45] Subsequent editors have eliminated **Tholosanus** from independent consideration by equating it with **Cuiacianus**. This left four (excluding β – see n. 25), until Ullman sought to restrict the number further to three: **Cuiacianus**, **Benedictinus**, and **Dalecampianus**. Yet his subsuming of **Memmianus** under **Benedictinus** (= *'vetus Pithoei'*) has been disproved by a better evaluation of **m** and the discovery of **dr** – all three deriving from a single manuscript with readings differentiated from **Benedictinus** but possessing ones attested for **Memmianus** elsewhere.[46]

In truth, Ullman was not very wide of the mark, but for a different reason than he supposed. A simple way to reconcile the references to a manuscript in the possession of both Pithou and de Mesmes, one which Pithou says he lent to de Mesmes, is to deduce that de Mesmes had Pithou's manuscript copied. This copy, then, is the **Memmianus** used and cited by our sources, not a medieval manuscript but a sixteenth-century apograph. It generated a further copy, the non-extant **Dalecampianus (Da)**, a sibling of **dmr**, which therefore dates also to the early 1560s.[47] Hence the sum of the missing ***L** manuscripts is four: two medieval and two sixteenth-century. It is by no means unlikely that they cross-referred to each others' readings and marginal variants.

THE 'PITHOU' CITATIONS IN **t**margine

My first topic in the sources of **t** is a review of the variants in the margin attributed to Pierre Pithou. As was seen in the last chapter, two manuscripts play a major role in the actual construction of the text: **Dalecampianus**, **t**'s only source for ***L** text up to about c. 112, and that manuscript together with **Cuiacianus** for the rest of it.[48] These not only added the exclusive ***L** material, but no doubt also controlled the content of the 1520 and 1565 editions (**c** and **s**) in the shared portions. This much is generally accepted. But, in addition to the above, de Tournes could apparently bring into consideration certain variants which he associates, in a way now to be decided, with Pithou. On the face of it, then, the method of attribution implies a source or sources for these variants independent of the sources listed in the preface of **t**, possibly verifiable from Pithou's own later editions. I cite the variants below, giving de Tournes' exact attributions, which are typically less than consistent:

[*LO]	4.5	*schedium* 'v.c. Pitth.'
	7.3	*titulos* 'v.c. Pit.'
[*LH]	30.1	*procurator rationes accipiebat* 'Pitth.'
	30.2	*VI viro* 'Pitth.'
	30.11	*quicquid ergo* 'Pitth.'
	36.6	*gesticulatus ita* 'Pitth.'
[*LOH]	55.6.15	*aequum est inducere* 'Pitth.'
[*L]	81.4	*venierunt* 'Pit.'
	94.15	*mimicam* 'leg. Pitth.'
	106.1	*mimicis* 'Pith. legit'
	117.2	*peram* 'Pith.'
	126.6	*mulio* 'Pith.'
	126.12	*daphnona* 'Pit.'
[*LO]	129.7	*tibicines* 'Pith.'
	133.3.12	*aura* 'Pith.'
	135.8.6	*mollis tilliae* 'Pith.'
	135.8.12	*sorba* 'Pith.'

Two of the above entries are overtly associated with a manuscript, and that belonging to Pithou; six are recorded with *Pith.*, five with *Pitth.*, two with *Pit.*, and one each with *leg. Pitth.* and *Pith. legit*.[49] Again on the face of it (and without yet testing collateral authority), unless de Tournes in **t** is being careless, misleading, or misled, we must understand two readings to be from manuscripts or a manuscript owned by Pithou and the other 15 to be conjectures by that scholar passed on to de Tournes (at a time before Pithou's own first edition was printed). I believe this to be the natural interpretation to satisfy the expectations of the day, as well as our own. Pellegrino, however, has a contrary view: he takes *Pitth.* and *Pith.* to equal *Pithoeanus*, i.e. a manuscript to be identified as the *v.c. Pithoei*; he therefore regards all the citations as manuscript variants. For him there is a consequence to this inference, that may serve as an object lesson in how scholars attempt to produce new information on the text. Mindful of the preface of **t**, where de Tournes lists among his manuscript sources **Dalecampianus** (or so we identify it), Pellegrino makes what he believes to be the inevitable assumption: *Pithoeanus* = **Dalecampianus**.[50]

Barring other considerations, the tenability of this view rests on several assumptions: one, that all the Pithou-flagged variants derive from a single source; two, that the source is a manuscript; and three, that the manuscript is cited misleadingly and differently from what one expects from the preface. This extremely indirect and ambiguous way of acknowledging the readings from the manuscript of his friend Dalechamps is advanced by de Tournes, according to Pellegrino, to declare that the **Dalecampianus** was sired by the *v.c. Pithoei* and that the readings are one and the same.[51]

There is much to take instructive issue with here, and I hope that I have interpreted Pellegrino's purport correctly. In the first place, given the consideration that the editor was using **Dalecampianus** extensively up to c. 112, and that he carried on using it, together with his second ***L** manuscript, the **Cuiacianus**, after that point, why would it have been necessary to make additional *marginal* citations of the **Dalecampianus** in the manner thus prescribed? For seven of these readings there was no other manuscript source available to de Tournes (i.e. the exclusive ***L** or ***LH** entries up to 106.1 *mimicis*), thus the readings in the *text* would then have to be conjectures. This is ruled out by independent manuscript substantiation for every one of them.[52] Actually, the reverse is more likely to be assumed by de Tournes' contemporaries as well as by us: the text-reading is manuscript-derived and the variant in the margin a conjecture by Pithou (where no '*v.c.*' is attached). Further, we should not infer from de Tournes' preface that all his readings, and particularly the marginalia, are confined to the listed manuscripts which are his major sources. To be noted, for instance, is that nine of them are said to come from a '*v.c. Br.*' or '*v.c. Brit.,*' and were evidently communicated individually by Pierre Pithou, since no qualifying manuscript is listed by de Tournes among the sources.[53]

The 17 marginal variants now under discussion must also have been secured from Pithou personally. Two of these de Tournes attributes to an actual manuscript of Pithou: there is no other evidence of an appreciation for a manuscript which Pithou certainly did not make available to him for his edition. We may now consider the affiliations of the above readings for the independent evidence bearing on the identity of the attributions.

The first two, 4.5 *schedium* and 7.3 *titulos*, occurring in the ***LO** context, are given the authority of a manuscript known to, or used by, Pithou; and indeed, the readings appear in a manuscript to which Pithou had access for his own edition of 1577 (a couple of years later), **Autissiodurensis**.[54] There is no reason, therefore, to posit another manuscript source here. 30.1 *procurator rationes* commences the readings given no manuscript attribution, and indeed, no manuscript available to de Tournes or Pithou has been found with that reading. Not the reading of any ***L** manuscript, it is no doubt a successful emendation, probably by the person to whom it has been assigned in the margin: Pithou.[55] We may argue similarly for 30.2 *VI viro* (successful emendation) and 30.11 *quicquid* (unsuccessful) – both carefully distinguished by Pithou in his own *varietas* from the readings of his own *vetus*, that is, **Benedictinus**. 36.6 *gesticulatus ita* is a successful transposition, though here Pithou prefers the reading of his *vetus* for his two editions' texts. 55.6.15 *aequum est inducere*, in that it is a reading of manuscripts available to Pithou (among them the *vetus*), is not a conjecture and is therefore cited inaccurately in t^margine. This could be the fault of either scholar, de Tournes or Pithou. With 81.4 *venierunt* we again have a unique reading in the successful conjecture, again spurned by the author of it for his manuscript's *venerunt*. At 94.15 *mimicam* and 106.1 *mimicis* Pithou emends his editions, citing the rejected readings of his *vetus*; while 117.2 *peram*, Pithou's conjecture for the *poenam* of his *vetus* which went into his first edition, supplants the manuscript authority in the second. 126.6 *mulio* has the same history but with the further interest of being the reading of Scaliger – denoting either some manuscript backing, or an informal sharing of variants.[56] 126.12 *daphnona* and 129.7 *tibicines* were unavailable in manuscripts; 133.3.12 *aura* has **Memmianus**' attestation. Yet Pithou ignores them all for his texts, and we should treat them too as conjectures.[57] Likewise 135.8.6 *mollis tilliae* is a conjecture given little credence by Pithou himself, though it finds favour with Müller and Ehlers 1983. Finally at 135.8.12 *aura* Pithou adopts his own conjecture, the reading used also by Scaliger after he first missed this verse in l and had to insert it in the margin.

With the exception of 55.6.15 all of the above examples commencing with 30.1 are grounded in Pithou-derived conjecture, verifiable from Pithou's own text, and it is thus encouraging to have confirmed the high standards of accuracy shown by de Tournes in citing in t^margine the Pithou-designated variants. The two assigned to a *v.c.* have Pithou-manuscript backing, and the rest, apart from the slip at 55.6.15, existed in no manuscript that we know of as being available to Pithou. They are, I reiterate, his conjectures. The **Dalecampianus** witness of this section of the *Satyrica* is relatively clear: it was the manuscript chosen by de Tournes for the *body* of his text. It is of course no accident that *these* readings bear a resemblance to *vetus Pithoei* (which gives the conjectural variants a contrasting interest), since **Dalecampianus** is a descendant.[58]

THE '*v.c.*,' '*al.*,' AND OTHER EVIDENT MS CITATIONS IN t^margine

In the margins of **t** there are a number of readings and other textual features that are given the authority of manuscripts – or so we have interpreted the conventional abbreviations, *v.c.* (*vetus codex*), *al.* (*alius* or *alii*, sc. *codex* or codices), *v.* (*vetus*), and *q.c.* (*quidam codex*). Of these designations the most prominent is *v.c.*, particularly since this is the term used to refer to the manuscript source from which 81 readings are cited in the list of *variae lectiones*, not in the margin but in a separate section at the end of **t** text. That manuscript has been identified, as we have seen, with the **Cuiacianus.** Are we entitled to expect that on the other occasions where *v.c.* is used it applies to the same manuscript, and thus conversely that the other terms are reserved for a different manuscript? This seems to be the crux of the problem, not only here, but in all the sixteenth-century efforts: the extent to which we may rely on any commitment to consistency. In our case now, as in others, the only way to answer the question is to gain a positive identification of the readings in both text and margins and test them against the citations for consistency.

It is perhaps no accident that the editor of **t** uses in his margins the *v.c.* designation chiefly (16 times out of 23; List A, below) to indicate the absence of words, or the presence of asterisks, in the observed manuscript or, in two cases, in his chosen text. The term *al.*, however, is used on all 12 occasions to cite a variant only (List B, below). In addition, *v.c.* is used of a manuscript which apparently transmitted the *Bellum Civile* poem in a different order of verses from that seen in the received **O** class. I shall treat this below separately and at greater length since its bearing on our view of the **L-class manuscripts might be considerable.

A

[*L]	22.5	coeperunt.*] <u>non est tamen in v.c.</u>
[*LH]	28.1	excipere*] <u>non est nota in v.c.</u>
	34.2	paropsis] etiam paropsis <u>in v.c.</u> legitur
	36.8	imperat*] <u>deest aster. in v.c.</u>
[*L]	98.1	tangebat.*] <u>deest in v.</u>
	98.9	hibernum] <u>v.</u> hiberum
[*LO]	110.8	sua memoria facta: quae expositurum] <u>v.c.</u> rem sua memoria factam expositurum
[*LOφ]	111.3	ab omnibus] <u>in v.c. deest</u> ab
	112.4	mulieris] <u>in v.c. abest</u>
	112.4	habere] <u>in v.c. abest</u>
	112.6	commodet ergo] <u>v.c.</u> commodaret modo
[*LO]	113.3	edile] <u>v.c.</u> hedile
[*L]	115.20	mittit*] <u>deest ast. in v.c.</u>
[*LO]	118.3	concipere] <u>v.c.</u> conspici
	118.6	quam poetae] <u>desunt haec duo verba in v.c.</u>

	118.6	tamquã] _v._ tamquam
	120.94	age] _deest_ age in _v.c._
	127.4	mihi] _deest_ mihi _in_ q.c
	130.6	iam] _deest_ iam
[*L]	131.7	alis] _v.c._ aliis
[*LO]	131.10	quid est] _deest_ est
[*L]	134.11	nocte] _deest_ nocte
[*LO]	135.6	spoliat] perite spo. _v.c._ pariter.

Leaving aside the asterisks for the present, let us evaluate the _v.c._ citations on word omissions and other variants. For identification purposes the portion of the text in which these occur takes on relevance. If we may take the term as the broad, rather neutral designation for any manuscript source, in specific distinction to a printed edition or a scholarly conjecture – the equivalent of 'manuscript' and nothing more – we infer from **t**'s preface that the available options, in the relevant segments of text, are **Cuiacianus**, **Dalecampianus** and a florilegium; I presume the latter to be couched in '_cetera, fragmenta._'[59] Thus in the text peculiar to ***L** there would seem to be only the two first-named manuscripts. However, in the ***LO** portions, where it can be demonstrated that **t** has leaned heavily on **s**, we must keep open the possibility that _v.c._ applies also to **O** manuscript readings attested by Sámboki, seen and quoted by de Tournes at second hand. Other **O** manuscript variants available to de Tournes are **Bituricus** citations, apparently borrowed from the owner of the manuscript, Pierre Pithou – or so we interpret the designations '_Br._' and '_Brit._' in the margins of **t** (see Chapter 2, n. 53). Hence, where **s** text exists, there are increased options for the meaning of _v.c._, with attendant difficulty in keeping the manuscripts apart.

In our list there are four non-asterisk _v.c._ citations in passages peculiar to ***L**: a word missing at 134.11, a word extra at 34.2, and two single-letter variants at 98.9 and 131.7. 131.7 and 134.11 occur after the point where we can expect the readings of **Cuiacianus** and **Dalecampianus** to have been mixed into the text and could theoretically be taken from either; while 34.2 and 98.9 should come from the only manuscript available, **Dalecampianus**. Thus we infer that the _v.c._ designation given to these variants that appear in the margin, and not the text, stands for **Dalecampianus**, here deficient enough, in the opinion of the editor, to be replaced in the text by what must only be successful conjectural emendations. In corroboration of a sort, there is no word in Pithou's or Scaliger's editions on these, an indication that they were not the reading of **Benedictinus** or **Cuiacianus**, while the former, Pithou's _vetus_, a manuscript which we know to be the forerunner of **Dalecampianus**, carries at 98.9 *hiberum* also. For his part, Scaliger writes *hiberum* in the text but then corrects to *hibernum* – no doubt a post-1575 addition dependent on **t**. This would seem to indicate that *hiberum* was also in **Cuiacianus** and is thus the *L representative.

If the readings at 131.7 and 134.11 are also conjectures, then the *v.c.* variants are now capable of standing for **Cuiacianus** or **Dalecampianus** readings. The former, *aliis*, is given by Pithou in his own *varietas* as the reading of *al.*, probably **Benedictinus**, now that **t** attests it as a manuscript variant. Here the editors print an erroneous conjecture; **t**'s source cannot be confirmed since *aliis* was likely the reading of *L.

The case at 134.11 *mecum nocte dormiat*, where *nocte* is attested as an omission in a manuscript (or so we must infer, though the actual *v.c.* designation is not used), offers these possibilities: it is the conjecture of de Tournes, absent in both his manuscript sources; or else it is the reading of one manuscript but not the other. Pithou's use of the word points to its presence in **Benedictinus** (though conceivably he could have lifted it from the text of **t**). Scaliger omits it, which suggests absence in **Cuiacianus**. If **Dalecampianus** had it, this would be the source of **t**'s text, with the marginal citation applying to **Cuiacianus**. At the end of this section, therefore, the tally is *v.c.* = **Dalecampianus** twice, and *v.c.* probably = **Cuiacianus** twice.

In turning to the *LO context we have 14 entries to consider, and it would be otiose to treat all at similar length, so I should like to summarize and to select. The first five, 110.8, 111.3, 112.4 (twice), and 112.6 were available to **t** from only one *L source, though there are now other options. For 110.8 de Tournes adopts the faulty reading straight from **c** or **s**, and the marginal variant is therefore that of **Dalecampianus**. In 111.3 the editor eschews the **s** order, following an incorrect, proleptic order for the prepositional phrase, taken probably from a florilegium. The attestation of the absence of *ab* is suspicious. I suspect it was simply a line further down in his *v.c.*, as part of the phrase correctly positioned as we see it in **O**. Here *v.c.* seems **s**-aligned. For 112.4 we have direct testimony that *mulieris* was not missing in **t**'s 'variae lectiones ex v.c.' (**Cuiacianus**), wherein the reading attested is *mulieris et secreto*.

This provides the clearest evidence possible that *v.c.* need not refer to that manuscript. The source of the error is problematic because **s** enters into consideration. Pithou and Scaliger silently have the word, and of course there is no other **Dalecampianus** source to support its absence there. It likely was in the *L manuscripts, the absence being a feature of the **O** manuscripts, transmitted into **s**. If **t** picked it up here the editor is deceiving us with the *v.c.* designation. One should note that **t** continues with **s** for its text in the same sentence, printing the otiose *habere*. Here the exact manuscript source to indicate the correct omission cannot be told: the possibilities are **Dalecampianus** and the florilegia. 112.6 *commodaret modo* offers something different. This correct reading is carried only in **BR** and is attested in Pithou's *varietas* as the reading of '*Autis.*' In all likelihood the editor of **t** obtained it from Pithou, and it should join this list despite its lack of attribution – a minor inconsistency. For 112.6 *modo* there are the usual suspects, **Dalecampianus** and the florilegia. To recapitulate, for the *v.c.* caption we now have some variety. Out of six examples there is one sure **Dalecampianus** source, two **s**-related sources, two from **Dalecampianus** or the florilegia, and one disguised contribution from Pierre Pithou.

There are nine further marginal attestations in contexts where the editor of **t** had a full range of sources to draw from: both ***L** manuscripts, the florilegia, and the **O** editions. The majority (118.6, 120.94, 127.4, 130.6, 131.10) concern missing words. In the first two the marginal variant supplies the correct reading, de Tournes having chosen his text from **s**. The interpolation at 118.6 is the reading of a cited '*codex Sambuci,*' and *age* at 120.94 could have come from a variety of manuscripts, either ***L** or **O**. At 127.4 the absence, in error, of *mihi* in *q.c.* is paralleled in the Leiden **Vossianus Lat. O. 81**, this reading having possibly come to de Tournes from there indirectly. The last two cases (130.6, 131.10) do not quote *v.c.* authority. The words are missing in **s**, which must therefore be the inspiration for the marginal note. Of the four remaining cases in this section three (113.3, 118.3, 118.6) show reading variants. *hedile*, the reading of the archetype, was probably obtained by de Tournes from **Dalecampianus**; *conspici* is the reading found in **O** and cited from a '*vet.*' in Pithou's *varietas*. Since **t** does not use any **O** manuscript directly, I take this reading to have been communicated by Pithou, like 112.6 *commodaret*. I suspect that this *vetus* was not the '*Benedictinum exemplar,*' which is an ***L** source. The source of *tamquam* is difficult: it has **O** associations but could also have been in ***L** abbreviated, as Scaliger's *tanq̄* seems to show. The last example in this section, *pariter*, occurs in the **O** manuscripts. **t** alone omits it from the text and offers in the margin alongside the *v.c.* caption the conjecture *perite*. The ***L** reading cannot be confirmed, but by implication it was also *pariter*; thus **t**'s source may not be determined.

From the above efforts to account for the origin of the *v.c.* variants in **t**^margine it emerges quite decisively that the term can be applied to a range of manuscript sources available to the editor, and also, in all likelihood, to the printed edition **s** and to readings obtained at second hand from Pierre

Pithou. Thus we may place little confidence in this designation for giving any specific single manuscript consistently when others are available. This consideration will not be forgotten when we review the asterisks said by de Tournes to be lacking in a *v.c.*, though in this case we can rule out **O** and florilegia sources, since there is no evidence that a manuscript from these classes carried them. The very idea of asterisks to denote lacunae seems to be an *L-class feature: the editors observed them in *L-class manuscripts and supplemented them or subtracted them as they saw fit.

In **t**'s case two *L manuscripts are our candidates, and on five occasions the editor signals the absence of asterisks in a *v.c.* which he now chooses to enter into his text to denote lacunae. Now that the concept of the asterisk to do this is established and exploitable, this gives us two possibilities: the asterisk either occurred in de Tournes' other manuscript, or else it occurred nowhere, being now inserted *per coniecturam*. The latter should probably be excluded because of the presence of asterisks in the same place in manuscripts of the **Memmianus** group, **m**, and **r**, sources independent of **t**. The absence of asterisks at 22.5, 28.1, and 36.8 in p^1 denotes that they were not in **Benedictinus**; they may thus be attributed to presence in **Memmianus**, entering **Dalecampianus** and then **t** from the parent source. This leaves **Cuiacianus** for the registered absences under the caption of *v.c.* We remember, however, that the editor received this manuscript after the text up to c. 113 had been printed, thus *v.c.* = **Cuiacianus** only if we accept that the citations could have been added to the margins subsequent to the printing of the first 67 pages but before publication. The multiple asterisks in **t** at 115.20 occur in **l** also, despite their putative absence in **Cuiacianus**, Scaliger's *L source. How may we then account for this? – only by surmising that some hint of them had been furnished to Scaliger less formally, perhaps in **Cuiacianus** margin (if we accept **l**'s prior date of composition). Nevertheless, where the asterisks are concerned, a good case may be made for the **Cuiacianus** being the *v.c.* from which they are reported by de Tournes to be absent.

B

[*LOφ]	5.1.8	*redemptus histrioniae*] <u>al.</u> *redemptus histrioniue*
[*LO]	6.1	*hunc*] <u>al.</u> *haec*
[*LOφ]	14.2.5	*ergo*] <u>al.</u> *iam nunc*
[*LH]	35.4	*lericulam*] <u>al.</u> *ficedulam*
[*LOH]	55.6.1	*luxuriae rictu*] <u>al. l.</u> *ritu*
	55.6.2	*clausus*] <u>al.</u> *lautus*
	55.6.5	*grata*] <u>al.</u> *Graeca*

[*Lφ]	100.1	*ducit*] <u>al.</u> *mittit*
[*LO]	118.3	*inundante*] <u>al.</u> *inundata*
	118.5	*rationis*] <u>al.</u> *corpus orationis*
	131.10	*venisti*] <u>al.</u> *totus venisti*
	132.15.7	*in arce*] <u>al.</u> *in arte*

In considering the above list of marginal variants ascribed to *al.* (*alius codex*, or possibly *alia lectio* or *aliter*), we note that, out of a dozen, only one occurs in text peculiar to *L, so far as de Tournes was concerned: 35.4 *ficedulam* was probably a conjecture communicated to the editor, hence occupying a position of authority somewhere between a manuscript citation and a conjecture of his own. In one other case there is no potential **O** source: 100.1 *mittit* is the reading of the florilegia. 5.1.8 *redemptus histrioniue* is not from **Cuiacianus**, as the reading *redimitus histrioni* cited in the *variae lectiones* of **t** makes clear; it is close to Pithou's *'vet.' redimitus histrionei*. If one takes this to be **Benedictinus**, *redemptus* appears to derive from an **O** source. 6.1 *haec* is not easily traceable. There is some support for it in **dr** (= **Memmianus**) that suggests for **t** a **Dalecampianus** origin, but palaeographic similarities to *hoc* and *hunc* rule out certainty. 14.2.5 *iam nunc* is the φ reading. 55.6.1 *ritu* is attested in **AH**, manuscripts unavailable to de Tournes. The source is therefore mysterious. In the next line *lautus* is given by Bücheler as a conjecture of Scaliger, though it is not in **l**. In line five of the poem, *Graeca* may have been inspired by Scaliger's *Graia*. 118.3 *inundata* has the respectable authority of the text of Pithou and Scaliger, and is accepted by the editors as correct. The inferior *inundante* entered **t** from **s**, driving what we may take as a genuine *L reading to the margin. Here the *v.c.* caption, if we seek consistency, would have been more appropriate. 118.5 *corpus orationis* is likewise a correct reading displaced by **s**. In that it was accepted into Pithou's second edition when the editor had access to **Tholosanus** (= **Cuiacianus**), in contrast to his first, there is grounds for believing that the editor of **t** obtained the variant from his newly acquired **Cuiacianus**. At 131.10 *'al.'* has added the word *totus*. Since this is a good reading in all the manuscripts its source may not be known. One wonders why de Tournes left it out of his text. He was clearly not satisfied with *lotus* either, which he saw in **s**, for it too was put in the margin. Finally, 132.15.7 *in arte* is again a manuscript reading displaced by **s**. Its exact origin may not be known, but an *L manuscript is the best prospect.

We see from the above that *'al.'* seems to be a kind of catch-all, with its use not necessarily confined to inferior, unauthenticated readings: the last four cited (one third of the total) appear to be genuine *L readings that have found favour with modern editors. Another two come from verifiable manuscript sources (florilegia). Some of the rest are conjectures. The proper significance of '*al.*' to the editor seems, therefore, not to be *aliud exemplar* or some such manuscript designation. It is an abbreviation for a vaguer term to take in, for convenience, readings from a variety of sources with no differentiation.

THE '*v.c.*' CITATIONS IN **t**margine OF THE *BELLUM CIVILE*

De Tournes carries opposite the text of the *Bellum Civile* poem (119–124.1) which he prints in **t** a remarkable set of indications of a disturbed order of verses, together with some omissions, observed in a '*v.c.*' The identity of this manuscript source (so we are invited to take it) and the possible implications for the textual history are tantalizing problems, made all the more mysterious because the transpositions are signalled by no other editor and there is not a shadow of the different order in any other source. I record below **t**'s indications:[60]

i	[ad v. 19]	In v.c. hi 13. versus sequuntur post illum [v. 57].
ii	[ad v. 27]	Ante hunc versum in v.c. leguntur illi [v. 61] et sequent.
iii	[ad v. 67]	Ante hunc versum legitur in v.c. [v. 79] etc.
iv	[ad v. 97]	Post hunc versum in v.c. leguntur [v. 105] et sequent.
v	[ad v. 110]	Hunc versum in v.c. sequitur [v. 116] et sequent.
vi	[ad v. 119]	haec desunt in v.c. usque ad vers. [v. 122].
vii	[ad v. 209]	haec leguntur in v.c. post illum ver. [v. 123], etc.
viii	[ad v. 213]	Desunt hi duo vers. in v.c. [vv. 213, 214].
ix	[ad v. 225]	Hi quatuor ver. in v.c. sequuntur post [v. 232].
x	[ad v. 245]	Post hunc versum in v.c. legitur [v. 253] etc.

We should separate these directions into those whose instructions are clear and those whose meaning is open to ambiguity. Only four fall into the first category: two (vi, viii) are precise *desunt*'s, while the other two (i, ix) give the exact number of verses to be shifted, with a specified block of verses following a single named verse. What principle, we may ask, underlies the directions for reordering the six other displaced sections when there is no indication of their extent? There are, unhappily, two possibilities, both of them susceptible to slight modification: either a single verse is to be moved (Option A, below), or else an entire passage, perhaps up to the next marginal indication, is to be relocated (Option B). A plausible modification of either option is that the transferred piece should fit in syntactically; thus we may talk of the relocation of the smallest 'sense unit.'

Otherwise too much violence would be done to the meaning of the poem
and we would be asked to believe that the *v.c.* carried a meaningless text.

It is clear that following the two options separately is capable of producing
radically different versions of the same poem, even if this is done consistently. If there were some inconsistency at work in the directions of the
editor, the situation would be hopeless since it could yield as many versions
as a Rubik's cube. One does assume, however, that de Tournes wished to
be understood by his contemporaries, who would then be having less
difficulty than we in following his directions. In the table below I have
reconstructions of the *Bellum Civile*, assaying both options and comparing
them with the version advanced by Pellegrino.[61]

OPTION A	OPTION B	PELLEGRINO
119.1–18	119.1–18	119.1–18
119.32–57	119.32–57	119.32–57
119.19–26	119.19–26	119.19–26
120.61, or 61, 62	120.61–66	120.61–66
119.27–31	119.27–31	—
119.58–60	119.58–60	—
120.62– or 63–66		
120.79		
120.67–78		
120.80–97	120.79–97	120.79–97
121.105	121.105–110	121.105–110
120.98–121.104	121.116–119	121.116–119
121.106–110	120.67–78	—
121.116	120.98–121.104	—
121.111–115	121.111–115	—
121.117–119		
<121.119–121>	<121.119–121>	<121.119–121>
122.122,123	122.122,123	122.122,123
123.209, or 209–211	123.209–212	123.209–212
122.124–123.208	122.124–123.208	—
123.210–212, or 212		
<123.213–214>	<123.213–214>	<123.213–214>
123.215–225	123.215–225	123.215–225
123.230–232	123.230–232	123.230–232
123.226–229	123.226–229	123.226–229
123.233–124.245	123.233–124.245	123.233–124.245
124.253	124.253–295	124.253–295

124.246–252   124.246–252   —
124.254–295

One sees from the above that Pellegrino follows Option B, but with the major difference that he does not resume the normal order after each transposition (119.27–31, 119.58–60, etc.). One assumes this to be a well-considered move, though one surely in error. Not observing the implicit task of resuming the running order of the poem produces seven substantial lacunae and a greatly exaggerated picture of the defects in *v.c.*[62] There is in fact no reason or need to infer any more lacunae than the ones that the editor takes pains to signal, on two occasions only (vi and viii), for a total of five verses. A strong implication exists that there are no others.

Even without lacunae the manuscript witnessed by de Tournes was severely defective in comparison with the 'normal' O-derived *Bellum Civile*, which the editor had printed. Assuming this section to be in one of his named sources, it is tempting of course to consider *v.c.* to be **Cuiacianus**, or perhaps **Dalecampianus**. The former is lent some support, as we have seen, by such a designation in the *variae lectiones* applying to it, while the best argument in favour of the latter is the above-described silence of the other editors, for we recall that only t has used this source.[63] But we should remember that an unknown O manuscript is also here a possibility. There is some other evidence for possible inferiority of **Cuiacianus**. When Pithou was preparing his second edition he thought so little of the newly acquired **Tholosanus** (= **Cuiacianus**) that, though he cited its variants 19 times in his *variae lectiones*, he adopted only one.[64] Pithou's preference for readings taken from his sources at the time of production of **p¹** indicates, surely, that the differences in **p²**, if they be uncatalogued, depend very little on **Tholosanus**.

Beyond taking the point that **Cuiacianus**, if this be the *v.c.* cited in the margins of t's *Bellum Civile*, may be a poor manuscript, there is very little to be said about the dislocations, far less explaining them. Option A is to be preferred because it does a bit less violence to the flow of the poem, but sense and syntax here too are often so mangled that it is still unintelligible as a poem, which would not say much for the literary responsibilities of the copyist.[65]

SUMMARY OF FINDINGS AND CONCLUSIONS

Principal information for the sources of t comes from the preface of the printer-editor, Jean de Tournes, and this has not now been reviewed or greatly modified, although I argue here and in the previous chapter for an adjustment to the standard view of when de Tournes actually began incorporating the readings of his two *L manuscripts into the text of **t**. At present I have concentrated on the attributions applied to a considerable number of variants found in the margins. These had never been studied extensively, and the difficulties in the task are well illustrated by the contradictory interpretations that have been put on the ascriptions. These then threaten to obscure not only the stemmatics of the principal manuscripts but even their number, putting modern editorial selection of readings on shaky ground.

In adjusting Ullman's view of **Memmianus** I believe I have found a way to reconcile conflicting testimony on the number of available *L texts in the sixteenth century, modifying Müller's stemma with four. In the marginal attributions to Pithou-derived variants I take the opposite view to Pellegrino's: I see the unattributed variants as conjectures and the few with *v.c.* captions as manuscript readings obtained from Pithou. A fortiori, I argue, the variants cannot present evidence that *Pithoeanus* = **Dalecampianus** or any *L manuscript other than **Benedictinus**. De Tournes' indirect use of Pithou's **Bituricus**, I find, is fully consistent with this practice. The evidence of affiliations, independently derived, confirms the character of these Pithou-derived variants, and they may now be dealt with appropriately.

A wider problem is the significance of the *v.c.* designation and its application: consistent or random, sometimes consistent, sometimes random? The belief, which I share, from the weight of the evidence, that the 81 variants in an addendum to **t** (see Chapter 7, page 122) so designated come from one manuscript, **Cuiacianus**, nurtures hopes for consistency in every application, but my evidence now suggests that this cannot be the case. Thus, again, it is pushing things much too far to assume that every *v.c.* reading provides evidence for the condition of **Cuiacianus.** My finding is that while *v.c.* carries proportionately more testimony of **Cuiacianus** than any other manuscript used by de Tournes, it has been applied also to **Dalecampianus, O**, and florilegia readings. While it is usually a serious term intended to signal the reading of a good or old manuscript, there is evidence also that de Tournes, out of convenience, occasionally uses it for a conjecture or for a reading out of **s**.

In the case of asterisks used to denote lacunae, with their apparent absence in a *v.c.* creating the impression of unbroken text, my evidence is, I believe, able to overcome the difficulties and support the view of consistent reference to a single *v.c.*, this being **Cuiacianus.**

Analysis of the *al.*-designated variants indicates, unsurprisingly, that it usually denotes other variants than good manuscript authority, though acquired at second hand and not conjectures. But on more than one occasion, I have found, it couches manuscript authority.

As for the *v.c.* captions in **t**^{margine} indicating a disturbed order of the *Bellum Civile* in the manuscript, de Tournes clearly implies (and this is the only thing clear) a single defective source. **Cuiacianus** offers itself, of course, but other citers of this manuscript bear no marks. The other possibility (it being an *L trait, evidently), is **Dalecampianus**. The silence of others lends it support, since it was not used by de Tournes' contemporaries. While the *v.c.*, if we believe de Tournes, is certainly in very poor condition, I argue that it is by no means so vastly lacunose as Pellegrino finds; this rests on a misunderstanding of de Tournes' marginal directions. While these are often ambiguous on the amount of material to be transposed, the extent of the lacunae is meticulously defined.

Though de Tournes' edition was an admirable effort for his day, we can see, therefore, how it was plagued with the problems afflicting most prototypes, and it is approached by the modern editor in full awareness of the intricacies involved.

3

Pierre Pithou and **p**

The two *Satyrica* editions prepared by Pierre Pithou were in several respects superior to their predecessor, **t**, the first edition to use ***L** manuscripts. In the first place, Pithou used more manuscripts: perhaps five for **p¹** and an additional one for **p²**. Second, four of these are actually provided with names: **Autissiodurensis, Bituricus, Benedictinus** and **Tholosanus** (the last for **p²** only). This information we derive not from an introduction listing materials, but from Pithou's *varietas lectionum* which follows his text; here, these names are attached both to readings accepted for the text, and to rejected variants.[66] Hence we have 60 citations from **Autissiodurensis** and 40 from **Bituricus**, both manuscripts finding favour with the editor on a number of occasions. In contrast, the 19 citations from **Tholosanus** are consistently rejected.

Despite these hopeful indications of precision, problems common to **t** remain: the readings or variants ascribed to the named sources are numerically inferior to the usual vague citations. For instance, in **p¹** there are no less than 75 rejected variants ascribed to *'al.,'* a designation, as we shall see, that might apply to almost any source whatsoever, including the very manuscripts cited elsewhere by name. There are a further 48 readings under the caption of *'vet.'* These too could couch the reading of one of the named manuscripts, as well as other 'old' sources not necessarily linked to **Benedictinus**.[67] Then there are the 27 variants in **p¹** tagged with *lege, scribe, deleatur,* and *addatur* – a number which declines markedly in **p²** because many have entered the text. These seem to be emendations.[68] Finally, we cannot be sure that many variants which would belong properly in the *varietas* have not silently entered the text.

The greater number of manuscripts used by Pithou increases the possibility that some of these may have survived and are known to us by another name. If this can be established, we are in a position to test the palaeographic skills of Pithou, and the typographical reliability of his editions; and we may also be able to isolate and confine some variants to other sources. Pithou's editions contain the so-called L-text of Petronius; thus it is reasonable to expect that at least one of his manuscript sources belongs to *L. A check of the readings cited for both **Benedictinus** and **Tholosanus**, particularly their contexts, shows that both qualify. The former is thus likely to be the main source, and the only manuscript source, for Pithou's *L material in p^1. In contrast, the readings cited for *Autis.* and *Bit.* never occur in an exclusive *L context; thus they must be O-class manuscripts.[69]

THE IDENTITY OF **Autissiodurensis**[70]

A comparison of the readings of *Autis.* with those contained in **B** (= **Bernensis 357** + **Vossianus Lat. Q. 30**) led Bücheler, first, to the confident assertion that they are one and the same manuscript. This was challenged by E.T. Sage on the basis of certain discrepancies; yet Sage's effort to raise a *germanus* of **B** for *Autis.*, despite the total lack of independent evidence for the existence of such a manuscript, won no converts – not until recently, when the vigorous effort of Pellegrino to revive Sage's doubts with a new look at the internal evidence demonstrates that the case is not yet closed.[71] I should like to commence this study of Pithou's sources with my own effort to end the controversy, using not only the internal evidence of the readings, but also the results of codicological study on the possessors of **B**, to prove beyond any reasonable doubt that *Autis. Pithoei* = **B**.

It is worth noting that if McClure, Sage, and Pellegrino were right, textual scholarship on Petronius would be in the sorry position of possessing not a single important manuscript, save for florilegia, verifiably surviving out of the many used by the sixteenth-century scholars; and, conversely, of having a set of our best manuscripts today, namely **BRP**, unknown to and unused by these same scholars. On the face of it, this is a situation both unsatisfactory and improbable. I shall try to determine, if in fact there are discrepancies in our equations, whether there might be another reason for them, possibly related to an insufficient understanding of the mental and editorial habits of the citers, together with mistakes, slips, typographical errors, and the like.

The identification of *Autis.* with **B** would be particularly useful, as is well recognized.[72] For **B**, by far the oldest and best of our Petronius manuscripts, is incomplete; a positive identification would provide us, via the citations of Pithou, with a dozen or so high-quality readings in the section today lost (taking into account the minor discrepancies which will be seen to emerge from the discussion, below). A further advantage, referred to already, is that it would present an almost unique opportunity to test with complete objectivity the quality of Pierre Pithou's scholarship and to understand better his methods of citation. In the latter regard, for example, it might be possible to establish that a proportion of *al.* and *vet.* variants are actually unacknowledged **Autissiodorensis** (= **B**) readings and eliminate other likely candidates from the Pithou source list.

It is therefore appropriate to study the evidence of Pithou's *varietates* (**p¹ᵛ** and **p²ᵛ**) with a greater thoroughness than has yet been attempted. In evaluating the links between Pithou's citations of *Autis.* in **p¹** and **p²** and **B**, I provide a list, below, of all the citations, collated against Pithou's text, with the readings of **B** shown. If the text reading (the lemma) is followed by a closed bracket, it indicates that Pithou rejected the *Autis.* reading (which then follows) in favour of another variant. Absence of the bracket indicates that the text reading is the one cited for *Autis.* In this way we may quickly discern and calculate the proportion of *Autis.* readings favoured by Pithou for his text. As a means of applying a modern and reasonably objective standard to Pithou's critical acumen and the *bonitas* of the **B** readings, I have underlined the reading found in Müller and Ehlers 1983. The results will be discussed after the section on the identification of the '*Autis.*' readings.

THE READINGS OF '*Autis.*' IN **p¹ᵛ** AND **p²ᵛ**, AND OF **B**, COMPARED

[*LOφ]	2.1	<u>in culina</u>] in coria '*Autis.*'**B**
[*LO]	2.8	<u>Thucydides</u>] Thucidides '*Autis.*': tuchidides **B**
[*LOφ]	3.4	<u>pisciculos</u>] discipulos '*Autis.*'**B**
	3.4	<u>moratur</u>] moritur '*Autis.*'**B**
[*LO]	4.2	propellunt] impellunt '*Autis.*'**B**: [<u>im</u>]pellunt
	4.3	mitigarentur] inrigarentur '*Autis.*'**B**: <u>irrigarentur</u>
	4.3	placent] <u>placeret</u> '*Autis.*'**B**
	4.5	<u>schedium</u>] schadium '*Autis.*'**B**
[*LOφ]	5.1.15	hunc] huic '*Autis.*'**B**: <u>hinc</u>
[*LO]	6.1	<u>dictorum aestu</u>] aestu rerum '*Autis.*'**B**
	7.3	<u>inter titulos</u> '*Autis.*'**B**
	7.4	aliam partem] <u>alteram partem</u> '*Autis.*'**B**
[*LOφ]	14.2.2	<u>nulla</u>] nuda '*Autis.*'**B**
[*LO]	14.2.4	<u>vendere verba solent</u>] verba solent emere '*Autis.*'**B**
	16.2	reclusaeque] remissaeque '*Autis.*'**B**
	16.3	sacrum '*Autis.*'<**B**> (see Plate 1)

	17.7	*timerem*] *timeam* '*Autis.*'**B**
	19.1	*mimico* '*Autis.*'**B**
	25.6	*ut dicatur* '*Autis.*'**B**: [...]
[*LOH]	55.6.11	*strato*] *sirato* '*Autis.*'**B**
	55.6.14	*probitas est*] *probita se* '*Autis.*'**B**: *probitas e*
[*LO]	81.1	*antescolanus* '*Autis.*': *antescholanus*
[*LOφ]	88.3	*Hercula* '*Autis.*': *hercule*
	88.4	*excellentissimi*] *excelsissimi* '*Autis.*'
	88.5	*convertar* '*Autis.*'
	88.5	*comprehenderat*] *comprehendit* '*Autis.*'
[*LO]	89.1.14	*mendacium*] *mens semper* '*Autis.*'
	89.1.22	*ictusque* '*Autis.*'
	95.8	*mulcāt exclusum* '*Autis.*'
	108.12	*tralaticium* '*Autis.*'
	108.14.2	*heros* '*Autis.*'
	108.14.8	*immittite*] *imponite* '*Autis.*'
	109.3	*ducentos*] *ducenos* '*Autis.*'
	109.6	*exultans* '*Autis.*': *exultantes*
[*LOφ]	111.10	*certe ab eo*] *certo ab eo* '*Autis.*': *certe in certa vel certo correctum, ut videtur,* **B**: [*certum ab eo*]
	111.12	*admonere debet* '*Autis.*': *ammonere debet* **B**
	112.3	*quisque* '*Autis.*'**B**: *quisquis*
	112.5	*cruciarii*] *cruciariae* '*Autis.*': *cruciaria* **B**
	112.6	*commodaret* '*Autis.*'**B**
[*LO]	113.3	*ele* '*Autis.*': *hedile* **B**: *Hedyle*
	118.5	*corpus rationis* '*Autis.*'**B**: *corpus orationis*
	119.9	*Aesepyrecum* '*Autis.*': *Aesepyre cum* **B**: *aes Ephyre* †*cum*†
	119.30	*sensim trahat*] *sensum trahat* '*Autis.*': *sensum trahant* **B**
	120.92	*usus*] *usum* '*Autis.*'**B**
	121.117	*Porthmeus* '*Autis.*': *porthmeus* **B**
	123.210	*pennis*] *pinnis* '*Autis.*'**B**
	126.17	*Parium*] *planum* '*Autis.*': *pharium* **B**
	127.7	*Poliaenum*] *Belienon* '*Autis.*': *polyae non* **B**: *Polyaenon*
	131.8.4	*errantibus* '*Autis.*'**B**
	131.8.8	*sua rura*] *suasura* '*Autis.*'**B**: †*sua rura*†
	133.3.4	*septifluus*] *semper fluvius* '*Autis.*': *semper flavius* **B**: †*semper flavius*†
[O]	133.3.14	*pecoris*] *decoris* '*Autis.*': *docoris* **B**
[*LO]	133.3.15	*lactens* '*Autis.*': *lactans* **B**
	134.12.7	*dracones* '*Autis.*'**B**
	135.8.5	*astu* '*Autis.*': *hastu* **B**: *actu*

135.8.6   *mollistillae 'Autis.' molli stillae* **B**: <u>*mollis tiliae*</u>
135.8.8   *et paries]* <u>*at paries*</u> *'Autis.'* **B**
135.8.13   <u>*texta*</u> *'Autis.'* **B**
135.8.14   *et timbrae]* *et ymbrae 'Autis.'* **B**: <u>*et thymbrae*</u>
135.8.16   *Hecates 'Autis.':* *haecates* **B**: <u>*Hecale*</u>

As we see, all 60 of the *Autis.* citations come from the *varietas* of **p¹**,
while there are three fewer in **p²**, where the readings at 88.4 and 135.8.8
vanish into the text, and 88.5 loses its attribution. The 13 citations between
81.1 and 109.6 may not be compared with the reading of **B** because this
section of the manuscript is missing today; thus they have no influence on
the identification argument.[73] Were evidence to exist that **B** had already
been dismembered by 1577, we should have a serious objection to the
equation *Autis.* = **B**. I know of none.[74] Of the remaining 46 citations, 30
(65 per cent) demonstrate an outright *Autis.* **B** agreement. This leaves 16
readings to exhibit some sort of difference, on which the entire debate on
the internal evidence must turn. In other words, the differences, in their
character, must either support the view of two separate manuscripts or be
capable of being attributed to other factors.

Nearly half of the differences (seven) have to do with the forms of proper
nouns. This would tend to reduce, perhaps even eliminate, their significance
in any divergence, in that they would be susceptible of individual adjustment
by an editor for spelling (cf. also at 111.12 *admonere/ammonere*), capitalization and conformity with norms and tastes of orthography, without
comment. In this category are to be included 2.8 *Thucidides/Tuchidides*,
121.117 *Porthmeus/porthmeus*, and 135.8.16 *Hecates/haecates*. The above
readings were silently adjusted by the editor for his lemma, I would argue;
thus the seeming discrepancy between what Pithou cited for *Autis.* and
what we see in **B** does not necessarily exist. 2.8 is harder to justify than
the others, but we may surmise that Pithou had his mind more on recording,
and correcting, the y/i spelling variant than the Th/t and c/ch distinctions.
119.9 *Aesepyre cum/Aesepyrecum* may also be part of this phenomenon.
We need not assume that Pithou would consider the slight adjustment of
the manuscript reading for his lemma worthy of note. The three other
proper nouns will be dealt with separately.

Another apparent divergence in word division occurs at 135.8.6. In **p¹**
Pithou prints *molli stillae*, the exact, verifiable reading of **B**; but in referring
to this reading and its source in the *varietas*, where any difference would
be unwarranted and perhaps unintended, *mollistillae* is printed and given
to *Autis.* To me the only explanation is a misprint in the lemma, which
Pithou meant to show as the approved *Autis.* reading. Hence there is no

discrepancy. In **p²** Pithou changes his text to *molli stilla*, apparently abandoning his *Autis.* reading for a conjecture in **t**; yet he again records the *Autis.* variant, now relegated to the *varietas*, as *mollistillae*. Why? Because the citation together with its attribution was simply copied from the previous *varietas*. The *astu*/*hastu* variation at 135.8.5 may be another of those silent adjustments undertaken for reasons of orthography. Pithou had no interest in recording the 'h' in *Autis.* since his object in citing the variant was to contrast his selection with the consonantally distinct *actu* that he saw in another source.

There are only nine remaining potentially significant discrepancies. I should like to suggest and demonstrate how this small number may all be due to various types of mistake. One class involves palaeographical errors, usually of such a minor nature that the differences between what modern scholars are able to observe in **B** and Pithou's attestations for *Autis.* may not even have been detected, were it not for our concentration on individual letters. For example, at 111.10 *certo ab eo 'Autis.'* the final letter of the first word in **B** is anybody's guess: to me it looks as if an 'e' has been changed to an 'a,' but not without leaving the impression that it could be an 'o' – which is what Pithou has for *Autis.* And at 112.5 *cruciariae 'Autis.,'* Pithou has for reasons of syntax anticipated a diphthong, which might reasonably be rendered only minutely distinct from the final 'a' we see today in **B**, given the method of forming diphthongs by mounting the 'e' against the 'a' downstroke. Pithou's reading, as we require it, of *planum* for *pharium* at 126.17 seems odd, for he has not recognized in the uncapitalized, misspelt proper noun **B**'s rendering of the correct *Parium*, available elsewhere. Yet they are palaeographically extremely close. 133.3.4 *semper fluvius 'Autis.'* is only one rather similar letter away from the unparalleled *semper flavius* of **B**, and the 'u' was likely to have been suggested to Pithou by the *-fluus* of other available variants.

Another type of error is indicated for 119.30 *sensum trahat/trahant*. Pithou's interest in recording the distinction between *sensim* of the **Bituricus** and *sensum* of *Autis.* has caused him to overlook another *Autis.* variant in *trahant*. The case of 133.3.14 *decoris/docoris* might be another palaeographic slip, or a conscious emendation by Pithou of the **B** reading. Both seem justified by the obscurity of *docoris*, while the 'corrected' manuscript reading leads to Pithou's excellent emendation, *pecoris*. 133.3.15 *lactens/lactans* is similarly founded: an unrecorded and perhaps inadvertent 'improvement' of the *Autis.* reading. The *lactans* reading is signalled in the **p²** *varietas* (**p²ᵛ**) (under '*al.*'!) as a kind of correction.

I have kept for last the two readings out of 16 whose apparent divergences cannot be justified as adjustments, palaeographic misreadings of **B** or small oversights: 113.3 *ele/hedile* and 127.7 *Belienon/polye.non*. In view of the small number, they are hardly good grounds for postulating separate manuscripts. In fact, the differences may again be imputed to errors by Pithou. In both cases I believe the editor has simply misreported **B**, attributing to it readings which came from elsewhere. It is clear from the combination of text readings and citations in the *varietas lectionum* that Pithou was familiar with the two readings that we see today in **B**: *hedile* is cited in the *varietas* for '*al.*'; and *Poliaenum* (the name confirmed to Pithou by Homer's *Odyssey*, to which his note refers), is, *mutatis mutandis*, not far from **B**'s *polye.non*. I believe that with *Belienon* Pithou has simply reported for *Autis.* the 'adjusted' reading of his **Bituricus**, a manuscript which is either **P** or closely related to it (see below), since **P**'s corrupt, late-medieval reading is *bolienon*. The 'b' characteristic of the readings of all the *deteriores* would be out of place in the ninth-century **B**.

Why Pithou should have printed *ele* in his text (cited in the *varietas* as coming from *Autis.*), instead of simply noting it as a variant, as with *Belienon*, is puzzling. One is obliged to infer that, however inadequate the reading, Pithou felt that it was closer to the actual word than the variants available to him. It is thus, I believe, a kind of emendation. *Edile* was available to the editor in his **Bituricus**, to judge from the presence of this form in **P** and the notation '<u>al.</u> *Edile*' in Pithou's *varietas*. I suspect that again Pithou has misrepresented his *Autis.* Let any scholar who believes that we should expect infallibility of Pithou attempt a sample text and apparatus, to gain an understanding of how mistakes creep into the most careful effort. In the hundreds of opportunities for inaccuracies that go into a detailed edition a tiny number of careless instances, even from so noted a scholar as Pithou, is quite feasible. To me they provide a far better explanation for these trivial discrepancies than the alternative: postulation of two separate manuscripts, the one neither surviving nor indeed known to have existed, the other not used by Pithou. These two manuscripts, we are supposed to believe, were conveniently very close, but remained distinct on the basis of a few divergences that we have at second hand, logged with perfect accuracy and precision.

The question of whether the manuscript known as **B** today could have been available to Pithou for intensive scholarly use is relevant to the identification problem. There is some risk of engaging in a circular argument, and this I shall try to avoid. During the relevant period (1575–87) it appears that the manuscript was in the possession of Pierre Daniel, of whom Pithou was a close friend. Also for this period, I have seen no evidence to suggest that it was in anything but an intact state: I argue in Chapter 8, in fact, that the dismemberment, today such a notable feature of **B**, occurred in 1604, as a direct result of Daniel's death and a division among his heirs.[75] In the 1570s, then, Pithou certainly had both the scholarly incentive as editor and the opportunity to borrow his friend Daniel's **B** – intact – for the purpose of putting it to exactly the sort of use that he made of a manuscript whose readings had, at the very least, a strong resemblance to **B** (as we have seen in this chapter). This manuscript Pithou elected to designate not, unfortunately, **Danielis** but **Autissio-durensis**, ostensibly in honour of its provenance.

The next lines of investigation would be to link **B** to Auxerre and Auxerre to Daniel, and an acknowledgment of his friend's manuscript by Pithou is as good as proven. As with many disputes in the manuscript history of Petronius, these points cannot be demonstrated to everyone's full satisfaction. Lindsay, Cary, and Sage favoured the neighbouring scriptorium of Fleury, on palaeographic grounds and for its manifest contemporary knowledge of Petronius. In turn, the case for Auxerre is largely made on the Petronius-related activities of Heiric. A Fleury provenance would presumably show Pithou, and perhaps also Daniel, to be mistaken with '*Autis.*,' if this in fact is **B**. In the event, in 1562 both Fleury and Auxerre were burnt by the Huguenots, and Daniel rescued manuscripts from these as well as from other monasteries.[76] The internal evidence of *Autis.* = **B** is to my mind very strong and needs only moderate backing in the realm of opportunity. This is amply provided by the circumstances of chronology and scholarly association. The only thing **B** lacks is the thing it could not have had: the signature of Pierre Pithou. It would be unreasonable to withhold credence that *Autis.* = **B** on that ground alone.

It remains in this section to appraise the critical acumen of Pithou on the basis of his choices, remembering that he had access not only to good manuscripts, but also to the editions **c**, **s**, and particularly **t**, the first edition of the so-called **L** material. On the yardstick of adoption into Müller and Ehlers 1983, about half of the 60 *Autis.* readings are correct; thus **B** for all its age is hardly as reliable as one would hope. Approximately half of these good readings are rejected by Pithou in favour of other variants; but these miscues are balanced by his choosing the same number of correct readings not found in *Autis.* Thus Pithou works out to being right half the time: he cannot improve on the performance of *Autis.* despite access to a large range of variants.

The chief statistical difference between the overall picture and the group of 13 *Autis.* readings that cannot be verified by presence in **B** is that only one variant, as opposed to 15 overall, is a successfully rejected *Autis.* reading: 108.14.8 *immittite*] *imponite* '*Autis.*' Otherwise, four *Autis.* variants are rejected in error, six more are adopted correctly, and the two remaining are adopted in error. But in this group the *Autis.* showing happens to be particularly good: 10 readings out of the 13 are correct, with only 88.3, 108.14.8 and 109.6 going astray. Pithou himself is rather less successful, at seven. While these patterns have no bearing on the identification of **B** they do show the value to the text of Pithou's *Autis.* citations. The dispute over the identity of *Autis.* becomes also, as we have seen, the ground for increasing our knowledge of the habits and reliability of Pithou. But in this regard Pithou's use of **Bituricus** and of the designations *'vet.'* and *'al.'* should be examined for the fullest picture.

THE IDENTITY OF **Bituricus**

As with the case of **B** and *Autis.*, there is a surviving Petronius manuscript, **P (Parisinus lat. 8049)**, to which citations by Pierre Pithou for a manuscript which he calls *Bit.* (**Bituricus**) bear a strong collective similarity. The issue to decide is again whether the manuscripts are the same or merely closely related. The list below follows the same format as above: Pithou's lemma, with closed bracket if it does not coincide with the reading of *Bit.*, the reading of *Bit.*, the reading of **P** (with routine abbreviations usually expanded), text of Müller and Ehlers 1983 underlined:

THE READINGS OF *'Bit.'* IN $\mathbf{p^{1v}}$ AND $\mathbf{p^{2v}}$, AND OF **P**, COMPARED

[*LO]	2.5–6	<u>ad hoc genus exercitationis accessisse</u>. et ideo [<u>video</u> Müller and Ehlers 1983] <u>grandis, et, ut ita dicam, pudica oratio non est maculosa, nec turgida</u>] adsignes exec. [sic] excessisse et ideo grandis et velut ita dicam pudica oratio non est masculosa sed turgida 'Bit.': ad hoc genus exercitationis accessisse. et ita grandis et velud ita dicam pudica oratio non est maculosa nec turgida **P** (see Plate 3)
	3.1	<u>ipse in schola sudaverat</u>] i. etiam s. fundaverat 'Bit.': etiam i. s. sudaverat **P** (see Plate 3)
	3.2	<u>Cicero</u>] Cicio 'Bit.': cic⁷o [cicero] **P** (see Plate 3)
	3.4	<u>moratur</u>] moriatur 'Bit.'**P**, 'i' <u>eadem manu ut videtur deleto</u> (see Plate 3)
[*LOφ]	5.1.9	<u>armigerae</u>] armigenae 'Bit.': armig⁷e [armigerae] **P**, 'e' <u>in</u> 'o' corr. (see Plate 3)
	5.1.14	<u>et ingentis</u>] ingenuus 'Bit.'**P** (see Plate 3)
[*LO]	7.3	<u>inter titulos nudasque meretrices furtim spatiantes</u>] intesticulos invidasque m. interspatiantes 'Bit.': int'ticlos. inundasque m. interspaciantes **P**
	17.3	<u>retexit</u>] detexit 'Bit.': retexit **P**

	17.5	*regio*] *regia* 'Bit.' **P**, *ex* 'o' *factum*, *ut videtur*
	25.1	*Pannichis*] *Parrathis* 'Bit.' (**p¹ᵛ**): *Parrhathis* 'Bit.' (**p²ᵛ**): *parrachis* 'ch' *deletis* **P**: *Pannychis*
	26.2	*iocantium*] *vocantium* 'Bit.': *iocantium* **P**
[*LOH]	55.4	*memorata est*] *deest in* 'Bit.': *memorata est* **P**
	55.5	*Publium*] *Publicum* 'Bit.': *publium* **P**: *Pub[li]lium*
	55.6.9	*cara tribacca*] *cara tibi bacca* 'Bit.': *cara t'baca* **P**: *caram tibi bacam*
[*LOφ]	84.2	*extruere*] *instruere* 'Bit.': *extruere* **P**
	88.7	*invenisset*] *attigisset* 'Bit.' **P**
[*LO]	95.3	*iam enim faxo*] *iam iam* 'Bit.' **P**
	95.8	*soleis ligneis*] *deest ligneis in* 'Bit.' **P**
	108.14.2	*Troius heros* 'Bit.': *troius eros* **P**
	108.14.4	*fraterno*] *superno* 'Bit.': *fr'no* **P**
	109.6	*exultans captabat* 'Bit.' (*sed legitur in* **p** *e. quaerebat) e.q.* **P**: *exultantes quaerebat*
	109.10.5	*times*] *paves* 'Bit.': *times* **P**
	118.3	*inundata*] *inundaverit* 'Bit.' **P**
	118.4	*ut fiat*] *itaque fiat* 'Bit.': *ut fiat* **P**
	119.9	*Aesepyrecum*] *Ac se pirecum* 'Bit.': *Ac sepyre cum* **P**: *aes Ephyre* †*cum*†
	119.11	*accusant*] *accusat* 'Bit.': *accusati* **P**: †*accusatius*†
	119.30	*sensim* 'Bit.': *sensum* **P**
	120.93	*iubentur*] *fatentur* 'Bit.' **P**
	121.117	*accerse*] *accresce* 'Bit.' **P**
	121.120	*mande*] *pande* 'Bit.' **P**
	122.133	*morientia*] *manantia* 'Bit.' **P**
	129.10	*fieri*] *frater* 'Bit.': *fi⁷* **P**
	131.8.4	*errantibus*] 'Bit.' **P**
	131.8.6	*Iasdon*] *yasdon* 'Bit.' **P**: *aedon*
	131.8.8	*sua rura*] *suasura* 'Bit.' **P**: †*sua rura* ...†
	132.7	*poteram confingere, languorem simulare coepi*] *poterat contingere, langorem simulavi* 'Bit.': *poteram contingere langorem simulavi* **P**
	132.8.7	*supplicio*] *supplicit* 'Bit.': *supplic'* **P**
	134.6	*moram*] *nomen* 'Bit.' **P**
	134.12.7	*dracones* 'Bit.' **P**
	135.8.5	*astu* 'Bit.' **P**: *actu*

Pithou's *varietas* provides a list of altogether 40 variants ascribed to **Bituricus.** Some of these we have met before in the margins of **t** under the same 'Bit.' (or 'Br.') ascription: 55.4 <*memorata est*>, 95.3 iam [iam],

95.8 *soleis* [*ligneis*], 108.14.2, *Troius heros*, 109.6 *captabat*, 118.3 *inunda-verit*, and 129.10 *frater*. Among these, as was noted (n. 53), there are two discrepancies: in t^margine only *est* at 55.4 is said to be missing in *Bit.*; and *heros* is quoted as *heres* – both minor slips. Interestingly, there are **Bituricus** variants in t^margine which do not take their place in the Pithou list: 96.4 *iniuriamque* and 109.6 *exsonat*. About half of all these **Bituricus** readings, including the last two, are also the readings of **P**. This leaves about 20 to be accounted for that exhibit some sort of difference.

My contention, as in the case of *Autis.* = **B**, is that *Bit.* and **P** are one and the same manuscript. In this instance I have the backing of neither Bücheler nor Müller, both of whom would rather believe that one manuscript descends from the other; thus the last scholar to review the evidence, Pellegrino, might be seen on firmer ground in refuting the equation.[77] The same two alternatives are presented: *Bit.* and **P** are clearly close, but do their alleged differences revert to their being separate manuscripts or to errors in the reported witness of **Bituricus**? I should like, in this fresh appraisal, to try to make the case firmly both on palaeographic and codicological grounds for the latter solution.

P is a manuscript not as easy to read, and quote, as **B**. The writing exhibits the typical lateral compression of Gothic script, and there are many abbreviations and ligatures – these by no means used consistently. The scribe has a tendency to copy corrupt bits of text and follow nonsensical order in the poems.[78] The discrepancies between the alleged witness of **Bituricus** and **P** are therefore to me quite understandable, especially if we go on to examine their character, though it does mean a quite lengthy and repetitious effort to impute slips and failings to an important scholar. Yet we do not know under what conditions Pithou worked, or what sort of a literary critic he was, or how skilled he was as a palaeographer, or how he interpreted his prerogative in this regard to make minor changes in the reporting of the readings of his manuscript. We should not assume that his conventions were as strict as ours are, with scholars today expecting to be given not only every variant word, but to be shown every distinct letter if it may be relevant to the transmission. As we can expect, and have seen with **B**, Pithou's standards were high, but in this task of punishing minuteness the opportunities for an error of record are plentiful. Given the condition of **P**, I should say these are well within the acceptable range.

As we proceed through the list we see, in fact, that many of the differences of opinion occur over the writing out of ligatures: at 2.5–6 *adsignes* (*ad h̄ gn̄s* run together looks very like this – see Plate 3) and *masculosa* must so derive; while *velut* is a spelling correction and *excessisse* was a slip by

Pithou, one argues, influenced by the previous word. To continue with this entry: *nec* had then to be changed by Pithou to *sed* in order to bring the subsequent *turgida* from series to contrast, since *masculosa* is a positive attribute. In 3.1 there has been a perhaps careless transposition of *etiam ipse*, and *fundaverat* has been read by Pithou for *sudaverat* through mistaken assumption of a ligature ('s' being similar to 'f'). 3.4 *Cicio* is certainly the ligature (which we see) oddly misread. 5.1.9 *armigenae* by Pithou is likewise a misreading of the correct *armigerae*, again in ligature, though we see today the correction of final 'e' to 'o' (see Plate 3). At 7.3 *intesticulos* is also the product of misreading a heavily ligatured word, *inundasque* arises from misreading, and *interspatiantes* is a spelling adjustment by Pithou. In this way almost every difference can be explained by the misreading of a ligature, a trivial error of spelling or word division, or an adjustment.

There are a few, however, which do not fit this mould. The apparent absence of 55.4 *memorata est* in *Bit.* would clearly be a problem if it were true, but the recorded loss only of *est* in the *Bit.* citation in **t**^margine invites much suspicion over what really was missing according to Pithou.[79] Some inaccuracy, I would say, has arisen in **p**^v, possibly as a result of failure to transcribe correctly the collation, either by Pithou himself or in typesetting: what should perhaps have been printed was *memorata est*] <u>*deest est in ex.*</u> <u>*Bitu.*</u> As for Pithou's original allegation of *est* being missing in **Bituricus**, this may be a kind of misattribution caused by the distraction of *commorata* in **s** (see below). A further confusion may have arisen over use of an asterisk – an ambiguous practice signifying either a lacuna (and here one could have been postulated by Pithou in his notes after *memorata est*, as does Bücheler) or a reference mark. On a couple of occasions the mistake seems attributable to miscopying from the previous line, as at 118.4 *itaque fiat* for *ut fiat*, under the influence of *ut ita dicam*, just above. I have little doubt that some other errors are due to misattribution, as at 132.7 *poterat*, where Pithou ascribes to his *Bit.* the reading found in **t**. Similarly at 135.8.5 *actu* there is the attribution to *Bit.* of a reading which Pithou was able to see in **s**. In short, I would say that there is hardly a single error of the scribal sort, which detractors of the *Bit.* = **P** equation would be having to impute to the scribe of the 'deriving' manuscript, that could not with equal facility and likelihood be attributed to Pithou himself as he read and cited **P**.

Now for the codicological evidence. May Pithou be linked, as either possesser or user, to **Parisinus lat. 8049**?[80] It is established that this manuscript entered the Bibliothèque Nationale from the Colbert Collection, having been acquired by Colbert from the library of Jacques-Auguste de

Thou, the famous historian, collector, and personal friend of Pierre Pithou, who acquired upon Pithou's death in 1596 a large number of his most valuable manuscripts. Now in an unpublished catalogue of manuscripts so derived there is a Petronius.[81] De Thou appears to have owned but a single manuscript of this author, for in the catalogue of his manuscripts prepared upon his own death in 1617 by Pierre Dupuy Petronius is listed only once, in a manuscript given the number of 'de Thou 781.' This happens to be a collection with a content the same as **Parisinus lat. 8049** and in the same order, except that the final item is to be found today in **Parisinus lat. 3358**.[82] There seems no question, then, that the Petronius in de Thou 781 is **P**, and only a little more doubt that **P** is the Petronius manuscript which came to de Thou from Pithou. This being so, it is entirely to be expected that the latter, owning it (or at least in possession of it upon his death), would have used it for his editions. Now Pithou quoted extensively from a manuscript, called by him **Bituricus**, extremely like **P** on the basis of readings, as we have seen. The external evidence points not to similarity but identity.

In his *varietas* Pithou mentions that this **Bituricus** had been owned by Jean, duc de Berri (1340–1416).[83] Admittedly, citation in one of the many catalogues of the duke's collections of a Petronius or some of the other texts of our three manuscripts is lacking.[84] But it seems reasonable to regard Pithou as not mistaken: the manuscript which would henceforth be his (though he did not sign it), was named by its new possessor after its earlier owner and is the one known to us as **P**.[85]

The quality of the readings of **Bituricus** apparently did not impress Pithou very much, since of the 40 which he wished to publicize he rejected 27 for his lemma – correctly, as it turned out. Two other readings were rejected by him which Müller and Ehlers 1983 judges to be right, and on three more occasions Pithou adopts readings of **Bituricus** which we deem to be correct also (yielding a total of five correct **Bituricus** readings). On the final eight occasions Pithou chooses neither the incorrect reading of **Bituricus** nor any other correct one. He thus emerges from this test with a score of 10 incorrect readings for his lemma out of 40 – quite a respectable showing.

COMPARISON OF READINGS AND VARIANTS IN $\mathbf{p^1}$ AND $\mathbf{p^2}$

Establishing the identity of the *Autis.* and *Bit.* citations in $\mathbf{p^v}$ is part of the broader problem of interpreting several different types of citation, and hence the value of the hundreds of variants that go with them. I believe a good way to do this is to trace the evolution of Pithou's texts by comparing reading and variant. In the two columns below, the first line of each citation shows the text and the *varietas* (if present) of **p¹**, including lemma when differing from the text (as e.g. at 2.8); the second line those of **p²**, where three dots (...) indicates that the text is the same as **p¹**. Minor inconsistencies of punctuation have been eliminated.

[*LO]	2.3	*quibus deberent loqui*	—
		...	<u>Thol.</u> *ex quibus loqui debemus*
	2.8	*qui Hyperidis*	*qui hyper.*] <u>lege</u>, *quis Hyp.*
		quis Hyperidis	—
	3.1	*ipse in schola*	*ipse in scola*] <u>Bitur.</u> *ipse etiam scola*
		ipse in scola	<u>Bitur.</u> *ipse etiã schola*
	4.5	*improbitatis*	<u>al.</u> *humilitatis* <u>recte</u>
		...	<u>al.</u> *humilitatis* <u>rectius</u>
[*LOφ]	5.1.3	*polleat*	<u>vet.</u> *palleat*
		...	<u>vet.</u> *palleat* <u>rectius</u>
	5.1.9.	*arces*	—
		...	<u>Thol.</u> *artes*
	5.1.18	*celeri*	—
		...	<u>Thol.</u> *sceleris*
[*LO]	6.1	*in porticum*	—
		...	<u>al.</u> *in hortis*
	7.1	*nunquid*	<u>scribe</u> *num quid*
		numquid	—
[*L]	10.7	* *hanc tam praecipite*	<u>deleatur</u> <u>asteriscus</u>
		hanc tam praecipite	—
[*LO]	16.3	*sacrum*	<u>Sic</u> <u>Autis.</u> <u>al.</u> *sacram*
		sacram	<u>vet.</u> *sacrum*
	17.3	*inter se ... contritis*	—
		...	<u>Thol.</u> *interius in ... constrictis*
	17.7	*lenire*	—
		...	<u>vet.</u> *lenire*
	17.9	*protendo*	—
		...	<u>Thol.</u> *obtendo*
	18.3	*tertianam*	—
		...	<u>al.</u> *temperata*
	18.3	*providentiam*	—
		...	<u>vet.</u> *prudentiam*
[*L]	20.4	*de sinu*	<u>Vetus</u> <u>glossar.</u> *de sura*
		...	<u>al.</u> *de sura*
	20.7	*Eucolpius*	—

			...	*lege ut in vet. cod.* Encolpius
	23.3.1	convenite spat.	*lege* convenite nunc spatalocinaedi
		convenite nunc spat.	nunc] *Thol.* vere
[*LH]	27.1	videmus senem	*Io. Salib* ... *Mart* ...
		...	—
	28.8	cerasino	—
		...	*Tholos.* Caesarino
	29.1	du omnia	*lege* dum omnia
		dum omnia	—
	29.3	tenia	*vet.* teńa
		...	*vet.* Temena
	31.9	bisaccio	—
		...	*Thol.* bisatrio
	34.5	* obīt ei	obit ei] *sic vet. unicum hac in parte exemplar*
		obīt ei	obit ei] *sic vet. Ben. exemplar.* *Tholos.* obiter
	35.3	ac rienes	—
		...	*sic vet. Thol.* aetienes
	35.4	odopetam	—
		...	[*Thol.*] adopetam
	36.3	utriculis	inticulis] *sic vet. non,* utriculis
		...	inticulis] *sic vet. non* utriculis *Thol.* intriculis
[*L]	79.6	invenisset	*sic vet. non* [sic] intervenisset
		intervenisset	
[*LOφ]	80.9.1	nomen amicitiae	*Io.Salis.Polic.lib.iii.c. vii.* *&.lib.viii.cap.iii.*
		...	—
	80.9.2	mobile	*sic vet. non* nobile
		nobile	*vet.* mobile
[*Lφ]	82.5.3–4	omnia late qui tenet	*al.* omnia cernens Qui timet
		o. cernens qui timet	*al.* omnia late qui tenet
[*L]	83.5	Ligurgo	—
		...	*Thol.* ligargo
	83.7	quos	—
		...	*al.* quod genus
[*LOφ]	83.10.3	vilis adulator	*Io.Salis.pol.iii.c.xiii*
		...	—
	88.4	excellentissimi	*Autis.* excelsissimi
		excelsissimi	*al.* excellentissimi

	88.4	*ter*	—
		...	*Vet. teter*
	88.5	*ad plastas convertar*	*Sic Autis. al. revertar*
		...	*Vet. l. [sic] revertar*
[*LO]	89.1.6	*figurarent*	—
		...	*vet. figurabant*
	89.1.21	*tradunt*	*sic vet. non tardant*
		tardant	*al. tradunt*
	89.1.30	*replevit*	—
		...	*al. repellit*
[*L]	92.4	*partem*	—
		...	*al. patrem*
[*LO]	95.1	*luditur, diversitor*	—
		...	*vet. ludit, deversitor*
	95.3	*Mannicii*	—
		mannicii	*Vet. Mamucii*
	95.8	*mulcant exclusum*	*Sic Autis. al. exclusum multant*
		mulcāt exclusum	...
[*L]	99.6	*in alt⁷*	—
		in alutam	*vet. in alt.*
	102.15	*barbā*	—
		...	*Thol. barbara*
	106.2	*contumeliarumque*	*Vet. iniuriarumque*
		iniuriarumque	—
	106.3	*prosit*	—
		...	*Thol. possit*
	107.1	*officium*	—
		...	*Thol. add. legatum*
[*LO]	108.12	*tralaticium*	*sic Autis al. stalatarium*
		...	*sic Aut. al stlatarium et statarium*
	108.13	*ex patrio more*	—
		...	*Vet. ex more patrio*
	109.6	*exsonat*	—
		...	*Vet. exsonat ergo*
	109.8	*capillorum*	—
		...	*Thol. in capillos suos*
[*LOφ]	111.11	*et quid*	—
		...	*al. ecquid*
	111.12	*curare*	—
		...	*vet. sentire*
	112.6	*circumscriptus*	*al. circunspectus*

		...	*al.* circumspectus dum residet
	113.4	praeoccupaverat	*lege* occupaverat
		occupaverat	—
[*L]	114.8	applicitus	*addatur nota asterisci*
		* applicitus	—
	115.8	ergo	*lege* ego
		...	*al.* ego
	117.1	* prudentior	*deleatur asteriscus*
		prudentior	—
	117.2	poenam ... differrem	—
		peram	*vet.* poenam ... deferrem
	117.4	in unum	—
		mimum	*vet.* in unum
[*LOφ]	118.1	multos	*addatur in margine* EUMOLPUS
		...	—
[*LO]	118.5	versum	—
		...	*al.* visam
	118.6	religiose	*scribe* religiose
		religiosae	—
	119.1	orbem iam totum	*Pompon. Sabin. in Virgil.*
		...	
	119.9	Aesepyrecum	*Sic. Aut. fortassis pro* Aes Ephyrae regum
		Aes Ephyrae regum	*Autis.* Aesepyrecum
	122.134	mortem	*scribe* Martem
		Martem	—
	122.144	pulsae	—
		...	*al.* pulso
	122.148	adulti	*al.* adusti
		...	*al.* adulti
	122.169	ita mei * comites	*deleatur stigma asterisci*
		ita mei comites	—
	123.188	rupit	*lege* rupti
		...	—
	123.212	attonito	*scribe ut in Vet.* tonitru
		tonitru	—
	123.212	fert	—
		...	*Vet.* ferit
	123.226	panda	—
		...	*al.* pavida
	124.252	sincera	*scribe* summissa

		summissa	—
	124.293	*Epidamni nomina*	*sic Vet. recte*
		epidamni nomina	—
[*L]	126.1	*commodos*	*al. commodas*
		commodas	—
	126.6	*mulio*	—
		...	*Vet. multo*
[*LO]	126.12	*rogavi ancillam*	*dele ancillam*
		rogavi	—
	127.1	*ornatam*	—
		hornam	*Vet. ornatam*
	127.4	*Quidni*	—
		quid tu	*Vet. Quidni*
	129.5	*quid tandem agas*	*scribe tamen*
		quid tamen agas	—
	130.1	*hunc*	—
		...	*vet. hanc*
	130.5	*invenio*	—
		...	*al. invideo*
[*L]	131.7	*alis*	*al. aliis*
		...	*aliis Vet. ex. fortassis rectius*
[*LO]	131.8.6	*silvester Iasdon*	*Bit. yasdon*
		silvester iasdon	*Thol. ex. silvestris hirundo nullum*
			ex. Aedon
	131.10	*quod*	*scribe ecquid*
		ecquid	—
	133.3.8–9	*egenis Attritus*	—
		egenus attritis	*Vet. egenis Attritus*
	133.3.15	*lactens*	—
		...	*al. lactans*
	134.3	*multavit*	*sic vet. non mulcavit*
		mulcavit	*vet. multavit*
[*L]	134.11	*cornu*	*al. corvum*
		...	*al. corvum for. cornum*
[*LO]	134.12.15	*Idaeo frutices*	*Sic Vet. ex. non latices*
		...	*sic Vet. ex. rectius*
	135.8.6	*molli stillae*	*mollistillae] sic Aut. al. molistilla*
		molli stilla	*Aut. mollistillae*
	135.8.8	*Et paries*	*Autis. At paries*
		At paries	—
	136.2	*frangitur ergo*	*Politian ...*

		...	—
	136.4	*foedoque*	—
		foedeque	*al.* foedoque
	137.1	*admisisti*	*al.* admiseris
		admiseris	*al.* admisisti
[*LOφ]	137.9.1	Quisquis habet	*Io. Salisb.Pol.lib.vii.c.xvi*
		...	—
[*L]	138.1	*veticae trito*	<u>Sic Vet.</u>
		urticae trito	—
	139.2.6	*cavit Ulixes*	<u>Vet.</u> pavit
		pavit Ulixes	—
	140.15	*levatores*	<u>Sic Vet. non</u> leccatores, <u>quos antiq.</u>
			<u>Gloss. gulosos & lenones interpret</u> ...
		...	<u>sic vet.</u>
	141.10	*Petavii*	<u>Sic. vet. Bened. exemp. quod unicum</u>
			<u>hac in parte habuimus</u>
		...	<u>Thol. cod.</u> Petausi
	141.10	*captabant*	—
		...	[<u>Thol. cod.</u>] captabatur

The above is not a complete list of the notes in the *varietates*, since I have omitted the ones wherein p^1 and p^2 agree in lemma (reflecting the same text), variants, and cited source. For it is in the exhibited differences, especially where the same variant is listed with a differing ascription, that useful information may be carried on the meaning of these citations. We are interested, particularly, in what we see as inconsistencies, for they must make us redefine Pithou's terms and in consequence the value of the readings according to their sources – manuscript or otherwise – behind them.

There are around 106 differences between p^{1v} and p^{2v}. As one would expect of a second edition separated from its predecessor by 10 years, p^{2v} is used to convey new information received, or a change of opinion in the mean time. One might expect also that a number of textual changes have been made in accordance with this. We see immediately from our list that there are in fact far fewer text changes than differences in the *varietas*: there are 46 alterations, most of them slight. In these cases we can expect to see the new direction signalled in p^{2v}, and this is done. But in many other instances a reading or suggestion in p^{1v} is adopted into the text, and reference to it does not occur in p^{2v}; thus at 2.8, 7.1, 10.7, 29.1, etc. This is done for several reasons. More than once (as possibly at 2.8 and at 29.1) it was to correct a misprint. On the other hand a new inconsistency emerges in 2.8, where the cited lemma fails to receive the capitalization occurring in the text. This is surely another printing or mechanical error. It, and the example at 3.1, where the lemma in **p¹** (*scola*) again differs from the text it purports to cite (*schola*), illustrate the extreme hazard of taking any such discrepancy as transmissional. In the latter we actually see the **Bituricus** reading cited as *scola* in **p¹ᵛ** and as *schola* in **p²ᵛ**. This is excellent evidence to show either some sort of inaccuracy, or, more likely, that Pithou regarded the spelling variant as immaterial. In either case, it demonstrates that we should place no reliance on similar spelling differences between **P** and the alleged citations by Pithou of his **Bituricus** in arguing for separate manuscripts.

There is a wealth of other inferences to be made from the comparisons, of which now I provide a selection. Some entries are relevant to the debate on the identity of **Autissiodurensis**: in **p¹ᵛ** at 16.3 Pithou clearly identifies *sacrum* as the reading of *Autis.*, but in the corresponding position in **p²** he notes it only as coming from *vet.* It seems reasonable to infer that the same manuscript is being referred to. In other words, it did not trouble Pithou to be vague now about a source which he had earlier named specifically. We must take it from this that not all the **Autissiodurensis** readings which Pithou uses are so labelled. In fact, we have seen above that **p²ᵛ**, particularly, has a tendency to delete the *Autis.* designation (at 88.4, 88.5, and 135.8.8) and replace it with a generality or not at all. Further, we are by no means entitled to expect that Pithou selected, clearly marked, every instance of an **Autissiodurensis** variant, to the extent that a variant not cited by Pithou but seen in **B** may be given as evidence, *ex silentio*, that the two sources are different. In the case of *sacrum*, for the unique reason given above, the reading of **B** cannot be verified.[86] At 80.9.2 also *vet.* couches the identity of a manuscript that may again be **Autissiodurensis**, since the reading cited, *mobile*, appears in **B**.

A third instance of the same phenomenon shows that *vet.* and *al.* are to Pithou synonyms. At 133.3.15 a reading seen by Pithou and cited from '*al.*,' *lactans*, is available to us in **B** and **P**. No doubt he saw it in either or both manuscripts and on this occasion was content to be unspecific about the source. A final instance of **Autissiodurensis** interest, which raises the question of typographical error, is 135.8.6 *molli stillae*, the text entry of **p** which unaccountably becomes a single word in the lemma, and in this form is given the authority of '*Aut.*' This is repeated for **p²ᵛ**, but can it be the reading of *Autis.* or is the version in the text meant? Can the fact that **B** has it in two words, like the text, be serious evidence that **B** is not the same as *Autis.*?

The conclusion to be drawn from all this is simply that we are not

entitled to hold Pithou to consistency and to make arguments for identification on that basis. Furthermore, it takes only a single instance of verified
looseness to establish change as a phenomenon likely to occur at any time.
On the subject of misprints, I should say that they must be few, but one
should keep their prospect in view also: 7.1 *num quid* in the $\mathbf{p^{1v}}$, approvingly
given under '*scribe*,' seems to enter the later text as a single word. Then
there is the case at 122.148, where *adulti* in the text of $\mathbf{p^2}$ is followed,
illogically, by '*al. adulti*' in the *varietas*. The convention would be satisfied
either by printing *adusti* (the 'al.' reading of $\mathbf{p^{1v}}$), or else by repeating the
$\mathbf{p^{1v}}$ entry. Of course the inconsistencies in the printing of the citing
conventions are legion and should not be seen as signifying anything.

Asterisks, however, appear to be treated less casually by Pithou. This
feature of the *L manuscripts is taken by him in more or less the same
way as we regard it: indication of something missing. Seeing it in their
manuscripts, the editors copied it to conjecture lacunae of their own (or
else they deleted the asterisk if disagreeing that a gap existed). Our instances
here are at 10.7, 117.1, and 122.169, where the suggested deletion of the
asterisk is acted upon in the ensuing edition; conversely, at 114.8 one is
added for the new text.

THE IDENTITY OF **Tholosanus**

The most celebrated appearance in $\mathbf{p^{2v}}$ is that of Pithou's **Tholosanus**, an
*L-class manuscript (as we know from certain exclusive contexts) whose
readings Pithou quoted 21 times, though adopting scarcely one for his text.
Only at 23.3.1 *nunc* does he accept the inclusion of this word from that
manuscript with approval – not that we can argue that it did not exist in
the only other manuscript source available to him, **Benedictinus**, since he
cited it in $\mathbf{p^{1v}}$ with '*lege*.' This might indicate that he followed the text of **t**
here for his own edition, and put the reading of **Benedictinus** in the
apparatus, only to admit it when it appeared also in **Tholosanus**. Alter-
natively, one would have to argue that *nunc* was a conjecture, happily
confirmed by the **Tholosanus** reading, which thus here differed from
Benedictinus. Since the term '*lege*' is often used for conjectures (cf.
Chapter 6), this option is preferred.

29.3 presents the possibility, also, that there may be even more **Tholosanus** readings in $\mathbf{p^{2v}}$, unacknowledged. In this context only one manuscript existed to Pithou for $\mathbf{p^{1v}}$: '*vet.*' *tema*. This was no doubt his
Benedictinus (Pithou prints in his text *tenia*, the reading of **t**). Whence
came the differing '*vet.*' *Temena* of $\mathbf{p^{2v}}$? **Tholosanus** is certainly one
prospect, though it could also be a rereading of his **Benedictinus**. Similarly
at 83.7 the '*al.*' which supplies *quod genus* could be a manuscript. We note
that 14 variants (of which 13 are rejected) out of the 21 in **Tholosanus**

are in the exclusive *L context. Thus Pithou's text reading comes either from his **Benedictinus** or from **t**, the edition which preceded his own.

We are challenged by the 21 *Thol.* citations in **p²ᵛ** to identify on their basis the manuscript from which they derive. Since it becomes clear very soon that this was an *L manuscript, we cannot hope to equate it with any manuscript surviving today. Our task is then to test for uses of this manuscript by comparing readings in other sixteenth-century editions, which, in defining their sources, help us to obtain further 'fixes' on the manuscript. It was Ullman who first suggested that this **Tholosanus** of Pithou was probably the manuscript used by de Tournes – hinted to have been supplied by Cujas – in **t**.[87] Ullman proceeds to equate a **Cuiacianus**, on external grounds, with a long manuscript used by Scaliger for his handwritten edition (**l**). The inference, on external grounds alone, is that all three editors used a single manuscript, and that therefore **Tholosanus = Cuiacianus**. For Ullman the identification was confirmed internally by **Tholosanus ltᵛ** agreements where the readings divided against the other possibilities. The case was well established and has been fully accepted by subsequent editors. I should like to review the data with a view to testing its quality and making a number of supplementary points pertaining to the editorial habits of the day.

THE READINGS OF '*Thol.*' IN **p²ᵛ**, AGAINST **p²**, WITH AGREEMENTS[88]

[*LO]	2.3	*deberent loqui* **lt**: *loqui debemus* **tᵛ**
[*LOφ]	5.1.9	*arces* **lt**: *artes*
	5.1.18	*celeri* **lt**: *sceleris*
[*LO]	17.3	*inter se usque ad* **t**: *interius in* **ltᵛ**
	17.3	*contritis* **t**: *constrictis*
	17.9	*protendo* **t**: *obtendo* **ltᵛ**
[*L]	23.3.1	*convenite spatalocinaedi* **tp¹**: *c. nunc s.* **lp¹ᵛp²**
[*LH]	28.8	*cerasino* **lt**: *Caesarino*
	31.9	*bisaccio* **lt**: *bisatrio*
	34.5	*obīt* (*obit* **pᵛ**): *obiter* **lt**
	35.3	*ac rienes* **lt**: *aetienes*
	35.4	*odopetam* **lt**: *adopetam*: *oclopetam*
	36.3	*utriculis* (*inticulis* **pᵛ**): *intriculis*: *interculis* **tᵛ**: *int culis* **t**: *int⁷culis* **l**
[*L]	83.6	*Ligurgo*: *ligargo*: *Lycurgo* **lt**
	102.15	*barbam* **t**: *barbara* **ltᵐᵃʳᵍⁱⁿᵉ**
	106.3	*prosit* **lt**: *possit*
	107.1	*ad hoc officium*: *ad hoc officium legatum* **lt**
[*LO]	109.8	*capillorum* **t**: *in capillos suos* **ltᵛ**

131.8.6   *silvester Iasdon* **t**: *silvestris hirundo* **l**: <u>*silvester aedon*</u>

[*L]   141.10   *Petavii* **lt**: *Petausi*: <u>*Petelini*</u>

141.10   <u>*captabant*</u> **lt**: *captabatur*

We note, first, outright **Tholosanus lt^v** agreement against all other sources at 17.3, 17.9, and 109.8, and may very well add the instance of 36.3, where the difference is in a ligature. Hence on all the occasions where the **Cuiacianus** reading can be found in all three sources there is agreement. It is worth noting that this small number of common **Cuiacianus** readings, when more of them were thus demonstrably available, in no way serves to call the identification into question. It simply means that de Tournes and Pithou employed the normal editorial practice (cf. Chapter 8 for Dupuy's use of **B**) of selecting only **Cuiacianus** variants which interested them for contrast, and ignored the rest. This amounts to de Tournes' ignoring 16 out of the above 21, and Pithou's, in citing 21 readings, ignoring the substantial number of 77 others that are to be found in **t^v**.

Scaliger's testimony must play a part, though the sources of his readings are not often easy to interpret. External evidence suggests, as we have seen, that he gained his **Cuiacianus** readings from a visit to Valence in 1571. In the ***LO** contexts, **Tholosanus** and **l** agree in five instances out of eight; here, of course, Scaliger had other manuscripts to choose from. Yet in the exclusive ***L** context elsewhere he differs from **Cuiacianus** clearly at least seven times. How can this be? Since he shares the readings of **t** on these occasions a ready explanation is that **l** was composed later, that is to say, after 1575.[89] Apparent influence of this sort from **t** but not from **p** may make one suspect that **l** was produced shortly after the *editio princeps* of the new, expanded *Satyrica* and was in fact stimulated by it. Attractive though this seems, there is good contrary evidence (see Chapter 1, n. 14), that **l** was made earlier, and if this is the case the explanation should have to be sought in another ***L** manuscript, or (more likely) readings or conjectures informally shared by Scaliger and de Tournes. Again, the identity of **Tholosanus** with **Cuiacianus** need not be threatened.

The two editions published by Pierre Pithou secure for this many-sided scholar the place of the most scrupulous Petronius editor of his age and the most valuable for our own. Here was a man in the happy position of being able to consult every important medieval Petronius manuscript that survived (with the exception of **R**). If, as I have argued in this chapter, we can share with him **B** and **P**, we may approach his testimony on the lost ***L**-class sources, **Benedictinus** and **Cuiacianus**, with something like confidence.

4

Pierre Daniel and
Bernensis 276

In a 1978 article M.D. Reeve and R.H. Rouse commenced an evaluation of the marginal annotations in a thirteenth-century Papias dictionary that today, together with a *Hugutionis Vocabularium*, makes up **Bernensis 276**.[90] The principal focus of this first study was citations from the commentary of Aelius Donatus on Terence. Subsequent efforts of these two scholars have greatly enlarged the number of citations identified, and an impressive set of authors and excerpts has emerged. It becomes clear that the interests of the annotator provide a curriculum and resource list of medieval learning, together with opportunities to evaluate the contemporary condition of classical texts and their transmission.[91]

It is no wonder, then, that the reporting of three citations from Petronius should have aroused interest.[92] For the medieval activity on this author is today quite obscure and not very well represented. A whole separate manuscript branch (***L**) has not survived. Altogether we possess: three representatives (**BRP**) of the class known as **O**; florilegia taken from a forerunner of ***L** (**Λ**; see stemma, Figure 1), but showing influence of **O**; and a single early Renaissance copy of the **Cena**, known as **H**.[93] Thus any new-found Petronius material in a manuscript of this era must immediately be tested for belonging in the extant or the non-extant branches, in both, or in neither.

These first three citations from the *Satyrica*, although containing book and title attributions of some interest and value, were textually unpromising: all three are in the medievally dominant and extant **O** branch, and two are in the florilegia – which at least showed that the anonymous compiler had gone beyond that collection. In point of fact, two were already known to scholars as citations, for it was possible to see them, taken from an apparent glossary and a *vetus liber*, in the apparatus of Bücheler 1862, that scholar having got them from the *Notae* of Pierre Daniel printed first in Goldast's 1610 Petronius edition.[94] The appearance of these same citations in a manuscript in Bern, with its well-known Daniel associations, indicates the need to determine whether in **Bernensis 276** we have the actual manuscript source of Daniel and to see where this finding may lead.

By 1983 five additional *Satyrica* citations had been remarked. Again, their content did not seem to merit focused scrutiny: the investigator's interest was drawn, rather, to the style of the attributions, and to one instance of a word apparently from outside the commoner ***LO** branches.[95] Most of these citations too had been found by Bücheler in the *Notae* of Pierre Daniel, attributed variously, including two which are now to be counted among the *Fragments* and thus lie outside not only ***LO** but also the *Cena* – beyond the early ninth-century archetype of our *Satyrica*. The present tally stands at eleven, a sufficient number at last to move toward a more definitive treatment of their possible connection with Daniel's scholarship and of their potential for adding to knowledge of the *Satyrica*'s textual history.[96]

The piecemeal way in which the evidence has accumulated over the last decade has served to disguise the suggestive link between the freshly revealed Petronius material in **Bernensis 276** and the citations recorded by Bücheler of Pierre Daniel: it has attracted virtually no direct attention despite the exactness of the correspondence and the well-attested possession of this manuscript by Daniel for something like 40 years.[97] If the identification can be established, some useful features follow: Daniel's method of referring to the manuscript, where present in the *Notae*, can be used to supply data both on its provenance and on Daniel's scholarly technique in matters of accuracy and consistency. In the former regard, there is the evidence to be dealt with of an immediate provenance different from the locale argued by Reeve and Rouse 1978.[98] Daniel's *Notae* therefore take on an importance that surpasses their interest to Petronian studies, since they offer this key to knowledge affecting the manuscript as a whole.

The immediate provenance of **Bernensis 276** (that is, prior to acquisition by Daniel) is of course not necessarily the same as its ultimate origin, or its location at the time of consultation by the mid-thirteenth-century lexicographer. There can be no reason here not to accept fully the persuasive case for the Orléanais, made on the basis of the curricular interests evinced from the texts cited, together with the occasional *ipse vidi* attesting a specific location.[99] Yet that still leaves 300 years to be accounted for. It would be normal to infer an unbroken sojourn until Daniel's time, but some evidence of possession by one John of Guignencourt, perhaps the man who was Chancellor of the University of Paris in the late fourteenth century, implies a break and a northward move.[100] We are not having to consider great distances, even in medieval France: Reeve and Rouse 1978, invoking a piece of evidence of Daniel's (on which see below), believed that the manuscript returned from Paris or Beauvais the hundred or so kilometres to the Orléanais, specifically Fleury. It is my contention that, if we accept the hitherto unused testimony of the *Notae*, **Bernensis 276** took the much shorter route to St. Denis, though I have not found any evidence yet to associate John of Guignencourt with the Abbey.

The very possession of **Bernensis 276** by Daniel exerts a strong pull for Fleury, but one which Rouse 1979 cognizantly seems to have resisted, since against his inclinations he must infer the Fleury antecedence not from any historical connection but out of specific evidence from Daniel himself.[101] This consists of a citation by the annotator of **Bernensis 276** ascribed to the *Aulularia* of Plautus but corrected by Daniel to the pseudo-Plautine *Querolus*, a play which is mentioned, as Daniel notes elsewhere, in an ancient glossary that was furnished by the monastery of St. Benoît, Fleury-sur-Loire.[102] One may still wonder at the ability of Fleury to impose itself with this single instance, despite the caveats which the authors themselves define: **Bernensis 276** is not especially old, thus a reference to it as *'vetustissimus'* is not really appropriate; and it may have left the Loire region at some point.

But a most important consideration is that **Bernensis 276** is not the only glossary that qualifies. There was at least one other, also containing Petronius material, as we may infer from a passage in his *Notae* where Daniel sets out evidence for the *Satyrica* being a fragment of a larger work divided into books: *'nisi fallunt veteres Glossarii, qui subinde Petronii testimonia citant et advocant è "libro primo Satyrarum"'*.[103] Daniel finds one instance of this in his glossary next to *excelsissimus* (88.4), and another next to the verse line *Et thymbrae veteres et passis uva racemis* (135.8.14). He continues: *'Quin et in veteri Glossario S. Benedicti Floriacensis habetur hic locus desumptus è Petronio Arbitro libro XV. "Sed video te totum in illa haerere tabula, quae Troiae halosin ostendit"'.* I interpret Daniel's way of introducing the third citation (*'Quin et'*) as implying that this last quote existed in a *separate* glossary, and that the provenance of the glossary containing the first two citations was not Fleury, like this last one. Support for the purely linguistic inferences comes from the presence of the first two quotes in **Bernensis 276** and of the third, the passage from Book XV, in another glossary once owned by Daniel, **Harleianus 2735** (see Plate 2).[104] This in turn affirms for **Harleianus 2735** a Fleury provenance – an important consideration when seeking a candidate for the Fleury glossary containing the mention of the pseudo-Plautine *Querolus*; and equally, it argues against a Fleury provenance for **Bernensis 276**.[105]

We should now try to determine whether **Bernensis 276** is the principal glossary authority for the Petronius citations in Daniel's *Notae*. Of the altogether eleven citations which I have seen in the manuscript, no less than seven turn up in Daniel's commentary.[106] Given that these references to our author do not occur in the fixed Papias text but in marginalia unlikely to be duplicated elsewhere, it seems highly likely that all seven derive from the single source that we have before us, **Bernensis 276**. A comparison of the language in the corresponding passages (see below) should put this beyond doubt. It is now that Daniel's attributions – his methods of attaching authority, manuscript or other, to the readings which he selects for his commentary – take on particular significance. Three attributions out of the seven (two from a *glossarium*, the other from a *codex*) advert to '*S. Dionysii*'; another is said simply to come from a '*vet. lexicon*,' another from a '*vetus glossarium*'; one more is quoted from a '*vetus grammaticus*'; and one last from Cornutus citing Juvenal (though the word is followed in Daniel's commentary by the manuscript annotator's exact definition of it).[107]

The three quotes given various, general sources without the detail of provenance do not, to my mind, weaken the St. Denis argument. Though they are imprecise they still qualify as descriptions of **Bernensis 276**, and Daniel's inconsistencies fall well within the bounds of sixteenth-century practice.[108] Before laying out the evidence, therefore, I should like to anticipate two conclusions: **Bernensis 276** is the single glossary source under the name of Petronius used by Pierre Daniel on seven occasions in his *Notae*; and the glossary manuscript, so far as Daniel was concerned, derived from the library of the Royal Abbey of St. Denis.

Since the latter removes **Bernensis 276** from consideration as the Fleury glossary with a *Querolus* mention, an alternative must be found to satisfy this requirement.[109] **Harleianus 2735** presents itself as the obvious prospect on grounds of Daniel's ownership and the Fleury provenance, as noted above. This manuscript, for being ninth-century, also accords better with Daniel's tag of '*vetustissimus*.' Now if a 'mention' of the *Querolus* were found in **Harleianus 2735**, it would go a long way to securing it as the glossary alluded to by Daniel in his *Querolus* edition, and at the same time strengthen the hold of St. Denis on **Bernensis 276**. My inspection has not turned up a reference to the *Querolus* by name, after the manner of the correction to the title of *Aulularia* by Daniel in **Bernensis 276**. However, on f. 7v, in reference to the entry '*apage*' and its definition, in the space above the column there is a medieval reference to '*Plaut. In aulularia*,' followed by the word in its context in the pseudo-Plautine *Querolus*.[110] Aside from this direct reference there are, scattered about the text of the manuscript, numerous single-word citations attributed simply to Plautus. On at least 30 occasions the author's name has been repeated in the margin by Daniel. As a rule, identification of the play from which these isolated words come has not been practised.[111]

A further corroboration of the link between the *'vetustissimus liber glossarum'* and **Harleianus 2735**, at the expense of **Bernensis 276**, is to be found in Daniel's same 1564 *editio princeps* of the *Querolus*. On page 18 of the text there is the word *patus*. In a note commenting on it Daniel writes: *'neque tamen praetereundum est quod in antelato vetustiss. lib. glossarum "patus," id est, pacem tenens, expositum repperi: et hanc interpretationem secutus est Papias in suo* [i.e. another; emphasis supplied] *Lexico.'* Now on f. 105v of **Harleianus 2735** there is the entry *Patus. Pacem tenens.* It should not escape us that Daniel has found this word from the *Querolus* in his glossary without any help from an attribution. In a further instance, to justify the selection of the spelling of *obaudire* (as against *oboedire*) for his *Querolus* text Daniel writes in his notes, *'ut in lexico manuscripto repperi.'* For this we compare **Harleianus 2735** f. 91v *'obaudiens: dictus ab aure eo quod audiat imperantem.'*

We are now free to return with some confidence to viewing **Bernensis 276** as the glossary ascribed by Daniel more than once to St. Denis. External corroboration is of course lacking; factual confirmation by way of a St. Denis shelfmark, or perhaps some entry in a library catalogue, would have been conclusive, though absence of this data does not in itself weaken the claim. Though books were catalogued at St. Denis under various administrations, no inventories for this period have survived.[112] Characteristics of writing and indications of origin or provenance of the manuscript before Johannes 'de guidincuria' do not enter into the argument. Further, commencing in the mid-fifteenth century, and continuing for a hundred years, a period of disorder settled on the monastery, caused by internal rivalries. This culminated in the sack by the Huguenots in 1567.[113] The external picture is therefore not conducive to finding good codicological demonstrations.

Daniel's connection with Fleury is admittedly stronger than that with St. Denis. His standing in Orléans and his Huguenot credentials, together with his scholarly interests, put him in an unrivalled position to effect the rescue of many ancient volumes from the Fleury manuscript collection when that monastery fell in 1562.[114] Though cynics may question his right to such good fortune, there can be no arguing that in this manner material was saved for posterity which could otherwise have been sold off to less responsible owners, stolen, or destroyed – all with the same result. He did not play quite such a role at St. Denis: at this abbey's sack in 1567 it was the turn of other scholars such as Lefèvre, de Thou, and Paul Petau to be on hand to secure through purchase and exchange the lion's share.[115]

But according to Daniel's ex-libris and the 1565 date, we should take it that **Bernensis 276**, a manuscript to which the marginal annotations must have lent a special value – I daresay, in the light of his *Notae*, not least for the Petronius citations – had already been acquired by Daniel and was safely in his hands.[116]

I have opted to set out in list form the full details of the Petronius citations in **Bernensis 276**, followed by an interpretation. The correspondence of the quotes, plus Daniel's repetition in many cases of the attribution used by the medieval marginal annotator, provides the backbone of the case for this manuscript being Daniel's source, and so Daniel's method of citing authority warrants especial scrutiny. This thirteenth-century material – both Petronius text and manner of attribution, with book numbers and the like – is a new, direct, and independent source for data, respectively on the contemporary condition of the manuscripts and on the evolution of the transmission. The interpretation seeks to lay out the uses and limitations of this data. Also, at one remove, Daniel's own reaction to this material, requiring careful extrapolation from his choice of lemma, choice of variant, and format of note and attribution, has its part to play. For all was governed by the different mix of manuscripts available to him together with the condition of the late-sixteenth-century *Satyrica* text and the assumptions upon which it was based.

CITATIONS ATTRIBUTED TO PETRONIUS IN MS, USED BY DANIEL

(a) Reference in **Bernensis 276**   f. 51
     Papias entry and definition   <u>cripta</u> *spelunca cuneus*
     Annotator's citation   *satis constaret eos nisi inclinatos non solere transire cryptam Neopolitanam*
     Petronius context   Fragment XVI
     Annotator's attribution   *Petronius*
     Daniel lemma   *satis constaret eos*
     Daniel attribution   *ex Glossario S. Dionysii*
     Daniel note   —
     Goldast 1610 reference   p. 96
     Bücheler 1862 note   *probabiliter illa libro qui quintum decimum antecessit attribueris*
     Bücheler reference to Daniel   p. 211

(b) Reference in **Bernensis 276**   f. 55v
     Papias entry and definition   <u>delicatus</u> *dicitur quod deliciis pastus*

Annotator's citation   *delicatus*
Petronius context   45.3 *non debemus delicati esse* [H]
                                             63.3 *ipsimi nostri delicatus decessit* [H]
Annotator's attribution   *Petronius in primo Satyrarum*
Daniel lemma   *num alio genere*
Daniel note   *contra delicatos lectores*
Daniel attribution   *Petronius in primo Satyrarum ... Ex vet.*
                                             Grammatico

Goldast reference   p. 79
Bücheler note   —
Bücheler reference to Daniel   p. 3

(c) Reference in **Bernensis 276**   f. 74v
     Papias entry and definition   *excelsus valde celsus elatus immensus*
                                             altus eminens

     Annotator's citation   *excelsissimus*
     Petronius context   88.4 *in cacumine excelsissimi montis*
                                             [*LOφ]

     Annotator's attribution   *Petronius in primo Satyrarum*
     Daniel lemma   *Eudoxus quidem in cacumen excelsissimi*
                                             montis conscendit

     Daniel note   *Excelsissimus dicitur à Petronio in primo*
                                             Satyrarum ...
     Daniel attribution   *vetus glossarium; Vet. Lexicon*
     Goldast reference   pp. 77, 84
     Bücheler note   *in Ī id est libro pro I reponendum censet*
                                             Wehlius
     Bücheler reference to Daniel   p. 103

(d) Reference in **Bernensis 276**   f. 153v
     Papias entry and definition   *obiter simul ... obiter dum in itinere est*
                                             ... obiter velociter

     Annotator's citation   *obiter id est interim*
     Petronius context   26.5 [*LO] (31.4, 34.5, 38.3 [H]; 92.2
                                             [*L])

     Annotator's attribution   *sic sumitur a Petronio in Satyris*
     Daniel lemma   *obiter labra* (26.5)
     Daniel note   *obiter, id est, interim*
     Daniel attribution   *sic apud Iuvenalem accipi notat Cornu-*
                                             tus ipsius interpres

     Goldast reference   p. 82

Bücheler note (p. 28)	*valgiter* [cf. (p), below] '*margo t, Goldastiana secundum Fulgentium ... (fragm. X)*'
Bücheler reference to Daniel	—

(e) Reference in **Bernensis 276**

	f. 173v
Papias entry and definition	<u>*petaurum*</u> *genus ludi*
Annotator's citation	*petauroque iubente modo superior*
Petronius context	Fragment XV
Annotator's attribution	*Petronius*
Daniel lemma	*petauroque iubente modo superior*
Daniel note	*Petaurus genus ludi. Petronius, &c.*
Daniel attribution	*Glossar. S. Dionysii*
Goldast reference	p. 96
Bücheler note	*expleri his oportet lacunam* [54.2: **H**] *petaurus formam commentus glossator est*
Bücheler reference to Daniel	p. 210

(f) Reference in **Bernensis 276**

	f. 180
Papias entry and definition	<u>*pondo*</u> *plurale indeclinabile neutrum genus ponderis libra*
Annotator's citation	*id est libra idem as vel assis: ipse senatus recti bonique preceptor mille pondo auri capitolio promittere solet*
Petronius context	88.9 [***LOφ**]
Annotator's attribution	*Petronius in libro Satyrarum*
Daniel lemma	*recti honestique* [reading of **s**]
Daniel note	*bonique*
Daniel attribution	*sic* [*bonique*] *habet V. Cod. S. Dionysii, sic & meus*
Goldast reference	p. 84
Bücheler note	—
Bücheler reference to Daniel	p. 105

(g) Reference in **Bernensis 276**

	f. 256v
Papias entry and definition	<u>*uva passa*</u> *uvae passae*
Annotator's citation	*et tymbrae veteres et passis uva racemis*
Petronius context	135.8.14 [***LO**]
Annotator's attribution	*Petronius in libro primo Satyrarum*

Daniel lemma	*Et thymbrae veteres, et passis uva racemis*
Daniel attribution	*vetus Glossarium ... è libro primo Satyrarum*
Daniel note	—
Goldast reference	p. 77
Bücheler note	—
Bücheler reference to Daniel	p. 194

CITATIONS ATTRIBUTED TO PETRONIUS IN MS, NOT USED BY DANIEL

(h) Reference in **Bernensis 276**   f. 82

Papias entry and definition   *flagrans splendens refulgens accensus furens olens pulchre* [cf. 85 v. *fraglare ardere olere bonum odorem olere*]

Annotator's citation   *innumerabilibus telis gravis atque flagranti stipite*

Petronius context   124.262–3 (*fragranti* **P**) [***LO**]

Annotator's attribution   *Petronius in libro Satyrarum*

(i) Reference in **Bernensis 276**   f. 135v

Papias entry and definition   *merces compendium luchrum redditus*

Annotator's citation   *ergo iudicium nisi publica merces*

Petronius context   14.2.5 *ergo iudicium nihil est nisi publica merces* [***LOφ**]

Annotator's attribution   *Petronius in libro Satyrarum*

(j) Reference in **Bernensis 276**   f. 231v

Papias entry and definition   *suffragium auxilium vel suffugium*

Annotator's citation   *ad predam strepitumque lucri suffragia vertunt*

Petronius context   119.40 [***LOφ**]

Annotator's attribution   *Petronius in libro Satyrarum*

(k) Reference in **Bernensis 276**   f. 232

Papias entry and definition   *sum es est inde dicitur ens futurus ... presens (pres)entia unde componitur inpresentiarum adverbium*

Annotator's citation   *depresentiarum*

Petronius context   58.3, 74.17 **[H]**
Annotator's attribution   *Petronius*

CITATIONS NOT ATTRIBUTED TO PETRONIUS IN MS, USED BY DANIEL

(l) Reference in **Bernensis 276**   f. 158
     Papias entry and definition   *opertus opertus et expertus ut a pario partus*

     Annotator's citation   —
     Petronius context   11.2 *opertum me amiculo evolvit* **[L]**
     Annotator's attribution   —
     Daniel lemma   *opertam me*
     Daniel citation   *opertum*
     Daniel attribution   *Glossarium sancti Dionysii*
     Daniel note   —
     Goldast reference   p. 81
     Bücheler note   *Daniel qui* opertam *in lemmate scripsit*
     Bücheler reference to Daniel   p. 13

(m) Reference in **Bernensis 276**   f. 219
     Papias entry and definition   *Sichel quod Latine siclus corrupte dicitur* [cf. f. 219v *siclus qui Graece dicitur stater xx obolos habet*]

     Annotator's citation   —
     Petronius context   14.3 *unum dipondium sicel lupinosque* **[*L]**

     Annotator's attribution   —
     Daniel lemma   *sicel, lupinosque*
     Daniel note   *Turneb. ... pro* sicel *legendum putat* scilicet. *Sed in vet. Lexico sic habetur;* Sicel Latino *sermone* siclus *appellatur* corruptè *... In alio Lexico legitur;* Siclus, *id* est, stater, *qui* habet obolos XX

     Daniel attribution   *in vet. Lexico*
     Goldast reference   p. 81
     Bücheler note   —
     Bücheler reference to Daniel   —

OTHER CITATIONS, OF LEXICA AND GLOSSARIES, BY DANIEL

(n) Reference in MS   ?
    Daniel lemma   *quibus deberent loqui*
    Petronius context   2.3 *invenerunt verba quibus deberent loqui* [***LO**]
    Daniel citation   *loqui debemus*
    Daniel attribution   *in v. Glossario S. Dionysii*
    Daniel note   —
    Goldast reference   p. 79
    Bücheler note   —
    Bücheler reference to Daniel   p. 4

(o) Reference in MS   ?
    Daniel lemma   *embasico aetas* [reading of **s**]
    Petronius context   26.1 *iam embasicoetas praeferebat facem* [***LO**]
    Daniel citation   *Embasicoeta, qui vel quae frequenter dat basia*
    Daniel attribution   *Vet. Lexicon*
    Daniel note   *Leg.* <u>*embasicoetas*</u>
    Goldast reference   p. 82
    Bücheler note   —
    Bücheler reference to Daniel   —

(p) Reference in MS   ?
    Daniel lemma   *obtorto valgiter labello*
    Petronius context   Fragment X
    Daniel citation   *Obtorto valgiter labello*
    Daniel attribution   *in vet. cod. & vet. Glossario*
    Daniel note   *vulgo apud Fulgentium,* <u>*Abrosa*</u> <u>*valgia*</u> <u>*labello*</u> ...
    Goldast reference   p. 95
    Bücheler note   —
    Bücheler reference to Daniel   p. 209

(q) Reference in MS   ?
    Daniel lemma   *dividias mentis*
    Petronius context   —
    Daniel citation   *Dividia, discordia, bellona* ...
    Daniel attribution   *In vet. Lexico*

Daniel note	*apud Fulgentium in verbo DIVIDIAE,* *citatur* <u>*Propertius*</u> *... leg.* <u>*Petronius*</u> *(quomodo ... Scaliger non malè iudi- cavit) ...*
Goldast reference	p. 97
Bücheler note	—
Bücheler reference to Daniel	—

(r) Reference in **Harleianus 2735**   f. 43 (Plate 2)

Daniel lemma	*sed video te totum in illa haerere tabula*
Petronius context	89.1 [***LO**]
Daniel citation	*sed video te totum in illa haerere tabula, quae Troiae halosin ostendit*
Daniel attribution	*in vet. Lexico S. Benedicti Floriacensis*
Daniel note	*citatur ex lib. XV. Petronii Arbitri ... in excussis extat fragmentis*
Goldast reference	pp. 77, 84
Bücheler note	—
Bücheler reference to Daniel	p. 105

OTHER *'PETRONIUS'* CITATIONS, IN **Harleianus 2735**

(s) Reference in **Harleianus 2735**   f. 8v

MS entry	*aumatium ...*
Annotator's citation	*in aumatium memet ipsum conieci*
Petronius context	Fragment XIII [Fulgentius]
Annotator's attribution	*Petronius Arbiter*
Daniel lemma	*in aumatium*
Daniel attribution	*sic Fulgentius*
Goldast reference	p. 95
Bücheler note	—
Bücheler reference to Daniel	p. 210

(t) Reference in **Harleianus 2735**   f. 21

MS entry	<u>*dolosus*</u> *insidiosus vel malignus ab eo quod deludit. aliud enim agit et aliud simulat Petronius aliud existimat dicens 'quid est, iudices, dolus? nimirum ubi aliquid factum est quod legi dolet: habe- tis dolum. accipite nunc malum.'*
Petronius context	Fragment XIV [Isidore]

Daniel lemma	*Quid est, Iudices, dolus*
Daniel attribution	*ex Isiod. [sic] ...*
Goldast reference	p. 98
Bücheler note	—
Bücheler reference to Daniel	p. 210

COMPARISON OF ATTRIBUTIONS IN **Bernensis 276** AND DANIEL

Bernensis 276	Daniel's *Notae* (Goldast)
Petronius in primo Satyrarum: (b), (c), (i)	*v. gram./v. gloss./v. lex.*: (b), (c)
Petronius in libro Satyrarum: (f), (h), (j)	*v. cod. S. Dionysii*: (f)
Petronius in libro primo Satyrarum: (g)	*v. gloss.*: (g)
Petronius in Satyris: (d)	*Juvenal apud Cornutum*: (d)
Petronius: (a), (e), (k)	*gloss. S. Dionysii*: (a), (e)

INTERPRETATIONS

Bernensis 276 = *Vet. Lex. Danielis*

The first list sets out the seven instances of correspondence between the Petronius citations in the margins of **Bernensis 276** and Daniel's citation, which generally appears as the lemma in his *Notae*. Since the context of the latter is a Petronius commentary, Daniel does not always find it necessary to specify Petronius or the *Satyrica* as his source or subject (although this information naturally was available to him here in **Bernensis 276** on every occasion of use). Thus the author is not mentioned in (a), (d), and (f), while his name is repeated by Daniel in (b) and (c) because of the importance of the reference to the *primus Satyrarum;* likewise, in (g) Daniel cites the title, though omitting the author's name; (e) simply presents an inconsistency, with Daniel running on with his citation.

In all the cases of attribution to Petronius – (b), (c), (e), and (g) – Daniel employs the same italic script as the quote, indicating that it is copied from his source and not supplied by himself. In contrast, in (a), (d), and (f), the physical source of the quote in Daniel is in normal type, indicating that *he* is providing the information. (c) is very instructive for giving a mix of his own attribution ('*vet. lexicon*') in normal type and the attribution found in **Bernensis 276** in italics. In this way the reader of the commentary is encouraged to take the italicized attributions as actual direct quotes of the manuscript source. In confirmation, **Bernensis 276** gives a very exact correlation between the annotator's attribution and Daniel's. Thus, in (b), (c), and (g), the evidence is of the highest quality; (e) is almost as good; and (a), (d), and (f) certainly offer no contradiction from the point of view of attribution.

The arrangement of the seven citations yields patterns that lead one to suspect that Daniel's methods of citing his physical authority are not as random as they appear.[117] For instance, the three 'St. Denis' attributions – (a), (e), and (f) – share the absence of reference to the 'first book'; while the vaguer attributions – (b), (c), and (g) – come with them; (d) is an oddity and is probably a misattribution by Daniel, having no effect on the patterns.

Two of the 'St. Denis' attributions – (a) and (e) – come from the *Fragments*, which is probably why the annotator did not cite them as deriving either *'e (primo) libro Satyrarum'* or *'in Satyris.'* Attached to them in the annotator's own source was the information that he could repeat: only that they were from *'Petronius.'* This leads to the important inference that these passages did not form part of any *Satyrica* manuscript used by the annotator, and this confirms what we know of the contemporary state of the transmission: the material had become detached from the text by the thirteenth century and was taken by the annotator from an earlier glossary or lexicon. It also supplies the reason for Daniel's specificity: this particular Petronius material was not to be seen elsewhere, in neither manuscripts nor editions available to Daniel or anyone else. It was hitherto unknown to the scholarly world; thus its source was interesting and might prompt a desire for authentication.

The reason for the 'St. Denis' specificity in the citation occurring in *LOφ – (f) – is different but discernible: it gave, in *bonique*, a variant of interest and quality, available in manuscripts but nonetheless rejected by Daniel's lemma in favour of *honestique*, the reading of **s**. Again, the authority was worth quoting with more precision.

In two of the three remaining instances – (c) and (g) – the attention of Daniel was not on textual matters but on the references in his glossary to a 'first book.' They illustrate an observation made in the preface to his commentary, and therefore call for a different and perhaps vaguer form of attribution in the body of the *Notae*.

The case of (b) is a great anomaly. The correspondence of Daniel's attribution with the annotator's confirms Daniel's source for an occurrence in Petronius of a single word, *delicatus*, which was (we now know) hitherto unexampled in the manuscript tradition. Daniel's desire to use it presented him with a problem: being unavailable in any text, its proper position as a lemma within the commentary would be impossible to establish. It could, of course, have been provided as an addendum like the *Fragments* citations (a) and (e), but as a single word it obviously lacked instructiveness. Instead, therefore, Daniel was constrained to find the next most convenient place: at the beginning, as a note to the first lemma of the *Satyrica, num alio genere ...*, and not in the lemma itself. The note reads rather like a Daniel-supplied gloss of the target audience of the opening harangue. However, the use of italics running into the attribution misleadingly implies that *contra delicatos lectores* is part of the citation of '*Petronius in primo Satyrarum.*' **Bernensis 276** confirms that only *delicatus* is vouched for by the annotator as Petronian.

Reference (d) demonstrates another curiosity: Daniel's failure to attribute in any manner to his glossary (**Bernensis 276**) the citation *obiter*. Petronius also is not acknowledged, though this latter, as was noted, would not be a requirement for a Petronius commentary. However, very good evidence for **Bernensis 276** being the source of *obiter* in the meaning approved by Daniel and supplied ostensibly without the assistance of it, as his note *id est interim* in normal type implies, is that this explanation appears in the manuscript as the annotator's gloss. In this case it has suited Daniel to avoid acknowledging his glossary, instead drawing attention to a sense allegedly found in Juvenal, according to Cornutus.

References to Book Division

As is shown from the introductory remarks to his commentary, Daniel was drawn to evidence in his glossary that the surviving *Satyrica* under the name of Petronius was but a fragment of a (longer) version divided up into books (Goldast 1610, p. 77). Daniel cites two examples, for instance, of testimony from '*veteres glossarii*' attributing their Petronius quotes to a '<*liber*> *primus Satyrarum*,' (c) and (g). Daniel does not evaluate this data, but, taking its place alongside other scraps of evidence for the length of the work, it has been generally disbelieved, and grounds have been sought for rejecting it. For it seems scarcely credible that the examples cited, which appear so far along in our version of the *Satyrica* (at 88.4 and 135.8.14) could still be from Book I. Indeed, none of our text may be from the first book.[118] Well before the discovery of **Bernensis 276**'s annotations and its present establishment as Daniel's glossary and hence the source for his evidence, a palaeographic answer to this puzzle had been suggested by Wehle: an abbreviation referring to the general '*liber*' may have been misinterpreted (by Daniel, it was assumed) for the first numeral (I).[119]

The plausibility of this explanation may now be tested from inspecting Daniel's actual source and evaluating all the citations available to him, of which the two given in his *Notae*, we see, were only a sample. It is appropriate to go to the full record, here (see p. 75), of all the allegedly Petronius-derived citations in **Bernensis 276** (11) observable by Daniel: three – (b), (c), and (i) – are under '*Petronius in primo Satyrarum*'; one, (g), under '*Petronius in libro primo Satyrarum*'; three – (f), (h), and (j) – under '*Petronius in libro Satyrarum*'; one – (d) – under '*Petronius in Satyris*'; and three – (a), (e), and (k) – under '*Petronius.*' The latter four may be dismissed from the evidence, of course, and the three '*in libro*' are of no positive help, although their wording may be instructive. **Bernensis 276** demonstrates, actually, that there is little room for palaeographic confusion by Daniel since the references of the annotator do not seem capable of being ambiguous. This has the effect, however, merely of shifting to the annotator the charge of misinterpreting *his* source or dealing with it inconsistently. If this source was an actual manuscript the first seems impossible because, from what we know of the tradition available, there would likely be no reference of this sort to misread: the annotator would be devising his own system of attribution, and inconsistency would be puzzling. It seems best to fall back on the explanation supplied by Wehle, that the references are general indications of a work or volume under the name of *Satirae* and that a numeral has crept in from a misunderstood abbreviation.[120]

The Citations as Evidence for the Textual Transmission

The Petronius material could have confronted the thirteenth-century annotator either in another compilation of short excerpts from which he made the selection which we see, or in an independent manuscript or manuscripts of the author, or perhaps in both. We have no independent evidence yet of another source, rather of the order of those to whom we are indebted for the *Fragments*, containing this specific mix of excerpts. The Petronius citations (and here I count all eleven – the seven taken up by Daniel plus the four others which he found it unnecessary to use) certainly do not depend on the florilegia, since only four are shared – (c), (f), (i), and (j). The majority – (c), (d), (f), (g), (h), (i), (j) – occur in passages common to the two branches of the tradition which emerged as hyparchetypes in the medieval period: ***L** and **O**.[121] Neither was very productive. Of **O** three members survive (**BRP**).[122] There are no extant witnesses of ***L**, but in the thirteenth century, according to our best sixteenth-century evidence, there were probably two such manuscripts, **Benedictinus** and **Cuiacianus**.[123] Other possibilities for texts available to the annotator could be the exemplar of **H** and the potential predecessors of our known branches, like a version of ***L** uncontaminated by **O**, or perhaps a representative of the entire archetype.

Under the above conditions it would seem impossible to choose between an ***L** and an **O** manuscript as the annotator's source for the six citations residing in both. An appeal to variants exhibited either in **BRP** or in the sources quoted by the sixteenth-century editors is not well served by the skimpy data, but there is one clue: the annotator's citation of 124.262–263 – (h) – does not share the variant *fragranti* (for *flagranti*) found in **P**. To what extent this acts as a counterweight to the suggestion of a source close to **P** for the glossary one does not know: in one instance **P** chooses for its title *'satirarum liber,'* a form not found elsewhere and which may have been responsible for the annotator's *'liber Satyrarum'*, but the base word is too capable of individual alteration – making it on different occasions a genre and a profession – to have transmissional value.[124] Useful new data on the tradition out of these seven citations themselves is not yet demonstrable.

The textual significance of the annotator's use of material from outside the ***LO** branches – (a), (b), (e), and (k) – is an intriguing problem. Two of the instances are but single words – *delicatus* and *depresentiarum* – that happen to exist today only in the hyparchetype represented by **H**, one apparently rarer still than ***L** and **O**. Thus when it comes to deciding whether the annotator saw them in a manuscript representative or as lexical items in some work of learning, one is going on very little.[125] To my mind their single-word format, alphabetical closeness, and value as unusual vocabulary all argue for the latter. The other two citations occur nowhere in the archetype, and **Bernensis 276**, as we now know, is the sole and original source for them – which alone places a high value on this glossary manuscript. As mentioned above, they – together with one of the quotes from the **H** hyparchetype – are cited only as *'Petronius,'* without the references to *Satyrae* which accompany the eight others (seven of which can be placed in our *Satyrica* text). This 'absence' is surely most significant and must point to their adoption by the annotator from a secondary source, and one hence without value for indicating the availability of a non-***LO** manuscript to the annotator in the late-thirteenth century.[126] Hence claims for **Bernensis 276** as a witness to the presence around Orléans of a Petronius manuscript other than one related to the dominant medieval branch (**O**) are premature.[127] Yet the case for access to a true manuscript of this latter type, one source in several, remains strong.

The Significance of the Citations Ignored by Daniel

If we take it, as I believe we must, that **Bernensis 276** was accessible to Daniel for his Petronius commentary, we are able to detect at least four Petronius citations that he apparently failed to use: (h), (i), (j), and (k). If, too, Goldast's 'Petri Danielis Notae' is a fair depiction, without omissions, of this commentary, we can only guess at the reasons for this. The citations appear to me as no less interesting and worthy of a lemma than the rest. Indeed (k), one would think, deserves a mention 'ex Glossario' because of its absence in the manuscripts and editions available to Daniel; but for the same reason its place in the text could not be fixed. Of the others, two – (h) and (j) – occur in the Bellum Civile. There would be an excellent reason for Daniel to cite **Bernensis 276** for (j) suffragia, since he does in fact use this in a lemma, but with a variant noted from Vincent of Beauvais. Thus an attribution formula such as the one at (f) would have well suited this entry too. We must assume that it was simply not wanted (or missed). The other Bellum Civile citation not taken up – (h) – occurs within an odd and unprecedented gap in Daniel's commentary (122.160–125.4) that includes the last half of the poem – the reason for which must remain unknown; a mechanical omission is certainly suggested by the size. But if this was deliberate, we can only conclude that Daniel saw little interest in the citations themselves, and nothing worth recounting in their attribution in **Bernensis 276**, where we note that 'Petronius in libro' and 'Petronius in primo' duplicate the method already remarked by Daniel in his preface.

Other Citations from **Bernensis 276** Used by Daniel

Daniel's commentary shows unmistakable indebtedness to **Bernensis 276** in two places – (l) and (m) – where he cites not a marginal annotation coming with Petronius attribution, but the Papias entry itself, which happens to offer etymologies of words found by Daniel in the Petronius text. Thus the context of the **Bernensis 276** usage is not Petronian, and no 'positive' evidence of the thirteenth-century tradition is derived. However, the very omission of a marginal expansion citing the author may be not without value in generating new knowledge of the transmission. For example, we note that these two citations by Daniel of his Satyrica text, reproducing words which he feels he should authenticate by reference to a glossarium and a vet. lexicon, occur in the exclusive *L class. This is evidence, albeit of the silent kind, that the late-thirteenth-century annotator's manuscript of Petronius belonged to the O class. He had no authority for connecting the words with Petronius; hence no marginal expansion appears.

Besides giving further proof of Daniel's use of **Bernensis 276** for his *Notae*, (l) and (m) offer a glimpse of flaws in his methodology. Daniel's lemma at 11.2 shows the interesting variant *opertam*, though he cites *opertum* for his '*glossarium S. Dionysii.*'[128] Actually, the Papias entry to my eyes is in the nominative case (albeit masculine) – more appropriate as an entry for a gloss. Yet final 's' is easily confused with final 'm,' and this is what Daniel seems to have done, even to the point of giving his glossary as the authority (despite its lack of Petronius attribution) for a variant which already had manuscript backing.[129]

There is less uncertainty over the other example, 14.3 *sicel* (m). Daniel reproduces from **Bernensis 276** Papias' gloss that adverts to a common corruption of the word, assigning it to a *vet. lexicon*. He then proceeds to quote a definition for the corrupt variant, which is itself listed, together with a gloss, on the verso of the same folio in **Bernensis 276**, as occurring '*in alio lexico*'! A little carelessness by Daniel with his sources should not detract from the corroborative value and interest of these entries.

Other Citations, of Lexica and Glossaries

In a number of instances Daniel's *Notae* cite old glossaries and lexica as the source for material which I have failed to find in **Bernensis 276**: (n), (o), (p), and (q). (n) gives to a St. Denis glossary the variant *loqui debemus* (2.3); and as long as it remained undetected in the manuscript it contributed to calling the identification into question.[130] But there is another explanation for its absence: mistaken attribution. The reading is available and well attested elsewhere: in t[v], and in p[2v] as *Thol.* It is hence the reading of **Cuiacianus**. It is extremely unlikely that this **L reading occurred in Daniel's St. Denis glossary, and no wonder that it cannot be found in **Bernensis 276**. The source of this familiar variant has simply been mis-remembered.

The three other entries – (o), (p), and (q) – alleging Petronian material under a general category like *vet. lexicon* in Daniel's *Notae* also seem to have no connection with **Bernensis 276**. (o) may owe its lemma to a Petronian source, and the entry may be lexical in character (and not 'modern'), but the definition, *per etymologiam*, is certainly inane. The last two are even more obscure: the one is Petronian on the authority of Fulgentius (Fragment X), while the other's connection depends on a Scaliger proposal to correct an attribution in Fulgentius to Propertius. We can have little use for them.

The Citations from Harleianus 2735

As we have seen, one of the genuine Petronius citations in Daniel's *Notae* – (r) – has served the commentator as evidence for the compass of the original *Satyrica*. It was to be seen, Daniel tells us, in a Fleury glossary, identifiable as **Harleianus 2735** both from the appearance of the citation therein and from proof of Daniel's former ownership. With this use of **Harleianus 2735** for the *Notae* attested, one might expect other echoes of it, where appropriate, in the commentary. The example of (t) may be one such, though Daniel seems familiar with the exact reference in Isidore himself, the source for the gloss. One may surmise, however, that its occurrence in the glossary played a role in causing it to be included in the *Notae*. Another link is (s), the citation of a word that Daniel includes as Petronian on the authority of Fulgentius again. Here too there is no direct proof of **Harleianus 2735**, but it should be safe to assume that Daniel had seen this form in his glossary, as its presence there may have dictated the choice of it over variants found in two '*veteres codices.*'

CONCLUSION

All new medieval material on Petronius in the form of direct citations verifiable by manuscripts contains intrinsic interest in high degree, and we have seen how **Bernensis 276** becomes the sole primary source for Fragments XV and XVI, which may be Petronian. Yet the value of all this in modifying our knowledge of the transmission remains limited, since the exact connection to the tradition, on the one hand, or independence from it, on the other, cannot be established. The material bears the marks of being taken by the medieval annotator from perhaps two sources: in the main, an **O**-based manuscript, plus a secondary or even tertiary source which early on had excerpted, for a collection, words of evident lexical interest.

On the positive side, **Bernensis 276** reveals itself as an important manuscript source for Daniel's commentary; and the commentary in turn provides codicological information on the manuscript. Our ability thus to confirm Daniel's source and to compare his commentary lemmata and citation record with the actual manuscript from which they derive adds significantly to knowledge of the methods of a sixteenth-century scholar with a pivotal place in the history of the text.

5

Pierre Daniel and **d**

The texts upon which we depend for our knowledge of the *L-class readings and variants have, in the modern apparatus, the status of manuscripts, though they are actually editions that either saw publication (**t, p¹**, and **p²**) or remained in longhand (**l, m, r**, and **d**). With the sole exception of **d**, as this chapter seeks to show, they are to varying degrees the product of a complex interaction of sources, inadequately identified and employed without consistency. The handwritten texts all predate the published editions, though the latest of them, **l**, seems to have some connection with the earliest printed source, **t**, which appeared in 1575. The preceding chapters have described the method and mix: basically, the editors subjected one or both of the newly appeared *L-class manuscripts, **Cuiacianus** and **Benedictinus**, and/or their apographs, **Memmianus** and **Dalecampianus**, to a comparison with the vulgate derived from **O**-class sources, namely manuscripts **B** and **P**, and printed editions **c** and **s**, not forgetting to consult the so-called **L** editions that immediately preceded their own. In this welter of choice it is no wonder that the *L readings are in danger of disappearing, especially since there is ample evidence that the editors had a fondness for **s**, in particular, outweighing its value.

The problem that this creates for the modern editor is in determining the genuine *L readings in the L texts, so that a true *L: O model may be drawn up for proper evaluation of readings in the text and variants in the apparatus criticus.[131] Even agreement on a variant in these *L sources does not always betoken the manuscript form, since palaeographic errors, conjectures, and even misprints may be shared. In order to separate this textual cocktail there may be no alternative but to isolate every ingredient, every communicated reading in the shared context where variants exist. It is in this that **d** performs some very useful functions and may be able to act as a control. For of all these *L-manuscript-based texts **d**, the *Schedae Danielis* (see Plates 5 to 8), appears to be the least touched by the sort of contamination outlined above, and hence may be the purest representative that we have of *L.[132]

In order to avoid a perpetuation of errors or misunderstandings that can come from an apparatus, **d** merits a full transcription; and it is greatly to be regretted that the manuscript is so short, containing only the first 15 chapters of the *L text. Yet for this amount at least, and in the interesting section that it covers, we may usually be confident that a reading in **d** differing from the **O** variant is an *L witness – though we must apply tests for individuality both in **d** and in its exemplar, **Memmianus** or intermediary. **d**'s role in providing the *L reading may be considered particularly secure if the reading is shared by **lmprt** against an **O** variant; and it is capable of signalling possible **s**-derived contamination in the same sources if they agree with the **O** variant against **d**.[133]

Two instances will illustrate the latter phenomenon: 1.3 *sed tyrannos* is the reading preferred by editors from Bücheler to Pellegrino; it appears in the text of **t**, in **p¹**, and in the manuscript editions **l** and **m**; however, it is also the reading of the **O**-class **s** (which preceded the above-named editions but fortunately not, it seems, **d**), the only **O** source to carry it: all the manuscripts, along with the 'L-class' **d** and **r**, have *et tyrannos*. It seems assured that this latter is the corrupt reading of the archetype, **O** hyparchetype and Λ hyparchetype (if shown by **dr**), while the correct reading in **s**, out of step with its **O** source, evinces a successful emendation adopted by **lmp¹t** to displace the manuscript reading (which, however, de Tournes notes in **t**ᵛ, the *variae lectiones* from the *L-class **Cuiacianus**).[134] The second instance is at 5.1.5 *impotentium*, where, from consultation of **c** or **s**, **lmpt** eschew the manuscript reading *impotentum* which shows up in **dr**. The depiction of this by Pellegrino in his apparatus as 'impotentium: Ls m p t *cum par.* s [**lmptcs**], impotentum φΩ [φO]' again lets one down by implying an *L: O division that simply does not exist.

It is to be seen from the above, I think, that **d** merits more careful attention than it has yet been given. To date, fullest treatment and the potential value of the readings is to be found in Müller 1961 and Müller and Ehlers 1983. Müller seems to be the first scholar to have studied **d** and fixed its readings as **Memmianus**-aligned, along with those of **r** – a manuscript which has a special reason for being kept in view when investigating **d**; in addition to the similarity of their texts through the common ancestor there is evidence in **r** to suggest that its scribe had access to the immediate source of **d** (see below and n. 139).[135] As for **Memmi-**

anus, no cited evidence exists that it was a medieval manuscript like **Cuiacianus** and **Benedictinus**; it was more likely an apograph of the latter, made around 1562. The *terminus post quem* for **d** is the following year, for its contents are transcribed in the four empty pages after the *Scholia* of Muret's 1562 edition of Cicero's *Philippics*, which was purchased by Daniel in Paris on 27 October 1563.[136] The immediate puzzle is the circumstances of the copying only of an introductory fragment of this **Memmianus**-aligned text at a time when we may presume the full manuscript to have been available (as witnessed by **r** and to a lesser extent **m**).[137]

One makes a number of inferences from the physical evidence itself. The room allotted by Daniel for **d** implies that he had but a short manuscript exemplar before him for the fit: he judged that he had sufficient space for it in a maximum of four empty leaves. He appears to have judged very well. After a little initial uncertainty caused him to write the first 20 lines conservatively, in a markedly smaller and more cramped hand, he settles confidently into a larger script, which he continues with a skilful consistency up to completion of the fragment, with a little room to spare, at 15.4 *tuberosissimae frontis.*

Either Daniel made this selection, discarding subsequent leaves which were available to him, or else he used an exemplar which corresponded exactly to **d** and contained no more text. In either case (I favour the latter) it would not be difficult to guess the value to him of the piece selected. In the rhetorical debate and the Affair of the Cloak, these 15 chapters present a couple of interesting self-contained vignettes (both for their presentation of material of possible professional interest to Daniel the advocate); and the text, for our *Satyrica* before the *Cena* preponderantly pure **L*, does not get salacious, vexed, and grossly lacunose until after this point – immediately after, one notes. There are also two of the most appealing and subsequently popular gnomic poems, 5.1 *Artes severae si quis amat* [*sic*] *effectus*, and 14.2 *Quid faciunt leges.*

Notwithstanding the abrupt ending at an unfinished sentence, there would be reason to believe, as does Müller 1961, p. xxiii, that Daniel is simply supplying himself with his own extract from the actual **Memmianus**, were it not for evidence in **r** that one of the copyist's sources was a manuscript which terminated in exactly the same place as **d**: in **r** f. 9v, in the margin opposite 15.4 *frontis* (or one line below, to be precise – which is not significant since on other occasions the marginal note is not quite opposite the word in the text to which it applies, as at 7v *nil/nihil*) is written, in the characteristic red ink used by the scribe for most of the marginal entries, *non plura habebat exemplaria.* Since **d** resides in such a personal, confined, and modest setting, we should deem it unlikely that **r** used **d** itself (though this would have been physically and chronologically possible in the Paris of the 1560s). In any case, **r** does not seem to be influenced by seeming peculiar errors in **d** (though these could have been corrected from another exemplar).[138] Thus it should be concluded, I think, that Daniel copied **d** from a **Memmianus** fragment that was available to the scribe of **r** also.[139] I shall pursue the identity of this manuscript further when treating **r** in Chapter 7: to be considered chiefly is whether it is the *'fragmentum Cuiacii'* against which the scribe says (f. 7 *supra*; see Plate 11) he has collated the 'first two folios' of **r**.

The manner in which Daniel chose to transcribe **d** apparently left no room for marginal or interlinear variants, and it was evidently to Daniel's scholarly fashion to produce, for its short length, an uncontaminated, unredacted manuscript, although of course we cannot be sure that variants to the **Memmianus**-type text were not available in the margins of Daniel's exemplar and seamlessly inserted. For extensive use by Turnèbe of **Memmianus** could have left it a variant carrier.[140] The alignment of **d** is established by the internal evidence: the affinity of its readings with **mr** and their common ancestry to the **Benedictinus** and **Memmianus** line of *L;[141] while divergences from **r** (i.e. **dm: r**) have a possible role in recording **Benedictinus**: **Cuiacianus** division in the exclusive *L passages, since **r** has been argued to show **Cuiacianus** influence.[142]

It is clear that successful demonstration of affinities for the accurate stemmatic picture requires the recording of readings with a fullness not attempted hitherto. In the history of textual scholarship on our author there are instructive illustrations of the pitfalls of anything less. A few manifest discrepancies of varying character and unclear origin between the citations by Pithou of his **Autissiodurensis** and the verifiable text of **B** have threatened the commonality of the source. Then there is the celebrated confusion caused by Otto Jahn's failure to record **E** accurately on 23 May 1839, which led to the *ex silentio* assumption that this manuscript showed a medieval text closer to his L-style collating copy than the poor Renaissance hyparchetype.[143] With regard to the present record on **d**, which of course escaped the exhaustive collation of Bücheler, Müller 1961 is reliable as far as it goes, but the apparatus is too selective to sustain detailed conclusions. Pellegrino's new edition, to date published in a first volume of text, full apparatus, and commentary up to 26.6 and thus encompassing all of **d**, well illustrates the difficulties encountered by editors ancient and modern in securing a true variant picture:

THE READINGS OF **d**, AGAINST **d** ACCORDING TO PELLEGRINO

2.8   *Thucydides*] *Thucididis* **d**: *thicididis* **d** P. [= Pellegrino]

2.8   *omnia*] *omnino* **d**: <u>*tacet*</u> P.

2.8   *usque*] <u>*om.*</u> **d**: <u>*tacet*</u> P.

3.2   *nisi*] *si* **d**: <u>*tacet*</u> P.

5.1.4   *trucem*] <u>*om.*</u> **d**: <u>*tacet*</u> P.

5.1.11 *Sirenumve*] *Sirenumque* <u>*codd.*</u>, *si renumque* **d**: <u>*tacet*</u> P.

5.1.11 *det*] *dat* **d**: <u>*tacet*</u> P.

5.1.15 *Graio*] *Orai* **d** <u>*ut*</u> <u>*videtur*</u>: <u>*tacet*</u> P.

6.1   *dum*] <u>*sic*</u> **d**: *cum* **d** P. <u>*ex silentio*</u>

7.1   *consurrexitque*] <u>*om.*</u> **d**: <u>*tacet*</u> P.

8.4   *iam ille*] *cum ille* **d**: *iam cum ille* **d** P.

9.1   *Gitona*] *Guitona* **d** <u>*dubitanter*</u> <u>*certe*</u>: *Gnitona* **d** P.

9.3   *habitu*] <u>*om.*</u> **d**: <u>*tacet*</u> P.

9.4   *accucurrit*] *acucurrit* **d**: <u>*tacet*</u> P.

9.10   *cuius*] *cumque* **d**: *cuius cumque* **d** P.

10.1   *interpretamenta*] *interpretes* <u>*in*</u> *interpreses* <u>*cum*</u> <u>*spatio*</u> <u>*correxit*</u> **d**: *interpres* **d** P.

10.7   *iam dudum*] *Tañ dudum* **d**: <u>*tacet*</u> P.

10.7   *Gitone*] *Critone* **d**: <u>*tacet*</u> P.

12.1   *tegeret*] *legeret* **d**: <u>*tacet*</u> P.

14.2.3 *pera*] *caera* **d**: *cera* **d** <u>*cum*</u> <u>*cett.*</u> P.

15.3   *quaeri*] *queri* **d**: <u>*tacet*</u> P. [cf. 9.2 *quaererem*, 9.3 *quaesivi* **d**]

Most of the discrepancies are due not to a palaeographic difference of opinion but to failure to cite the **d** variant or omission, leaving an impression of orthodoxy which is disastrous for tracing **d**'s exact affiliation. For although many of the **d** variants are peculiar to it – errors without transmissional significance – in other instances they are recorded in **r**, either in the text (as at 10.7 *Critone*, thus probably the reading of **Memmianus**), or as a correction (as at 5.1.11 *dat* **dr**ᶜ), or in the margin (as at 6.1 *doctorum* **dr**ᵐ). *Ex silentio* orthodoxy (i.e. implicit disagreement with **r**) restricts **d**'s role as a guide to **Memmianus** variants and diminishes its ability to distinguish **Cuiacianus** variants. For example, 7.1 *consurrexitque* is recorded in Pellegrino's apparatus as omitted by **r** only: *ex silentio* presence in **d** indicates correct transmission in **Memmianus**, with absence in **r** alone thus due to individual error. But confirmed absence also in **d** turns this reasoning on its head: it points to a separative error in **Memmianus** itself, or possibly in the **Memmianus**-aligned fragment which was **d**'s exemplar.

There is a useful irony in observing these difficulties encountered by the scholar who has sought to overturn the **Autissiodurensis** = **B** equation and whose influence might be the same as Jahn's were it not for the fact that the manuscript survives to be verified.[144] Were Pellegrino to have chosen a different name for the manuscript which he used, such as *fragmentum veteris libri Petr. Danielis*, the 20 or so differences exhibited explicitly or implicitly against **d** in the space of 15 chapters would be quite sufficient to argue that it was an apograph or a *germanus* and not the same manuscript.

The above has been raised not as criticism for its own sake but for instructive value. Since absolute accuracy with the citation of manuscript variants in a task of this scope and complexity is probably beyond human ability, I believe I have the excuse to provide a remedy, which in the case of **d** is fortunately quite practical: a complete transcription to show the basis for my subsequent collation.

TRANSCRIPTION OF **d**

Petronii Arbitri Satiricon

[***LO**] *Num alio genere declamatores inquietantur, qui clamant Haec vulnera pro libertate publica excepi, Hunc oculum pro vobis impendi, Date mihi ducem qui me ducat ad liberos meos nam succisi poplites membra non sustinent. Haec ipsa tolerabilia essent, si ad eloquentiam ituris viam facerent. Nunc et rerum tumore et sententiarum vanissimo strepitu hoc tantum proficiunt, ut cum in forum venerint, putent se in alium orbem terrarum delatos.* [***LOφ**] *Et ideo ego adolescentulos existimo in scholis stultissimos fieri, quia nihil ex iis quae in usu habemus aut audiunt aut vident:* [***LO**] *sed piratas cum catenis in littore stantes et tyrannos edicta scribentes, quibus imperent filiis ut patrum suorum capita praecidant, sed responsa in pestilentiam data ut virgines tres aut plures immolentur, sed mellitos verborum globulos, et omnia dicta factaque quasi papavere et sesamo sparsa.* [***LOφ**] *Qui inter haec nutriuntur, non magis sapere possunt quam bene olere qui in culina habitant.* [***LO**] *Pace vestra liceat dixisse, primi omnem eloquentiam perdidistis. Levibus enim atque inanibus sonis ludibria quaedam excitando effecistis ut corpus orationis enervaretur et caderet. Nondum iuvenes declamationibus continebantur, cum Sophocles aut Euripides invenerunt verba quibus deberent loqui. Nondum umbraticus doctor ingenia deleverat, cum Pindarus novemque Lyrici Homericis versibus canere invenerunt. Et ne poetas quidem citem, certe neque Platona nec Demosthenem ad hoc genus exercitationis accessisse. Et ideo grandis, et ut ita dicam, pudica oratio non est maculosa, nec turgida, sed naturali pulchritudine exurgit. Nuper ventosa isthaec et enormis loquacitas Athenas ex Asia commigravit animosque iuvenum ad magna surgentes, veluti pestilenti quodam sydere afflavit; semelque corrupta eloquentiae regula stetit et obmutuit. quis postea ad summam*

Thucididis, quis Hiperidis ad famam processit Ac ne carmen quidem sani coloris enituit, sed omnino quasi eodem cibo pasta, non potuerunt ad senectutem canescere. Pictura quoque non alium exitum fecit, postquam Aegyptiorum audacia, tam magnae artis compendiariam invenit. Non est passus Agamemnon me diutius declamare in porticu, quam ipse in schola sudaverat. Sed, adolescens inquit, quoniam sermonem habes non publici saporis, et quod rarissimum est amas bonam mentem, non fraudabo te arte secreta. Nimirum in his exercitationibus doctores peccant, qui necesse habent, cum insanientibus furere. [***LOφ**] *Nam si dixerint quae adolescentuli probent, ut ait Cicero soli in scholis relinquentur.* [***LO**] *Sicut* [***LOφ**] *ficti adulatores, cum caenas divitum captant, nihil prius meditantur, quam id quod putant gratissimum auditoribus fore. Nec enim aliter impetrabunt quod petunt, nisi quasdam insidias auribus fecerint,* [***LO**] *sic eloquentiae magister nisi tamquam* [***LOφ**] *piscator eam imposuerit hamis escam, quam scierit appetituros esse pisciculos, sine spe praede moratur in scopulo.* [***LO**] *Quid ergo est? Parentes obiurgatione digni sunt, qui nolunt liberos suos severa lege proficere. Primum enim sicut omnia, spes quoque suas ambitione donant. Deinde cum ad vota properant, cruda adhuc studia in forum propellunt, et eloquentiam qua nihil esse maius confitentur, pueris induunt adhuc nascentibus, quod si paterentur laborum gradus fieri, ut studiosi iuvenes lectione severa mitigarentur ut sapientiae praeceptis animos componerent, ut verba atroci stilo effoderent, ut quod vellent imitari diu audirent, sibi nihil esse magnificum, quod pueris placent. Iam illa grandis oratio haberet maiestatis suae pondus. Nunc pueri in scholis ludunt, iuvenes videntur in foro; et quod utroque turpius est, quod quisque perperam discit, in senectute confiteri non vult. Sed ne me putes improbasse studium Lucinianae humilitatis quod sentio et ipse carmine effingam:*

[***LOφ**]

> *Artis severae si quis amat effectus*
> *Mentemque magnis applicat, prius*
> *More frugalitatis, lege polleat exacta*
> *Nec, curet alto regiam <...> vultu*
> *Cliensque caenas impotentum ne captet*
> *Nec perditis addictus obruat vino*
> *Mentis calorem, neve plausor in scena*
> *Sedeat redemptus histrionei addictus*
> *Sed sive Armigerae rident Tritonidis arces*
> *Seu Lacedaemonio tellus habitata colono*
> *Si renumque domus dat primos versibus annos*
> *Maeoniumque bibat felici pectore fontem*
> *Mox et Socratico plenus grege mittat habenas*
> *Hunc Romana manus circumfluat et modo Orai*
> *Exonerata sono, mutet suffusa saporem*
> *Interdum subducta foro det pagina cursum*

Et fortuna sonet celeri distincta meatu
Dent epulas, et bella truci memorata canore
Grandiaque indomiti Ciceronis verba minentur
His animum succinge bonis, sic flumine largo
Plenus Pierio diffundes pectore verba

[***LO**] *Dum haec diligentius audio, et dum in hoc doctorum aestu motus incedo, non notavi Ascylti fugam, et dum in porticum venit, ut apparebat ab extemporali decla-matione nescio, cuius qui Agamemnonis suasionem exceperat. Dum ergo iuvenes sententias rident, ordinemque totius dictionis infamant, opportune subduxi me, et cursim Ascyltum persequi coepi. Sed nec viam diligenter tenebam, quia nec quo stabulum esset, sciebam. Itaque quocumque ieram, eodem revertebar, donec in cursu fatigatus, et sudore iam madens accedo ad aniculam quandam, quae agreste olus vendebat, et rogo inquam mater numquid scis ego habitem. Delectata illa urbanitate tam stulta Et quidni sciam inquit et coepit me procedere. Divinam ergo putabam. et subinde ut in locum secretum venimus, centonem anus urbana reiecit et hic inquit, debes habitare, Cum ego negarem me cognoscere domum, video quosdam inter viculos nudasque meretrices furtim spatiantes. Tandem immo iam sero intellexi me in fornicem esse deductum. Execratus itaque anicula insidias, operui caput et per medium lupanar fugiens, coepi in aliam partem, cum ecce in ipso aditu occurrit mihi aeque lapsus ac moriens Ascylto Putares ab eadem anicula esse deductum. Itaque ut ridens eum consalutavi, quid in loco tam deformi faceret quaesivi Sudorem ille manibus detersit, et si scires, inquit, quae mihi acciderunt, quid novi inquam Ego? At ille deficiens, cum errarem inquit per totam civitatem nec invenirem quo loco stabulum reliquissem, accessit ad me Paterfamilias, et ducem se itineris humanissime promisit. Per anfractus deinde obscurissimos egressus, in hunc locum me perduxit, prolatoque peculio, coepit rogare stuprum* [***L**] *Iam pro sella meretrix assem exegerat,* [***LO**] *cum ille mihi iniecerat manum, et nisi valentior fuissem, dedissem poenas.* [***L**] *Adeo omnes ubique mihi videbantur satirdon bibisse* * *Iunctis viribus molestum contempsimus* * *[quasi per caliginem vidi Guitona in crepidine semitae stantem, et in eundem locum me conieci. Cum quaererem numquid nobis in prandium frater parasset, consedit puer super lectum, et manantes lachrimas pollice expressit. Perturbatus ergo* <...> *fratris, quid accidisset quaesivi. At ille tarde quidem et invitus sed postquam precibus et iracundiam miscui. Tuus inquit iste frater seu comes paulo ante in conductum acucurrit, cepitque mihi velle pudorem extorquere,* [***LO**] *cum ego proclamarem gladium strinxit. Et si Lucretia es inquit, Tarquinium invenisti,* [***L**] *quibus ego auditus intentavi in oculos Ascylti manus, et quid dicis inquam muliebris patientiae scortum cuius ne spiritus purus est inhorrescere se finxit Ascyltos, mox sublatis fortius manibus, longe maiore nisu clamavit, Non taces, inquit, gladiator obscaene, quem de ruina arena dimisit. Non taces nocturne percussor, qui ne tum quidem cum fortiter faceres, cum pura muliere pugnasti, cumque eadem ratione in viridario frater fui qua nunc in diversorio puer est. Subduxisti te (inquam) a praeceptoris colloquio. quid ergo homo stultissime* *facere debui, cum fame morerer? An videlicet audirem sententias id est vitream fractam et somniorum interpretes <...> Multo me turpior es tu hercule qui ut foris coenares, poetam laudasti. Itaque ex turpissima lite in risum diffusi pacatius ad reliqua secessimus * Rursus in memoriam revocatus iniuriae, Ascylte, inquam, intelligo nobis convenire non posse. Itaque communes sarcinulas partiamur, ac paupertatem nostram privatis quaestibus tentemus expellere Et tu litteras scis et ego. Ne quaestibus tuis obstem aliquid aliud promittam. Alioqui mille causae nos quotidie collident et per totam urbem rumoribus deferent. Non recusavit Ascyltos, et hodie inquit quia tanquam scholastici ad caenam promisimus, non perdamus noctem. Cras autem quia hoc libet, et habitationem mihi prospiciam, et aliquem fratrem.* [***Lφ**] *Tardum est inquam differre quod placet ** [***L**] *Hanc tam praecipitem divisionem libido faciebat. Tamen dudum enim amoliri cupiebam custodem molestum, ut veterem cum Critone meo rationem diducerem * Postquam lustravi oculis totam urbem in cellulam redii, oculisque tandem bona fide exactis, alligo artissimis complexibus puerum, fruorque votis usque ad invidiam foelicibus. Nec adhuc quidem omnia erant facta, cum Ascyltos furtim se foribus admovit, discussisque fortissime claustris invenit me cum fratre ludentem. Risu itaque plausuque cellam implevit, opertam me amiculo evolvit, et quid agebas inquit frater sanctissime? quid verti contubernium facis? Nec se solum intra verba continuit sed lorum de pera solvit, et me coepit non perfunctorie verberare, adiectis etiam petulantibus dictis: sic dividere cum fratre nolito xxx veniebamus in forum deficiente iam die, in quo notavimus frequentiam rerum venalium, non quidem preciosarum, sed tamen quarum fidem male ambulantem obscuritas temporis facillime legeret. Cum ergo et ipsi raptum latrocinio pallium detulissemus uti occasione oportunissima cepimus, atque in quodam angulo laciniam extremam concutere, si quem fortem emptorem, splendida vestis posset adducere. Nec diu moratus rusticus quidam familiaris oculis meis cum muliercula comite propius accessit ac considerare pallium coepit Invicem Ascyltos iniecit contemplationem super humeros rustici emptoris ac subito examinatus conticuit. Ac ne ipse quidem sine aliquo metu hominem conspexi. Non videbatur ille mihi esse qui tuniculam in solitudine invenerat. Plane is ipse erat. sed cum Ascyltus timeret fidem oculorum ne quid temere faceret: prius tanquam emptor propius accessit detraxitque humeris laciniam et diligentius tenuit. O lusum fortunae mirabilem. Nam adhuc nec suturae quidem attulerat rusticus curiosas manus sed tanquam mendici spolium etiam fastidiose venditabat. Ascyltos postquam depositum esse inviolatum vidit et personam vendentis contemptam seduxit me paululum a turba, et scis inquit frater rediisse ad nos thesaurum de quo querebar Illa est tunicula adhuc ut apparet intactis aureis plena. quid ergo facimus? aut quo iure rem nostram vindicamus? Exhilaratus ego non tantum quia praedam videbam, sed etiam quod fortuna me a turpissima suspitione dimiserat negavi circuitu agendum, sed plane iure civili dimicandum ut, si nollet alienam rem reddere, ad interdictum veniret.*

[***LOφ**]   *Quid faciunt leges ubi sola pecunia regnat*
                Aut ubi paupertas vincere nulla potest

[*LO]   *Ipsi qui Cynica traducunt tempora caera*
                 Nonnumquam nummis vendere verba solent
[*LOφ]   *Ergo iudicium nihil est, nisi publica merces*
[*LO]   *Atque eques in causa qui sedet, empta probat*

[*L] *Contra Ascyltos leges timebat, et quis aiebat, hoc loco nos novit, aut quis habebit dicentibus fidem? Mihi plane placet emere, quamvis nostrum sit quod agnoscimus, et* [*Lφ] *parvo aere recuperare potius thesaurum, quam in ambiguam litem descendere* [*L] *sed praeter unum dipondium sicel lupinosque quibus destinaveramus mercari, nihil ad manum erat, ne interim praeda discederet. Itaque vel minoris pallium addicere placuit, ut pretium maioris compendii leviorem faceret iacturam: Cum primum ergo explicuimus mercem, mulier aperto capite, quae cum rustico steterat inspectis diligentius signis, iniecit utramque laciniae manum magnaque vociferatione latrones tenere clamavit. Contra nos perturbati, ne videremur nihil agere, et ipsi scissam et sordidam tenere caepimus tunicam, atque eadem invidia proclamare nostra esse spolia quae illi possiderent. sed nullo genere par erat causa nostra, et conciones quae ad clamorem confluxerant nostram scilicet de more ridebant invidiam, quod pro illa parte vendicabant preciosissimum vestem, pro hac pannuciam, ne centonibus quidem bonis dignam. Hinc ascyltos pene risum discussit qui silentio facto, videamus inquit, suam cuique rem esse charissimam, reddant nobis tunicam nostram et pallium suum recipiant, Et si rustico mulierique placebat permutatio advocati tamen iam pene nocturni qui volebant pallium lucri facere flagitabant uti apud se utraque deponerentur ac postero die Iudex querelam inspiceret. Neque enim res tantum quae videretur in controversiam esse, sed longe aliud queri in utraque parte scilicet latrocinii suspitio traheretur. Iam sequestri placebant, et nescioquis ex concionibus calvus tuberosissimae frontis*

In the above we have the best witness available, in its limited context, of an *L manuscript, blessedly free of contamination from s by the simple expedient of having preceded it, and untouched by any O or **Cuiacianus** alignment via the editions of de Tournes and Pithou for the same reason.[145] d is thus the purest exponent of the medieval *L text, and in addition is apparently of value in resembling a second **Memmianus**-aligned source used by the scribe of r to construct his text (see below). The abundant genuine *L readings supplied by d are able to provide a fair test of the value of the Λ branch of our stemma against O, where they differ. The division reverts to the ninth century.[146]

COLLATION OF **d** ON MÜLLER AND EHLERS 1983, WITH
AGREEMENTS

[*LO]   1.1   *furiarum*: om.
[*LOφ]   1.3   *his* Oφ: *iis* *L *cum* m

[*LO]   1.3   *sed tyrannos* **s**, *ex quo* **m**: *et tyrannos libri*

          2.2   *omnium* **s** [*e codice deteriori*], *ex quo* **m**: *omnem libri*

          2.4   *timuerunt: invenerunt cum* **r** *ex Memmiano*

          2.5   *ad testimonium: om., expungit* **r**, *Memmianum fortasse secuti*

          2.5   *video Turnèbe, ex quo* **m**^margine: *et ideo libri*

          2.8   *omnia: omnino*

          2.8   *usque: om. cum* **r** *ex Memmiano*

          3.2   *nil mirum si Muret, Leo: nimirum libri*

          3.2   *nisi: si*

          4.2   *ambitioni impr. priores, ex quibus* **m**: *ambitione libri*

          4.2   [*im*]*pellunt Bücheler ex impellunt* Ω: *propellunt* **lmrtp** *propter*
                  Benedictinum, puto

          4.3   *irrigarentur: mitigarentur cum* **r** *et* **p** *Benedictini gratia, puto*

          4.3   <*si persuaderent*>: *add. Winterbottom*

          4.3   *nihil esse* **O**: *nihil esset* ***L**

          4.3   *placeret: placent cum* **r** *et* **p** *Benedictini gratia, puto*

          4.4   *ridentur: videntur*

          4.4   <*di*>*dicit* **A**: *dicit* **O**: *discit* ***L**

          4.5   *schedium Pithou de schadium* **B**: *studium* Ω

          4.5   *Lucilianae* **O**: *Lucinianae* ***L**

[*LOφ]   5.1.1   *ambit* **t**^margine: *amat libri*

          5.1.2   *mores* **O**: *more* ***L**

          5.1.3   *poliat Heinse: polleat libri praeter Cuiac. qui palleat*

          5.1.4   *trucem: om., spatio relicto*

          5.1.5   *impotentium impr. priores: impotentum* **O**: *impotentum ne* ***L**

          5.1.7   *scaenam Heinse: scena libri*

          5.1.8   *histrionis Turnèbe, ex quo* **m**^margine: *histrionei* Ω

          5.1.8   *ad rictus Ribbeck: addictus libri*

          5.1.11 *Sirenumve Bücheler: si renumque: sirenumque* Ω

          5.1.11 *det: dat cum* **r**^c, *Memmianum secuti*

          5.1.14 *versum totum om. cum* **r**, *Memmianum secuti: add.* **r**^m

          5.1.15 *hinc impr. priores, ex quib.* **m**: *huic* **O**: *hunc* ***L**

          5.1.15 *Graio: Orai, sed aliquod post 'i' deletum videtur*

          5.1.22 *defundes Scaliger: diffundes* Ω

[*LO]   6.1   *hunc* **O**: *haec* ***L**

          6.1   *audio ... in porticum:* [*locus valde perturbatus in* **d** *cum* **r**, *scribae*
                  Memmiani culpa, sic:] *audio et dum ... incedo non notavi Ascylti*
                  fugam et dum in porticum. omittitur mihi cum ingens scholastic-
                  orum turba; additur alterum et dum ante in porticum; fugam om.
                  r, *habet* **r**^m

          6.1   *dictorum: doctorum cum* **r**^m, *ex Memmiano sumptum*

          6.1   *suasoriam: suasionem cum* **r**^m, *ex Memmiano sumptum*

	6.4	[quia] *del. Goldast*: quia *libri*
	6.4	nec quod *Bücheler*: nec quo Ω
	6.4	et cursu: in cursu **rtp** *ex* *L *probabiliter*
	7.1	delectata est **B**, *haud scio an* **O**: *om.* est *ceteri ordinis* **O** *cum* *L
	7.1	consurrexitque: *om. cum* **r**, *Memmiani culpa*
	7.2	ego: ergo
	7.2	inter titulos: inter viculos **rtp**^v *ex Benedictino, ut puto*
	7.4	tarde: tandem *cum* **r**^m
	7.4	aniculae: anicula *ut videtur*
	7.4	fugere: fugiens *cum* **r**^m
	7.4	alteram **O**: aliam *L
	7.4	lassus **O**: lapsus *L
	7.4	Ascyltos: Ascylto, *alii aliter*
	8.2	pater familiae **O**: pater familias *L
[*L]	8.4	cella **lrp**: sella **mt**, *Memmiani lectio*
[*LO]	8.4	iam ille: cum ille
[*L]	8.4	satyrion: satirdon: satireon **r**
	9.1	Gitona: Guitona **r**: Guitona [sic] **m**: Gnitona **l**
	9.2	extersit *F. Pithou*: expressit *libri*
	9.3	ego: ergo **mrp**² *ex Benedictino, ut puto*
	9.3	etiam **l**: et **mpt**: *om.* **r**, *add.* **r**^m, *inserendum*
	9.4	accucurrit: acucurrit *cum* **r**^m: accurrit **r**
	9.8	harena: arena **m**: *om.* **r**
	9.10	cuius eadem: cumque eadem: cuius in eadem **r**
	9.10	deversorio: diversorio Ω
	10.1	ego **lrpt**^{margine}: ergo **mtr**^m
	10.1	vitrea fracta *Scaliger*: vitream fractam *libri*
	10.1	interpretamenta: interpretes *ex* interpres *correctum, spatio post relicto*
	10.4	intellego: intelligo *libri*
	10.4	temptemus: tentemus *libri*
	10.5	different **l**^{margine}**p**²: deferent *libri plerumque*
	10.7	iam dudum: Tañ dudum
	10.7	Gitone: Critone
	10.7	reducerem *Bücheler*: diducerem *libri*
	11.1	osculisque: oculisque *cum* **r** *ex Memmiano*
	11.2	cellulam: cellam *cum* **mr**^m *ex Memmiano*
	11.2	opertum: opertam **m** *ex Memmiano*
	12.1	pretiosarum: preciosarum *libri*
	12.1	tegeret: legeret
	12.2	forte: fortem *cum* **r** *ex Memmiano*

| | 12.3 | *diligentius*: <u>om</u>. **mt**, <u>*expungendum notat*</u> **r**, <u>*e vetere Cuiacii libro*</u>, <u>*puto*</u> |

12.3   *diligentius*: <u>om</u>. **mt**, <u>*expungendum*</u> <u>*notat*</u> **r**, <u>*e vetere Cuiacii libro*</u>, <u>*puto*</u>

12.4   *exanimatus*: *examinatus* <u>*cum*</u> **r**^m <u>*ex Memmiano*</u>

12.5   *nam*: *non*

12.6   *temptavit* <u>*Burman*</u>: *tenuit* <u>*libri*</u>

13.4   *domino*: <u>om</u>. **mt**, <u>*expungendum notat*</u> **r**^m <u>*ex Memmiano*</u>

14.1   *Ascyltos*: *Asciltos*

[*LOφ]   14.2.3   *pera* <u>*Heinse*</u>: *cera* <u>*vel*</u> *caera* <u>*libri*</u>

[*L]   14.4   *itaque ne interim praeda discederet, vel* **t**^{margine} <u>*ex*</u> <u>*coniectura*</u>: *ne ... discederet, itaque vel* <u>*libri*</u>

14.7   *cociones qui* <u>*Saumaise*</u>: *conciones quae* <u>*libri*</u>

14.7   *vindicabant*: *vendicabant* **rt**

14.7   *pretiosissimam*: *preciosissimam* **lr**

15.1   *videmus* <u>*Jungermann*</u>: *videamus* <u>*libri*</u>

15.2   *querellam*: *querelam* <u>*libri*</u>

15.3   *viderentur*: *videretur* **t**

15.3   *quaeri*: *queri* **r**

15.3   <*quod*> <u>*add*</u>. **t**^{margine} <u>*ex*</u> <u>*coniectura*</u>: <u>om</u>. *libri*

15.3   *haberetur*: *traheretur*

15.4   *cocionibus* <u>*Saumaise*</u>: *concionibus libri*

INTERPRETATIONS

The irregularities of **d** set against the correct readings must be interpreted in their context to avoid conveying certain misleading notions. They do not necessarily imply, for example, that **d** is a poorer manuscript or copy than others. The collation only shows the weaknesses of **d** when judged against the full combined authority of the rest of the tradition and the best of conjectures. One service, in fact, performed by such a collation is to show that the variants in **d** are shared, in the great majority of cases, by other witnesses to the *L class; beyond that, **d** gives the distinct impression of being a more faithful copy of its exemplar, **Memmianus**, and hence of the *L class, than the other exponents of this class, **lmrpt**. These other texts contribute variants that are on some occasions better, on others worse, than **d**, in conformity with the quality of their source: access to **O** material older than *L, such as **B** (in the case of **p**) or to *L material giving a better reading than **Memmianus** (all texts) accounts for superiority; conversely, dependence on younger **O** material such as **c** and **s**, or of course on a predecessor carrying this material, accounts for inferiority of these other texts when measured against **d**. The above collation makes quantification of all this possible.

A major consideration is ambience. We observe that all the variants listed up to 8.4, roughly half of **d**, fall within the *LO or *LOφ context, necessitating the application of different analysis from the variants in the *L context of the second half. For example, the estimable value of **d** variants in the first half is in providing an accurate comparison of **O**: *L *bonitas*. Naturally, in the way the above collation is constructed, neither **d** nor the *L class is done justice, since the reading is only logged where it shows an inferior variant; thus at 1.3 *his*, 4.3 *nihil esse*, 4.5 *Lucilianae*, 5.1.2 *mores*, 6.1 *hunc*, 6.4 *et cursu*, 7.1 *delectata est*, 7.4 *alteram*, 7.4 *lassus*, 8.2 *pater familiae*. All the other instances of improvement on the *L source are due not to **O** superiority (since **O** shares the faults) but to conjectures: 1.3 *sed tyrannos*, 2.2 *omnium*, 2.5 *video*, 3.2 *nil mirum si*, 4.2 *ambitioni*, 4.2 *pellunt*, 4.3 *si persuaderent*, 4.4 *didicit*, 4.5 *schedium*, 5.1.1 *ambit*, 5.1.3 *poliat*, 5.1.5 *impotentium*, 5.1.7 *scaenam*, 5.1.8 *histrionis*, 5.1.8 *ad rictus*, 5.1.11 *Sirenumve*, 5.1.15 *hinc*, 5.1.22 *defundes*, 6.4 *[quia]*, 6.4 *nec quod*. These are in the nature of palaeographical adjustments, minor in scope. Balanced against the first list of **O** superiorities are the 'invisible' instances of a better reading in *L, not to be found in the above collation: 2.1 *culina*, 2.6 *et ut*, 2.7 *istaec* (*isthaec* **d**), 2.8 *quis*, 3.4 *pisciculos*, 3.4 *spe praedae*, 3.4 *moratur*, 4.5 *humilitatis*. **d** partakes of all of these. They could be instances of the reading behind *L – Λ – being better than its sibling **O**; whereas the first examples (where **O** is better) evince an inferiority in *L due to contamination of it from an inferior **O** source not much different from **P**, since that manuscript shares many of these errors.[147]

There remain two categories of **d** variant in the *LO context now being treated: those which revert to errors in its immediate source, **Memmianus** or excerpt apograph – here out of step with the other *L witnesses – and those which are peculiar to **d**. In the *LO context the former are by no means always easy to detect, for their confirmed identity as a variant depends on better evidence than *ex silentio* differentiation in other *L sources like the **lmprt** texts, since the readings there may come from **O**. Ideally, here and in the remainder of **d** where the context is supplied by *L manuscripts, there should be a positive indication somewhere in our sources of variants in **Cuiacianus**, **Benedictinus**, or **Dalecampianus** that differ from the **Memmianus** option.

Normally, however, one is constrained to posit **Memmianus** as the source of the variant if it is in **dmr** or in **dr** and resides or is cited nowhere else. Such is often the case in the **d** collation, above: 2.4, 2.5, 2.8, 5.1.11, 6.1 (3x), 7.1, 7.4 (2x), 9.3, 9.4, 11.1, 11.2 (2x), 12.4, 15.3. We see that in *LO **m** is less useful for this exercise, since the scribe has rejected his manuscript source with remarkable frequency in favour of **s**: 1.3, 2.2, 2.4,

2.5, 2.8, 4.2, 4.3, etc. In the limited context of **d** I find only a couple of instances of **dm** or secure **Memmianus** influence: at 11.2 *cellam and* 11.2 *opertam*. The value of **r** too for this purpose would have been rather circumscribed, since it may be something of an edition, like **m**, with potential access to at least one other source and its variants for the text, were it not for the scribe's invaluable habit of entering the rejected variant in the margin. In fact, as we see in the collation, the bulk of *ex Memmiano* variants are secured on the **dr**^m basis. I shall study the **dr** connection more closely in the next chapter.

Some of the errors of **d** derived from **Memmianus** are not the fault of the exemplar but of an antecedent. This may be determined if they are shared by **p** and/or other so-called **L** texts, as at 4.2, 4.3 (2x), 8.4, 9.3, 10.1, 12.3, 14.7. The source of the error becomes speculative, resting more on opportunity (as with the case of Pithou's texts and **Benedictinus**, for example) than on proof, and is quite tenuous in the ***LO** context. But here too it is possible to isolate the conditions in the apparatus for reasonable suppositions, as I believe I have done.

The remaining errors of **d**, scattered throughout the manuscript, are of individual provenance, and are few. Among them I count 1.1 *furiarum om.*, 2.8 *omnino*, 3.2 *si*, 4.4 *videntur*, 5.1.4 *trucem om.*, 5.1.15 *Orai*, 7.2 *ergo*, 8.4 *cum ille*, 8.4 *satirdon*, 9.3 *habitu om.*, 10.1 *interpretes*, 10.7 *Tañ dudum*, 10.7 *Critone*, 12.1 *legeret*, 12.5 *non*, 14.1 *Asciltos*, 15.3 *traheretur*. Very few of these are through straight carelessness, since even most of the omissions have the interesting feature of a left space, signifying illegibility in the exemplar; this and the direction of the errors demonstrate caution, and it is safe to say that Pierre Daniel has executed this text, brief though it is, with great skill. It is the most carefully done of the sixteenth-century texts, by perhaps the most responsible scholar. In any new edition, **d**'s readings will require more consideration.

For the last half of **d**'s text ***L** manuscripts are the only source, and their witnesses, **dlmprt**, are thrown back on one or two ***L** manuscripts for the production of their so-called **L** texts. The collation continues to demonstrate separative traits of **d** where they are deemed inferior, no matter the reason. Unique variants in **d** appear to be individual errors, while the extent and manner in which these are shared, and are in turn differentiated from the correct reading, reveal the family history. I have tried to trace the source of the errors. If, however, as is likely, **d** had for its exemplar the '*fragmentum veteris libri qui fuerat Cuiacii*' (see Plate 11 and Chapter 7, n. 189), it is possible that some of its individualities revert to this source. Yet they are not confirmed by the scribe of **r** (in **r**^c), and I assume good **Memmianus** authority in the '*fragmentum*.'

In some cases a correct reading – as against **d** – is an emendation, but in the others it demonstrates superiority of **Cuiacianus** over **Benedictinus** (lt^v divide against the rest), or else degeneration of **Memmianus** if the correct reading in **Benedictinus** is evinced by **p**^{1}. Yet an incorrect reading shared with **p**^{1} does not necessarily revert to **Benedictinus**, since it could have entered **p**^{1} from **t** and its **Dalecampianus**, and so revert to **Memmianus**. On the whole, the collation reveals, in this limited compass, a good degree of uniformity in the *L manuscripts and some success in their transcription by the editors of the L texts, with shared mistakes due to minor palaeographic differences of opinion. It is still not really possible to come to an opinion on the relative superiority of the two major long manuscripts, **Cuiacianus** and **Benedictinus**, from this perspective. No L text here is based solely on **Cuiacianus**, so a head-to-head comparison with **d** would not serve the purpose. I shall try to get closer to the witness of **Cuiacianus** in Chapters 6 and 7.

6

François Daniel and the *Notae*

The *Satyrica* commentary left under the name of the *Notae* of François Daniel, brother of Pierre, has gained a place in the textual history of Petronius from its preservation of readings, often ascribed to a '*vetus* <*codex*>,' that have been linked to **Cuiacianus**, though its capacity for recovering such readings, together with its other features, has not really been explained or developed.[148] There is sufficient material for such an investigation: close to 150 lemmata and variants, constituting a kind of skeleton of a sixteenth-century Petronius edition constructed from several sources, both manuscript and printed, as the compiler's methods of citation make clear.[149] The aim, then, is to classify Daniel's material according to the sources and to identify these with the aid of the modern apparatus.

A glance at the commentary tells us that the number of variants offered is not uniform throughout, and that it is a function of the context of the lemma. As one would expect, for the parts covered by *LO Daniel is inclined to cite more variants than for those carried in *L only. Specifically, in the former we find that he uses more than one manuscript, as the designation '*unus ex veteribus*' shows. The term *vetus* seems to be generic and not confined to the same manuscript each time.[150] However, in the entries belonging in the *L passages there is no good evidence, as we shall see below, of more than one documentary origin, the single source being a manuscript. Meshing context with variant is the key to distinguishing the number and the identity of the sources, and the ultimate purpose is, with Daniel's help, to systematize for our full text and apparatus the readings that are reliably formed.

Thus in the *Notae* we have a source, a 'manuscript,' for the text of Petronius not dissimilar in character to the definitive so-called **L**-class printed and manuscript editions of the same century, though of course far more limited in scope. As is usual with such second-hand (or worse) sources, the value of the cited variants will depend on the design, consistency, scholarship and even honesty of the compiler of the scholarly exemplar, and on freedom from typographical errors in the production of the book, if applicable. This is all a matter for investigation.

Of these attributes a strong measure of consistency is surely one of the most important, for without some trust in it separation and alignment of named variants into categories for a source examination would be impossible, and information on the constituents of the text or commentary would be quite beyond control.

Inhibiting considerations of this sort may have caused previous researchers to take the *Notae* no further, and perhaps that was fair for the rewards offered; but what has tempted me to try to extend the evaluation is a new test for accuracy and consistency: discrepancies between the 'received' text of the commentary in Goldast 1610 (hereinafter *FDG*) and the handwritten copy of the same commentary to be found in the back of r (r^{comm} – see Plate 13).[151] I shall try to illustrate how the differences in the two available copies help both to validate the variants in Daniel's sources and to point up the shortcomings shared by all the derivative 'manuscript' texts upon which we must rely for constructing a modern edition.

Another inconvenience of the *Notae* is uncertainty over the precise date of composition of it and its exemplar. This is a serious limitation in the specialized context of Petronian textual investigation since a date close to its 1610 printing would have Daniel's text and commentary *follow* all the formative editions. The opportunity of seeing them would make any independent use of manuscripts by Daniel virtually impossible to prove. Here indeed r^{comm} is of special use, for it is capable of being dated quite accurately – accurately enough to fix the exemplar of the *Notae* to the period *preceding* the publication of the first 'long' editions. This greatly contributes to its potential value, since its manuscript witness and all its other readings are now free from the powerful influence of those complex mixes. If the readings in the *Notae* are to have this validity, it will be important to be able to sort out and account for the discrepancies in the two purported copies and fix the correct version – if necessary revising the variant witness provided by Daniel for our textual apparatus.

The scholar-copyists who made *FDG* and r^{comm} were faced with primarily a palaeographic problem: faithfully transcribing a text containing a number of unfamiliar and even unprecedented words in a hand, albeit contemporary, that bears the marks of being difficult to read. Their successes and failures, conveniently measurable, may well have their less visible counterparts in **dlmr** and **pt.** We have tended to take the manuscript and variant citations in these editions at face value, attributing differences to a different manuscript source, yet it might be well to see a bigger role for the sorts of slips and palaeographic errors that are demonstrated by the present comparison. This would have the practical effect of reducing the number of manuscript-derived *L variants, simplifying the stemma.[152]

FDG AND r^{comm}, COMPARED

Before commencing the search for Daniel's sources we should secure the text of the *Notae* by accounting for the differences in the two copies. The relative reliability of these independent transcriptions can be evaluated in various ways. In the main, the fuller version of an exemplar is the more authentic, and here FDG wins hands down: r^{comm} has not a few shortfalls or omissions – sometimes careless, sometimes deliberate – ranging in length from a single word to several lines.[153] Conversely, in the differing points of detail, the rival words will have to be checked against the full external apparatus for relative plausibility, taking into account setting (lemma or variant) and such details of attribution as may be provided. Simple carelessness and copying blunders can usually be detected swiftly from a glance at the parallel text.

The version of the *Notae* in Goldast 1610 is superior overall to r^{comm}, as we might expect. For it was a professional copy destined for printing; r^{comm} remains as an earlier draft, for personal use, and has clearly gone without a good proof-reading. FDG gives the appearance of being as faithful as possible in all particulars to Daniel's exemplar, while r^{comm}, aside from unintentional error, has executed certain deliberate though trivial changes. For r^{comm}, in its own way, is also seeking to be faithful: there is no evidence of independent scholarly sallies or self-indulgence.

We may classify the differences from Daniel in r^{comm} according to whether they were deliberate or accidental. In the first category fall the instances of manifest shortening of some of the longer of Daniel's exegetical notes – usually where no variants are cited – to get rid of parallel citations in other authors and other unwanted detail.[154] Also here belong what appear to be minor adjustments in citation practice; for instance, *unus ex veteribus* may be replaced by *vetus unus*. The other category includes obvious copying blunders that may be detected all the more readily for having nothing to do with possible disagreement over interpretation of a word in the exemplar: lemmata that are out of sequence (a couple), words that have migrated from notes into lemmata (two occasions), notes appearing in the wrong lemmata (two), illogical omission or alteration of small parts of a note (several instances), and omission of lemmata together with their notes.[155]

Far more interesting are the differences of opinion between FDG and r^{comm} on the text of the exemplar where both scribes were seeking to reproduce it faithfully. Some of these have nothing to do with the tradition because they happen to be retailing a note or instruction and not a reading or variant. Nevertheless, their unwitting role is to contribute direct evidence of the problematic character (especially to the scribe of r^{comm}) of Daniel's handwriting, and are almost droll for their ineptness and failure to follow sense. I include here '*de tali sane*,' anagram gibberish for the '*deleatur sane*' instruction in the note at 89.1.4., and two instances of '*imprimis*' for '*impressi*' (at 2.5 and 3.2).

FDG : r^{comm} differences, where they purport to cite the actual tradition, are clearly the most significant of our concerns. In the majority we may again put more trust in FDG (reading in lemma if followed by closed bracket, in note if not): 3.1 *quam ipse: qua ipse*, 5.1.5 *impotentum: impotentium*], 5.1.13 *imitet: imiter*, 8.4 *Satyrion: Satyreon*], 55.4 *morsum: mersu*, 55.6.5 *ciconiam etiam: ciconia e.*], 55.6.14 *nisi ut: nisi si ut*, 79.3 *scirpos: scrirpos*], 81.3 *iudicium: indicium*], 88.4 *excelsissimi: excellentissimum*, 89.1.4 *Cum Delio: Cuna delio*], 89.1.19 *Crimen solutus: Limen solitus*], 89.1.38 *liberae: liberes*], 89.1.43 *Laconti: Lacanti*], 89.1.60 *iubas: vitas*], 93.2.6 *arata: acata*], 93.3 *Aminothecam: Aumolteram*], 94.3 *quem animum: quere annum*], 99.6 *in allene: in altra*, 109.6 *et quo: ex quo*], 109.7 *pennas per manas: plumas pennas per macras*, 112.5 *cruciati: cruciam*], 116.9 *audebitis: adebitis*], 119.8 *plebeio: plebleio*], 119.9 *ac sepiretum: ac se piratum*] *ac sepyrecion: ac se pyrae cion.*

This is a mixed bag of errors (miscopying Daniel: the version in FDG is by no means necessarily 'correct' – just the more accurate reproduction of the exemplar – for it was not the task of the copyist to emend Daniel). Many are easy to detect from misspelling or ungrammaticality. Others are more plausible, even to the point of rivalling the reading in FDG, because they happen to offer a 'traditional' variant. The following give pause: *impotentum: impotentium, iudicium: indicium,* and *audebitis: adebitis. Impotentum* seems secured by the implication in the note that *impotentium* is also possible; *iudicium* is preferred for being more accessible to Daniel (in an *L passage, the reading of his *vetus* = **Cuiacianus** [see below]); *audebitis* appears indicated because *adebitis* is misspelled, and FDG cites in the note *adibitis* as one of two conjectures; r^{comm} truncates the note by giving only the second conjecture, *videbitis*, perhaps confusing his lemma with the first. Also in the *L section, *audebitis* has good **Cuiacianus** credentials for being in the text of l (*adibitis. videbitis* l^{margine}).

None of the foregoing FDG : r^{comm} superiorities materially affects the text as we know it since they only confirm the canon available in a detailed apparatus, such as that of Bücheler. Investigation of the foregoing is therefore in a sense preliminary, and we may now turn with our new perceptions to the most important contribution of r^{comm}: the instances where it redeems itself by possessing a record of Daniel's *Notae* that is more accurate than *FDG*. Here a modification of textual knowledge is indeed in the offing – as potential for contradicting the established record – and I would give pride of place to any adjustment or cleansing of readings purported to belong to Daniel's *L manuscript source, **Cuiacianus**.

SUPERIOR READINGS OF r^{comm} OVER *FDG*[156]

[*LO]	14.2.4	*nonnunquam nummis: nonnunquam numinis*]
[*L]	14.3	*dispondium sicel lupinosque: dispondium sicel supinosque*] *siser: sisier*
[*LO]	17.4	<u>*alias*</u> *etiam antecessuras:* <u>*alias*</u> *etiam antecessuros*
[*LOH]	55.5	*publicium: Publicum*
	55.6.4	*Numidica: Numicida,* <u>*al.*</u> *numicida: municida*
[*LO]	55.6.9	*Tribacca indica:* <u>*om.*</u>]
[*L]	79.4	*prudens enim prudens: prudens enim prude*]
[*LO]	89.1.7	*obducti specis: obductum specis*
	89.1.50	*iam morte pasti: iam morte pacti*]
[*Lφ]	93.2.9	*Roza Cynamomum: Rosa Cynannomum*]
[*LO]	94.2	*Eucolpius: Eucalpius*] *euclopius: Enclopius*
	94.3	*Eumopso: Eumospo*
[*L]	107.11	*et maiora: ut maiora*]

The inferior readings and variants in *FDG* are not necessarily the fault of the scholarly copyist of Daniel's *Notae*. As a printed source *FDG* – in contrast to r^{comm} – provides a second point of entry for error in the mechanics of book production. The result is the same: an impostor with a false pedigree – the apparent sanction of a sixteenth-century scholar in possession of many source options for his text. A goodly number of the above savour of the *vitium typographi*, though it may not be proved. The example at 55.5 demonstrates the problem: neither form is what it purports to be, the reading of '*impr.*' (*Publium* c), yet r^{comm} must have the version of Daniel because, unlike *FDG*, its note is differentiated from the lemma, which already carries *publicum*. Entries that do not pass the test of sense or grammar are likely to be misprints, since the preparer of Daniel's copy for publication (Goldast himself?) would be more constrained to interpret it credibly than the scribe of r^{comm}. Yet there are few clear-cut instances where palaeography could not lend a hand if the scholar chose to race or nod. At any rate, *FDG* is suspect largely because the readings are unattested elsewhere:

numinis, siser (here Bücheler saddles his apparatus with this ghost word), *sisier, antecessuros, numicida, municida, prude* (again Bücheler *app.*), *obductum* (Bücheler *app.*), *ut.*

I have indicated that Daniel had access to only one *L source, a manuscript. The three cases in the above table with an exclusive *L content are presumed to be taken from it. Adding to them the reading *etiam antecessuras*, we may conduct a small test with a reciprocal value: to demonstrate Daniel's reading (i.e. the correctness of r^{comm} or FDG) and to point to his source. FDG's *etiam antecessuros*, I have noted, is elsewhere not found despite a context in *LO – a poor indicator of genuineness; in contrast, r^{comm}'s note variant *etiam antecessuras* happens to be the reading of **l**, which has *et antecessura*, Daniel's lemma, in its upper margin. Our evidence attests that this latter form is confined to the **O**-class manuscripts and their derived text **s** (not **c**, which is missing here), readily available to Daniel and Scaliger and no doubt thence obtained. Though the scholars have opposite views on reading and variant, we may be sure from their joint witness to *etiam antecessuras* that it is the attested form, *L class, and the reading of **Cuiacianus**, a known **l** source.

In the three divergent cases above where the context is *L it is r^{comm}'s showing that is identical to **l** while the 'received' FDG's is at variance. In the first two Daniel cites a *'vet.'* as his source, and in the third ('*et maiora*' in lemma) this is implicit from the variant in the note, which is carefully labelled a conjecture (*lego eo meliora*). Scaliger's authority again points to **Cuiacianus**. Thus r^{comm} performs the invaluable service of banishing three ghost readings that are in confusing conflict with **l** as they stand in FDG, and of corroborating the **Cuiacianus** authority of Scaliger's text at these points.[157]

SOURCES, 1: PRINTED EDITIONS

The first step in the search for the source constituents of the *Notae* is to isolate the ones with the greatest potential for independent, objective verification – those purporting to be printed editions. There are in all 62 variants that we may deem, on the basis of their attribution, to come from printed editions. Thus we have *impr.* (54x), *imp.* (2x), *in pr.* (1x), *impress.* (3x), *impressi* and *impressi cod.* (1x each). Helpful inferences may be drawn from the bare nomenclature and accidents of occurrence. All these variants occur in the **O** portion of the text; none shows any knowledge of the *L context, though such a context is well represented elsewhere in the commentary with variants said to come from a manuscript source (*vetus*). In this way, in fact, we may determine that Daniel's original commentary was composed prior to the appearance of the first 'long' printed text (**t**) in 1575 and that any ***L** influence in the *Notae* reverts to an actual manuscript.

To this *terminus ante quem* we may supply the *terminus post quem*. The method of citation indicated above, if truthful, refers with complete unambiguity on a couple of occasions to more than one edition. The maximum possible was four (**a**, **b**, **c**, **s**), though only two would be needed to qualify for the plural in the citation language. We can in all likelihood rule out the first two, the fifteenth-century Italian editions: to Daniel and his brethren north of the Alps the 1520 **c** enjoyed first edition status.[158] This being so, **s** qualifies as the only remaining edition consultable, and the *terminus post quem* for the *Notae* is set at 1565. The date of compilation of the commentary (and the text upon which it was based, which does not survive) is 1565–75.

The above could have been hypothesized from the contextual data in FDG alone; but by now using the evidence of **r^comm** we may substantiate this time frame and even narrow it. As I noted above (Chapter 1, n. 18), composition of **r** itself is fixed at prior to 1572 from a reference to van der Does' borrowing it from the owner, his friend Daniel Rogers, that year while on a visit to England. There seems every reason to believe, though it was then in England, that **r** was actually acquired by Rogers a year or two earlier, when he was in Paris on diplomatic business. Such an inference is based on the accessibility to manuscripts (both **O**- and ***L**-class) of Petronius and to the scholars working on them that only France and the French capital in this decade could provide. Of course **r^comm** is not spoken to by van der Does, and its compilation, if by Rogers, would be possible theoretically in any year up to Rogers' death in 1591. However, two considerations militate against putting it any later than Rogers' Paris period: first, there is some evidence that the commentary was available to the composer of **r** when it was written; and second (here I take a position contrary to that of Müller and others), I am sure that the scribe of **r** and **r^comm** was not Rogers himself. This being the case, the full manuscript (**Lambethanus 693**) was a commission or acquisition by him in Paris in the late 1560s or 1570.[159]

To return to the *Notae*'s citation of printed editions: while the few plural references are all that is needed to prove the availability of the two printed sources, one cannot count on the use of both on each occasion, and in fact the citation practice quickly lapses into ambiguity in the vast majority of cases. A logical (but utopian) expectation would have been to cite the variant under *impressi* if both **c** and **s** agreed on it (this would be the majority, as we know from the intimate resemblance of the two texts), and to reserve another word, such as *impressus* or *impr.*, for any desired variant that occurred in only one of the texts. If mention of a different variant was warranted, it could have been cited under *alter impr.*

To what extent has this scheme or some such unambiguous pattern been followed? The only way to tell is to compare the citations of Daniel with the record, which thankfully is available with **c** and **s**. We are obliged, however, to consider how Goldast 1610 might have altered the citing practices of his exemplar, employing his own in preference to those of Daniel. Here too we might try to employ the versions in r^{comm} as a control. A swift check of r^{comm} and FDG for this feature shows that the two scholars' methods of alluding to a 'printed' origin for the variant (an indication essentially copyable from Daniel's exemplar) is just as likely to be different as the same; thus *impr.* may exist opposite *imp.*, *impressi*, *impress.*, and so on. We shall certainly have to abandon seeing beyond this tangle to Daniel's own habit on all occasions. While both copyists seem to have felt less need to be as faithful to the citation style as to the variant itself, it is likely that the more formal, printed text retained better accuracy than r^{comm}.

As evidence for this we note an oddity in r^{comm} that in fact could tell something of Daniel's own formula: at 2.5 and 3.2 r^{comm} gives as the source for the variant *imprimis*, while FDG has *impressi* and *impress.* Behind this one sees Daniel's citation in fuller format (not *impr.*), apparently misread by r^{comm}. This and numerous other examples in r^{comm} demonstrate that the copyist had difficulty reading Daniel's longhand original.

It would be appropriate to abandon too the logical ideal above defined that specific information on the number of printed sources resides in the citation formula, although a few unusual variations may convey useful specific information and will be looked at later. For now we should turn to the variants themselves, verify them against the printed sources and check the citations for consistency.

Of the 62 variants given the authority of a printed edition, 52 agree outright (or differ insignificantly in a spelling detail) with the text of **c**. As one would expect, the common variants show the text of **s**, in most cases, though in all the match-up is somewhat better with **c**:

THE READINGS OF FDG**c** AGAINST **s**[160]

1.3	*sansuco* '*impressi cod. habent*': *sam psucho*
5.1.8	*histrionea* '*Impr.*': *histrioniae*
5.1.13	*imitet* '*Impr.*': *mutet*
55.6.6	*e tota lystria* [*vel listria*] '*Impr.*': *crotalistria*
55.6.7	*trepidi* '*Imp.*': *tepidi*
88.6	*tamen* '*impr.*': *tantum*

89.1.43   *Laconti 'impr.':* Lacoonti
89.1.46   *pias 'impr.':* pietas
111.2   *funeris sparsis 'impr.':* funeris officium sparsis
111.3   *se alimento subtrahebat 'Impr.':* sine a. trahebat
111.6   *ibi 'impr.':* ibi sibi
119.9   *Ac spireum 'Impr.':* Aes pyreum

In the above examples FDG is silent on naming the **s** variant, though often having it in his lemma – for which the **c** reading is consistently rejected. One might easily infer that Daniel consulted only one printed edition throughout, despite the citation formula (as at 1.3; slightly inaccurate and misleading). This makes practical sense, though we are still entitled to infer, if not from the lemmata (since the better **s** may be agreeing with another, manuscript, source), the availability of **s** for consultation from the following instance:

THE READINGS OF FDG**s** AGAINST **c**

5.1.6   *perditis addictus 'impr.'* [*praedictis abdictus 'alter'*]: *per dictis abditus*

The evidence is admittedly sparse, and made less reliable by the fact that *perditis addictus* is given to a manuscript also ('*sic habet unus ex veterib.*'). The ambiguous *alter* (sc. *'vet.'* or *'impr.'?*) is interesting. Although the variant so cited does not conform exactly to the reading of **c**, I would suggest that **c** is indeed the source; somewhere along the way an abbreviation and ligature have been mistaken, perhaps wrongly transcribed from Daniel's own notes. We may now examine the other instances of discrepancy between Daniel's apparent record of the printed variant and the version verifiable in the editions.

THE READINGS OF FDG *'impr.'/'Impr.'* AGAINST **cs**

4.3   *quem:* quod
7.1   *dicturam:* ducturam
25.7   *in furto:* in scorto
55.5   *Publicum vel publicium* [**r**^comm]: *Publium*
55.6.10   *aut ut matrona ornata:* an ut m. o.
89.1.50   *in morte passi:* i. m. pasci
94.3   *alioquin quoque adversus quem:* a. q. animum q. a
109.7   *macria inani spira:* inania i. s.
118.5   *extra orationis mudace expressi* [al. *extra rationis modum expressi* FDG:
           al. *extra rationis mudice expressae* **r**^comm]: *e. r. modum expressae*

These unexpected divisions require explaining. Taking the verifiable discrepancies from the last two lists, we see that the instances of outright disagreement between the alleged and the actual reading of the printed editions yield an error rate of about one citation in six. This may or may not seem high, but it leaves the suspicion of error in Daniel's citations of manuscripts also – and these are far harder to verify. Before we proceed to them it is well to review the above list to determine how the discrepancy may have come about.

Since we receive these readings at second hand in FDG and r^comm, there are two stages in each instance where an error could have occurred. The first is through the agency of Daniel himself, either by a mistake in transcription of c or s into his notes (this would be uncommon since printed editions are not difficult to read), or through misattribution or carelessness in copying his own notes from one version to another. The second stage of potential error is in the misreading of Daniel's longhand notes by the preparers of the two independent versions that survive: one, the copy (or even original) typeset for publication in Goldast 1610, and the other, the longhand copy in its informal situation in r after the *Satyrica* text. It is here that having two copies of Daniel's *Notae* proves useful, for their agreement on the erroneous variant is inclined to put the blame on the exemplar and not on misreading by the two copyists or typographic error.

One suspects that the *quem* for *quod* error at 4.3 is due to the writing out of an abbreviation incorrectly. The word is in fact abbreviated in c, but routinely. It seems to be an elementary slip by Daniel. 7.1 *dicturam* for *ducturam* must again be Daniel-derived, though I can see no special reason for it beyond his misreading his own handwriting. The instance at 55.5 *Publicum* for *Publium* is more complicated, both because r^comm differs, with *publicium*, and because *publicum* was apparently available elsewhere, for it is in the text of r, and it is selected for the lemma on the strength of a '*vet. lib.*' I am inclined to trust Goldast's copying of another slip of Daniel. 55.6.10 *aut ut* for *an ut is* simple carelessness by Daniel: the note's format prepares one for a variant on the lemma, such indeed as *an ut* would provide; instead the lemma is repeated *per dittographiam*. At 89.1.50 *passi* for *pasci* is obviously caused by a misreading of the word in longhand, since there would be no mistaking *pasci* in c. I assume, since it is in both FDG and r^comm, that Daniel mistranscribed his own note at an intermediate stage.

The last three entries in the last list would present no difficulty to the attentive transcriber, but they share by their jingly, repetitious, or convoluted format a potential for causing trouble to the hasty one. The problem at 94.3 is a difficult syntax adding to the likelihood of a copying error: Daniel's eye jumped from *quoq;* to *que*, missing out *aīum* (as these words are printed in **c**). The *macria* at 109.7 common to FDG and **r**^{comm} may have been the result of Daniel's eye straying over three lines in **c**, where word divisions at line ends are a pitfall for the careless copier: we have ... *ad ma/nus ... ina/nia īani spira .../ coeperat*; and *macria* is the hybrid result. Finally, we have the triple error at 118.5 *extra orationis mudace expressi*, for *extra rationis modum expressae*. Again replicated in both our sources, the blame is partly Daniel's and partly the printer's. It is clear from the variant cited under '*al.*' that Daniel has access to the text of **c**, and he may even have transcribed it correctly; ungrammatical '*i*' in FDG (as we may tell from the correct **r**^{comm}) is due to a misprint in Goldast 1610; *orationis* arrived from the lemma, *extra corpus orationis; mudace* (or *mudice* **r**^{comm}, possibly with a stroke over the '*m*') is mysterious, Daniel-derived.

The 62 variants from Daniel's printed source (**c**) are almost always in the position of the rejected error. Exceptions are at 5.1.6 *Nec perditis addictus*] ('*sic habet unus ex veterib. & impr.*'); 7.3 *inter viculos*] ('*sic habent impr.*'); and in one case Daniel likes a printed variant but still will not adopt it: 89.1.21 *uterum notavit*] ('*in pr. uteri, quod probo*'). We should not assume that he gave equally small credence to **c** in his Petronius edition as a whole. On the contrary: it should be surmised that where the printed variant is cited against a lemma it is specifically to show the superiority only in these instances of the manuscript-grounded authority for his text.

Thus Daniel's unflattering opinion of the *impressi* should be put in a fuller context. The bulk of the lemmata, we note, silently carry the reading of **c** and **s**. In these instances Daniel means to set off in his notes an opposite facet, an interesting but rejected variant from a manuscript or conjecture, without drawing attention to the printed source, especially if it agreed with another manuscript.[161] Indeed, he sometimes cites a variant only from a manuscript when we may see it in the *impressi*, as at 4.2 *quae nihil esse maius*] '*unus ex veteribus magis*' (also in **c**). This is potentially troubling because misattribution may be present, though here we need not suspect it because *magis* is read in the older **O** manuscripts such as **B** and **P**, to which Daniel could have had access.

SOURCES, 2: MANUSCRIPTS

As we turn to the manuscripts, our challenge is to determine their number and identity, using as clues Daniel's citation practices, the context of occurrence and of course the named variant itself. The formulas '*unus ex veteribus*' and '*vetus unus*,' invoked on many occasions, make it clear that he had the use of more than one; and sometimes our scholar seems obliged to take pains to show that there were exactly two at the operative point (e.g. at 14.2.4 *nonnunquam nummis*] '*alter ex veteribus*'). Unfortunately we may not assume that when Daniel uses only '*vet.*' he does so for contrast and that only one manuscript source is available. Such an interpretation simply cannot be made to square with our knowledge of context and manuscript history, and we should recognize in '*vet.*' only another way, of equivalent sense to the above, of citing a manuscript reading.

There are, however, instances of punctiliousness in drawing attention to the use (not the possession, which is a different thing) of a single manuscript source. Thus at 13.1 *nec futurae* [*L*]] we find the note '*sic habet vetus exempl. quo uno hac in parte, ut in aliis pluribus, usi sumus.*' I emphasize that Daniel does not actually state, as does Pierre Pithou in reminiscent language in his *varietas* (e.g. at 141.10 '*unicum hac in parte habuimus*') that he had no other manuscript source for the passage, though we must so take it for this *L example. But for the poem at 55.6, with its *LOH provenance, we have the note '*nos a veteri exemplari in exscribendis his versibus numquam discessimus.*' No real conflict here: Daniel merely states an adherence to *a* (not *the*) manuscript, implicitly against the printed text which is also available. The case at 44.17 *nemo ieiunium servat* [*LφH*]] '*sic habet vet. lib. quo unico hac in parte usi sumus*' is unclear. *L and a florilegium carry the text without differing on the wording. Daniel, I would say, used the former, for so the order in the commentary implies. It cannot be determined if the florilegium was at his side (see below).

The final reference to a single manuscript source is odd. For 7.3 *inter viculos* [*LO*]] Daniel, after citing a debt to the printed edition for this lemma, proclaims, '*vetus liber, quo solo hac in parte uti potui, habet, inter titulos.*' Here he uncharacteristically adverts to the possession of a sole manuscript reading. *Inter titulos* is an O-class reading, carried in the manuscripts that Daniel is most likely to have seen of this class, **B** and **P**. If he saw the reading in one of these, are we entitled to infer that it was missing in his *L source, **Cuiacianus**? If this be true, we must accept it *ex silentio*, since two of our other sources for this manuscript, **t**[v] and **Tholosanus**, decline comment. However, a third source, Scaliger's **l**, carries *internuculos*, testily exposed by **p**[2v] as a conjecture. May we take this apparent foray of Scaliger's as evidence that the reading was indeed absent or obscured in **Cuiacianus** and so meet Daniel's note with full comprehension?

The *L Context

We may be most confident of recovering the other readings from the unique *L-class manuscript (**Cuiacianus**) in the lemmata and notes derived from the exclusive *L context, hence the merit of a separate list of Daniel's entries in this setting.

FDG ENTRIES IN THE *L CONTEXT[162]

8.4	*Satyrion*]
13.1	*nec futurae*] *Sic habet vetus exempl. quo uno hac in parte, ut in aliis pluribus, usi sumus. fortasse leg. est furtive.*
14.3	*dispondium sicel lupinosque*] *Erat hoc ita emendatum in vet. lib. Quid si legatur dupondium quibus sicelion lupinosque vel, quibus siser lupinosque, &c. quod longe verius puto. Imo legend. dupondium sicel lupinosque ...*
20.4	*duas institas protulit e sinu*] *in vet. Lexico scriptum est de sura. ... Vide Papiam & Fratris Notas.*
30.1	*procursator rationis*] *Sic vet. Lego, procurator rationes accipiebat.*
30.2	*VIRO AUG*] *Sic vet. Lego VIVIRO AUG.*
30.11	*quid ergo est*] *Leg. puto quicquid ergo est.*
31.3	*paronicia*] *Malim scribere, paronichia*
79.3	*per omnes scirpos*] *Lego, scruptos. Apud Gellium lib. 12 cap. 6. vet. lib.* [*libri* **r^comm**] *habent scriptos, ut & apud Fabium & Cicer.*
79.4	*prudens enim prudens*] *Sic vet. Puto legendum prudens enim pridie cum luce, &c. Prudens enim ptis.*
79.4	*notaverat certaque*] *Sic vet. Lego, notaverat creta, quae linea.*
79.6	*invenisset*] *Lego, intervenisset.*
81.3	*iudicium harenae: indicium harenae* **r^comm**]
81.4	*cuius anni ad tesseram venerunt*] *Lego, venierunt.*
81.5	*quid ille alter die qui*] *Malim, qui togae virilis die stolam sumpsit. nisi tanquam toga virilis, pro, togae virilis loco positum est.*
82.3	*phaecasiati*] *Quid si legas, phocaliati*
83.5	*et hylari*] *Leg. puto, et Hylam nympha praedata.*
83.9	*amor ingenii neminem inquam*] *Quid si leg. unquam*
87.6	*usque beneficio*] *Lego, ususque.*
91.4	*contero*] *Quid si legas, contergo?*
92.4	*Ascylti partem*] *id est, Ascylto similem*
92.6	*ad solium*]
93.3	*Aminothecam*] *Malo, pinacothecam*
97.3	*...*] *Discoloria etiam veste*

97.8   *insertans commissuras*] <u>Si</u> <u>quid</u> <u>hic</u> <u>locus</u> <u>emendatione</u> indiget, <u>malim</u> <u>ita</u>
         <u>legere</u>, insertans commissuris digitos.

99.6   *in altum compono*] <u>Fortasse</u> <u>leg.</u> in allene: *in altra* **r**^{comm}

101.3   *nec ullius dolum*] <u>Leg.</u> ullum.

104.1   *Eucolpium quid quaeris*] <u>Lego</u>, quem quaeris.

107.11   *et maiora*] <u>Lego</u>, eo maiora.

115.5   *portam mugientem*] <u>Puto</u> <u>leg.</u> porcam.

116.9   *audebitis oppidum*] <u>Leg.</u> adibitis, <u>vel</u> <u>potius</u>, videbitis.

117.2   *poenam istam differrem*] <u>Quid</u> <u>si</u> <u>legatur</u>, peram?

This list contains 32 readings, in almost all cases adopted as lemmata, from the exclusive ***L** context of the tradition. They are quite beyond the reach of contamination from any **O** source, whether manuscript or printed edition. The readings are usually said explicitly to come from a manuscript (*vetus*), but where a notation does not occur we are still entitled to infer that the lemma was derived therefrom. The arrangement of the commentary is almost perfectly consistent with the presence of only one such source, since alternatives are not cited with a *vetus* designation (in marked contrast to the material from the ***LO** portions).[163] However, a feature of this segment of the *Notae*, amounting to only about one-fifth of the total, is something like three-quarters of Daniel's sallies into conjectural emendation, scrupulously marked as *lego, malo, malim scribere, quid si legas*, etc. (representing differing shades of conviction?), all relegated to the notes.[164] This corroborates the absence of the documentary variant. We may surmise, in fact, that the conjecture is the reason for the lemma's selection – in contrast to the ***LO** examples, whose presence was due to the availability of an interesting alternative. We may thus credit Daniel with the preservation of at least 32 likely readings from **Cuiacianus** and take them into account in an apparatus.

Although **Cuiacianus** was used to help formulate other editions of the day, notably l, **p²**, and **t** after c. 112, these texts may have had access to another ***L** source, and the compilers were not disposed to recording them apart.[165] No doubt many readings were taken from **Cuiacianus**: they simply cannot be identified positively. However, two of our sources, found in the above editions, seem to take pains to distinguish a number of readings from a single ***L** manuscript which, on external grounds, has been taken to be the **Cuiacianus**. These are the 81 variants of **t**^v, which preserved their individuality by the accident of being unavailable until the editor had printed the bulk of his edition; and 21 citations (mostly rejects) by Pierre Pithou of a **Tholosanus** in the *variae lectiones* of his second edition of 1587 (hereinafter **p²**^{v'Thol.'}).[166]

To 'prove' mutual use of **Cuiacianus** we are set the task of collating Daniel's lemmata from the above list against this rather sparse material. Commencing with **t^v**, we lose about two-thirds of our potential 'tests' simply from their being in the ***LO** context, which we have now excluded from consideration. Of the remainder, only one variant, 13.1 *futurae* (so, Daniel), is treated by both sources, and it is a problematic one. If this is the reading of **Cuiacianus**, it is flatly contradicted by **t^v**'s *furtive*. Fortunately, help is at hand in Daniel's commentary, where *furtive* happens to be offered as a conjecture. I contend that it is not a conjecture (by Daniel, that is) but a variant carried in the margin of **Cuiacianus**. Both readings could therefore be seen in the manuscript by the two scholars: Daniel selected the text of **Cuiacianus**, *futurae*, for his lemma and let someone else's conjecture, *furtive*, be taken as his own, while **t^v** offered a view of this variant and ignored *futurae*, perhaps because it (or something very like it, *suturae*, which **t** prints) was in his other ***L** manuscript.[167]

In **p^{2v'Thol.'}** also, for this test, we must eliminate the ***LO** context. Of the 13 remaining variants cited in this source, not one is picked up by Daniel as well. **Tholosanus** is not useless, however. The readings of it, **t^v**, and other sources of **Cuiacianus** such as **l** and **r**, will be worth comparing with Daniel's lemmata in the ***LO** context. Agreements with a manuscript citation in Daniel will point, in many cases, to common consultation of **Cuiacianus**, the success of the equation depending on the ability to eliminate from consideration the reading from any shared **O**-class manuscript or edition.

The Florilegia Context

Was a florilegium available to Daniel? The *Notae* uses 25 lemmata containing φ material, though in all instances but three it is shared by ***L** and **O**. In the absence of φ-derived separative errors in these lemmata (and I have found none) we shall have to dismiss from our evidence the ***LOφ** context, since here either a lemma or a manuscript variant (under *vetus*) in Daniel's notes might always refer to something *other* than a florilegium. This leaves only the three occasions where a florilegium reading could be set off against one other manuscript source.

FDG ENTRIES IN THE ***Lφ** CONTEXT

44.17   *nemo ieiunium servat*] *Sic habet vet. lib. quo unico hac in parte usi sumus.*
         Ceterum ut id, quod sentio, libere dicam, vereor ne hoc nobis verbum
         Monachus exscriptor pro iusiurandum ex ingenio reposuerit.

93.2.6   *atque arata sitis*] <u>Leg</u>. <u>puto</u> *arata Syrtis.*

93.2.9   *Roza Cynamomum* **r**^{comm}: *Rosa Cynnannomum* FDG] <u>Ratio</u> <u>carminis</u>
           <u>postulat</u> <u>ut</u> <u>legatur</u>, *cynnamum. Cinnamomum* <u>porro</u> & *cinnamum* <u>legitur</u>.

The case of 44.17 is instructive, even in its potential for causing
uncertainty. Daniel is at pains to show both that he was following one
manuscript at this point, and that he can offer an original conjecture. It so
happens that *ius iurandum* is added in the margin of a florilegium (**Parisinus lat. 7647 = par**), in a later hand. Its author could of course have
been Daniel (and this would prove that he had access to the florilegium
reading, which was *ieiunium*, as in his lemma – in which case **par** could
have been his *unicum*); but *ius iurandum* could equally have been entered
(given its undatability) by anyone who had seen it in **p** and **t**, into which
texts it may have come from Daniel – as his conjecture – in the first place.
Further, we have the clear authority of **t**^v that *ieiunium* was the reading of
Cuiacianus. As Daniel's single source for the text at this point, **Cuiacianus** would do very well.

In the other two instances we again have the lemma set off against a
seeming conjecture (or vice versa), though the apparatus of Bücheler seems
to assign *Syrtis* to a florilegium ('*Syrtis* pt, *margo* L [**ptl**^{margine}] *cum
florilegio*'), if I understand it rightly – or does he mean the reading is in
the florilegium's margin also (as above)?[168] Here again *sitis* is vouched for
in a **Cuiacianus**-aligned text, **l**, and it is reasonable to suppose that *Syrtis*
entered **ptl**^{margine} and **par**^{margine} (the latter either directly or at one
remove) from Daniel.[169] With *cinnamomum* and *cinnamum* '*legitur*' may
refer to a manuscript, but we have seen how the absence of the term *vetus*
signals a non-manuscript source.[170] In no case is it *necessary* to believe,
therefore, that Daniel had access to florilegia, and in fact the order assigned
in his commentary to these lemmata and notes is consistent with their
place in the **L* texts.[171] Absence of florilegium consultation certainly puts
us in a better position to recover his sources in the **LOφ* portion.

The **LO* Context

In this the major setting for the lemmata, the rewards will come from
being able to distinguish between **L* and **O** readings. We have established
that all genuine **L* readings revert to **Cuiacianus** and, in the appropriate
circumstance, we may hold the corollary to be true: that **Cuiacianus**
readings carry the witness of **L* against **O**. The condition to which I refer
is the requirement that the reading against which the **Cuiacianus** variant
is assigned as contrast not be likely to come from another **L* source.

Essentially, we are looking for separative errors in **Cuiacianus** against **O** and Ω, or for separative errors in the **O** class against Ω and **Cuiacianus**. We must reapply the test of t^v and **Tholosanus** against the range of Daniel's complete entries (lemma and note) in the ***LO** context, paying close attention to the mode of designation.

FDG ENTRIES IN THE ***LO** AND ***LO**φ CONTEXTS, COMPARED
WITH **t, t^v**, AND $\mathbf{p^{2v'\textit{Thol.}'}}$

[***LO**]	2.3	*deberent*] *unus ex veteribus deberemus*: *debemus* **$t^v p^{2v'\textit{Thol.}'}$**
	2.5	*certe neque Platona &c.*] *aliquid deesse videtur*: *deest certe* **t^v**
	3.4	*magister*] *unus ex veteribus, magistri* **t^v**
[***LO**φ]	5.1.2	*prius more*] *unus ex vet. merae* **t^v**
	5.1.3	*polleat*] *vetus unus, palleat* **t^v**
	5.1.8	*sedeat redemptus histr\<ionea\>*] *vetus unus, redimitus histrioni* **t^v**
	5.1.9	*armigerae*] *vet. crinigerae* **t^v**
[***LO**]	8.3	*perduxit*] *vet. produxit* **t^v**
	14.2.6	*\<causa\>*] *\<alter ex veterib.\>*, *cera* **t^v**
	80.9.5	*nimium* **t^v**] *ego legend. censeo, mimum* **t**
[***LO**φ]	83.10.6	*disertas* **t^v**] *vet. unus desertas* **t**
	88.4	*excellentissimi* **t^v**] *unus ex veterib. excelsissimi* **t**
	88.7	*invenisset* **t^v**] *unus ex veterib. attigisset*: *pervenisset* **t**
[***LO**]	109.8	*capillorum*] *alias, in capillos suos* **$t^v p^{2v'\textit{Thol.}'}$**
[***LO**φ]	111.6	*ergo*] *alias, vero* **t^v**

The above is the full record of *FDG* **$t^v p^{2v'\textit{Thol.}'}$** interaction, with the correspondences – the readings of **Cuiacianus** – shown. These are usually in the position of rejected variant from a *vetus*, although in two instances they are given as *alias*, a less precise designation. I can see no significance to the use of this term. Every entry, including 11 lemmata of the 15, has a variant in it that could have been provided by **c**, and I have little doubt that the printed edition was the basis for Daniel's text here (as largely in ***LO**). Thus Daniel cites a variant in a *vetus* that is meant to be different from **c** and perhaps also distinct from the reading in another available manuscript (for there were at least two, as the terms *unus ex veteribus* and *alter ex veteribus* show). This, being of the **O** class, was very likely to have been the same as the reading of **c**, hence 'confirming' it for his lemma. What we have is an **Oc**: ***L** division, and the identity of the **O** *vetus* cannot be known (but see below).

In four cases Daniel selects what appears to be the **Cuiacianus** reading for his lemma (*nimium, disertas, excellentissimi, invenisset*), yet without informing us of the manuscript origin. Again, the rejected variant is assigned to a *vetus* (except for *mimum*, which poses as a conjecture), with the difference that this time it was available to Daniel in **c**. We may preserve our belief in his honesty by positing the same variant's presence in the **O** manuscript at his disposal. The variant is too commonplace to identify its manuscript source: only a separative error in **B** or **P** would narrow the search.

There is one seeming violation of the FDG $t^v p^{2v\,'Thol.'}$ agreement that requires explaining: the case of 2.3 *deberent*: *deberemus/debemus*. The variant alleged by Daniel for his *vetus* has no support from either the *L or the **O** tradition. I see it as unlikely to have been in his manuscript; we have a differing opinion on a ligature or assumed ligature. Since it occurs in r^{comm} as well as FDG it is not a printing error but comes from Daniel himself.

2.5 *certe*] is also a special case. It appears that what we have here are two differing accounts of the same phenomenon in **Cuiacianus**. I suspect that the reference in t^v to *certe*'s absence in **Cuiacianus** is wrong – a misunderstanding by de Tournes of a marginal suggestion in it that was taken up correctly by Daniel (see also n. 164, above). The case of 14.2.6 is important, with certain implications. The entry is hampered by accidental omission of the lemma, but in the note Daniel cites a fuller variant, *cera, qui probat empta, sedet*, that occurs elsewhere: in p^{1v}, cited under '*al.*'. If this is the **Cuiacianus** reading, as I believe, we are faced with Pithou's access to it in some way years before his supposed first systematic use of **Cuiacianus**, as $p^{2v\,'Thol.'}$ (see Chapter 2, n. 64, and further discussion in the next chapter).

It remains for us to consider the readings of **l**, a known **Cuiacianus** user, in support of other **Cuiacianus** material in FDG . The debt of FDG to **Cuiacianus** may be proposed where the shared reading is contrasted with other identifiable testimony. For example, the 18 entries below have the best chance of containing **Cuiacianus** readings, usually in lemma.

Cuiacianus READINGS FROM FDG AND l, WITH AGREEMENTS

[*LO]	4.2	*maius*] *magis* <u>*vetus*</u> **Oc**	
	4.3	*mitigarentur*] *irrigarentur* <u>*vetus*</u> **Ocl**	
	4.5	*Lucinianae*] *Lucianae* <u>*impr.*</u> **Ocl**	
[*LOφ]	5.1.6	*nec perditis addictus*]	
	5.1.15	*huc* <u>*vetus*</u> **l**	
[*LO]	6.1	<*mihi*>] *mihi* <u>*impr.*</u> **Ocl**	

6.4   *in cursu*] *et cursu* <u>*impr.*</u> **Ocl**

16.2   *reclusaeque* **l**^{margine}] *remissaeque* <u>*vetus*</u> **Ol**, <u>*om.*</u> **c**

80.9.5   *agit*] *ait* <u>*vetus*</u> **Oc**

81.2   *sollicitudine* <u>*vetus*</u> **l**

89.1.7   *antrum* **l**^{margine}] *castrum* <u>*impr.*</u> **Oc**

108.12   *non stlatarium*]

109.6   *exonerat*] *exsonat ergo* <u>*vetus*</u> *LOl*^{margine}

109.7   *inanis pluma*] *inani spuma* <u>*alias*</u> **O**

118.3   *inundata*] *inundanter* <u>*vetus*</u> **O**

118.5   *orationis*] *rationis* <u>*al.*</u> **O**

119.8   *risu* <u>*vetus*</u> **l**

119.9   *ac sepiretum*] <u>*vetus*</u> *ac sepyrecion* **P**

All the other manuscript-derived entries in *FDG* are shared too promiscuously for ready assignation to **Cuiacianus**.

The **O** Context

As above indicated, regular **O** readings, for being carried in more than one source, cannot be attributed, and the *vetus* term is usually no help. The few unique features of an **O** manuscript that turn up on occasion show a relation to **P**.

P READINGS FROM *FDG*

2.1   *curia* <u>*unus ex veterib. lib.*</u>

4.4   *quisquis*]

89.1.7   *obducti specis* [<u>*vel*</u> *obductis pecis*] <u>*vet.*</u>

89.1.19 *crimen*]

109.6   *et quo*]

Contemporary use by Pithou and Scaliger of this manuscript, known to them as '*Bit.*,' attests to its ready availability in the period (see Chapter 3). An acceptable minimum set of sources for the Petronius edition of Daniel would then be **c**, **Cuiacianus** (the presumed stimulus for the task), and **P**.

In conclusion, it may be stated that the quality of scholarship exhibited in *FDG* is high – probably comparable to or better than that of **t** – with the level of errors we have detected representative of our good *L* sources. In support of this view we may note how Daniel's emendations were shared eagerly by scholars of the day, if we can believe, with Müller, that the frequent appearance of the same material in the margins of **lmrt** reverts to him. With the aid of FDG we may confirm, which is to say 'recover,' close to 70 **Cuiacianus** variants – not necessarily ones that we should print in the text, but whose positive identification as worthy medieval exponents surely helps to fix the text and purify the apparatus.

7

Daniel Rogers and r

Petronius manuscript r (see Plates 11 to 13) appears first to have been investigated by Konrad Müller in the late 1950s for Müller 1961; a comparison of readings with those quoted by Lambin and Turnèbe from a manuscript belonging to Henri de Mesmes established for the Swiss scholar that it was a scion of the so-called **Memmianus** and a sibling of **d** and **m**.[172] r's full-length *L-text makes it at once the most important **Memmianus** witness, since the quotes in the secondary sources are in their nature selective and not always reliable, **d** is a mere beginning, and **m** is likewise a fragment, strongly infiltrated by **s** in the **O** context. As seen in the last chapter, **r** was written in France – probably in Paris – close to 1570, the time when its first owner Daniel Rogers (who was not the scribe; see below) was posted there in the employ of Sir Henry Norris, the English ambassador.[173] This makes **r** also the earliest surviving text including *L, its age ensuring a better homogeneity than the other full *L-based versions of the next decade, **l**, **t** and **p**, which show the pull of interdependence.

Memmianus certainly went the rounds, with consequences for the stemma that are still not fully clear. De Mesmes, we know, was generous to the point of rashness in lending from his famous library.[174] In the case of his *Satyrica* manuscript (of which the indications are that it was a sixteenth-century exemplar, possibly annotated, and not medieval) his liberality seems to have had two results: first, the production of the handwritten manuscripts and dissemination of readings referred to above, augmented by an exemplar of **d**, which I should relate to a *fragmentum veteris libri Cuiacii*, a manuscript 'collated' by the scribe of **r** (see Plate 11, and below), and possibly by an exemplar of **m** used by an *incertus auctor* of conjectures to be found in Lotich 1629;[175] and second, the association of this manuscript no longer with de Mesmes but with other scholars who evidently borrowed it for considerable periods of time.

CHARACTER OF **r** AND CONTEMPORARY MANUSCRIPTS

For his part, Rogers obtained and possessed in **r** a handsomely written text for which the newly produced **Memmianus** Petronius must have been both the reason for production and the centrepiece. The very modest role of consultation of other material should be inferred from the scribe's single overt reference to collation – with a manuscript fragment formerly owned by Cujas – in the top margin of the first folio.[176] An ambitious editor would not have omitted to use, in the manner of the rest – the makers of **lmtp** and **r**^{comm} (but not **d**) – the printed editions **c** and particularly the recently appeared **s**. This the scribe of **r** does not seem to have done. We can also rule out direct influence from the first printed editions that like **r** itself carried the ***L** material, since it predated them, though as always during this period isolated readings going the rounds prior to publication may have been picked up.

 r contains in its text dots and underlines, sometimes keyed to marginalia in differing hands and inks. One hand is that of the scribe, and another important one is also sixteenth century.[177] These interventions would appear to denote comparison with other texts. There is no sure way of telling when they were applied. If the scribe was not Rogers, the variants in the scribe's hand (**r**^m and **r**^c, plus **r**^{comm}) are more or less concurrent with the date of production. But if Rogers did write **r**, such entries in the same hand could have been made over the ensuing 20 years as contrasting material became available (notably the printed editions of the 1570s); and later application of the variants would argue for a great measure of uniformity of the text in respect to its source. However, the adding of variants in the scribal hand in a body at the time of production (and there is no reason to suppose that this could not have happened) would provide a picture of sources more appropriate to the 1560s. If in fact the primary hand of **r** is not (as I believe) that of Rogers, we should at least be sure that it provided no variants after Rogers' return to England.[178]

 r therefore carries in smaller measure some of the uncertainties of that other, more notorious example of a 'marked-up' text, Scaliger's hand-produced **l**. This undeniably complex 'edition' appears to have been collated – fashioned – on at least one major manuscript from each of the three available classes (***L**, **O** and φ) as well as on the **O**-text in **s**.[179] That is for starters, as it were. Next there is the question of readings shared by it and **t**.[180] Into the mix add Scaliger's own conjectures and those of others, usually not distinguished or acknowledged, together with the potential for additions and alterations in both margin and text by the author over the next 30 years, and we have a textual omelette to defy unscrambling. I should like to attempt the task, but not here, since the undertaking would require a monograph of its own. In this chapter 1 will interest me largely as a **Cuiacianus**-witness and hence as an aid in determining **r**'s own sources.

At the other end of the scale of complexity is **d**, carrying, as I have argued in Chapter 5, a very pure text of an *L manuscript via **Memmianus**, but whose value is sharply curtailed by its discontinuance at 15.4.

r has been thought to lie between these two extremes, though closer to **d**. Apart from the above-mentioned *vetus Cuiacii*, also **Memmianus**-aligned (hence not **Cuiacianus** itself – see n. 189), we shall see that certain readings are linked to florilegia, and some are said to come from **Cuiacianus**.[181] **r**[comm] too should not be ruled out as an indirect source of the latter, since, as we saw in the last chapter, François Daniel's *Satyrica* commentary provides not a few readings from this manuscript.

Cuiacianus AND ITS INFLUENCE

François Daniel used **Cuiacianus** prior to the late 1560s (of that we can be fairly sure from the date of **r**[comm] – see Chapter 6, n. 148), and is thus the first surviving witness. The alignment of **r**[comm] after **r** in the same manuscript, in the same hand, puts any putative use for **r** within the same period. This was a time when, as a convergence of contemporary evidence indicates, **Cuiacianus** was still under the control of Cujas himself. For it was on a visit to Cujas in 1571 that Scaliger gratefully attests to having seen it for the first time, and to making a collation which we assume became the basis for **l**. It was in Cujas' library in 1574.[182] In 1575 de Tournes used it, with an acknowledgment to Cujas, for part of the text of **t** and for *variae lectiones*, in the manner described in Chapter 2. Pierre Pithou does not admit to using it for **p**[1] in 1577, and we see no widespread evidence of it in his text, though a few of its readings may be lurking anonymously in **p**[1v] (see below). It was about then – and this is no coincidence – that the great era of sharing for mostly private use, which had begun in the early 1560s, came to an end. One may wonder how, in the highly competitive atmosphere of the day, with scholars avid for new manuscripts to serve as the centrepieces for displays of exegetical skills in new editions of classical authors, the pre-publication period had lasted for so long.

The 15-year lag must have had something to do with the content of *L. Editors would have been unwilling to expose themselves to charges of immorality brought by enemies in this era of rivalry intensified by dangerous sectarian conflict. One need only point to the fate of Muret, forced to flee France some years earlier after a brief imprisonment on a charge of sodomy. Given that the new passages of the *Satyrica* abundantly depicted the 'immoral' (i.e. homoerotic) situations that had not since Carolingian times been part of the familiar *Satyrica*, Petronius' work in its new and 'full' incarnation had to be handled with circumspection and some sanctimony.[183] It was under these fertile conditions, then, that manuscripts such as **Memmianus** and **Cuiacianus** circulated privately and generated underground copies like **dlmr** and commentaries – some anonymous – assembled by the likes of Goldast 1610.

Then there was a purely practical consideration impelling contemporary scholars to go to the considerable trouble of either transcribing an entire manuscript or constructing a fresh edition instead of just collating it: in a time preceding a printed *L edition, annotating the printed vulgate with the collation of the much longer *L text was a nigh-impossible task. **s**, of this exact period, though a great improvement over the three earlier printed editions thanks to use of a better **O** manuscript and superior critical method and production, was an anachronism from the day of publication precisely because it did not attempt it.[184] Thus until 1575 handwritten transcripts and conflations were the preferred vehicles for recording the new Petronius text, represented by as few as two manuscripts of medieval vintage.

r AND **Cuiacianus**

A convenient first means to assess **r**'s readings comes from comparing them to the **t**: **t^v** oppositions. For these appear diligently to preserve a distinction between a **Benedictinus**-aligned edition (to c. 112), with a multiplicity of variant options, and a text purporting to carry the readings of a single, integral *L manuscript, **Cuiacianus** (reading of Müller and Ehlers 1983 underlined).

THE READINGS OF **r** IN RELATION TO **t**: **t^v**

[*LO]	1.3	*sed tyrannos*: *et tyrannos* **r**
	2.3	*quibus deberent loqui* **r**: *quibus loqui debemus*
	2.5	*certe neque Platona* **r**: *neque Platona*
	2.7	*ex Asia commigravit* **r**: *ex Asia emigravit*
	2.8	*ad senectutem* **r**: *usque ad senectutem*
[*LOφ]	3.3	*quam quod*: *quam id quod* **r**
[*LO/	3.4	*sic eloquentiae magister nisi, tanquam / piscator, eam imposu-*
*LOφ]		*erit hamis escam* **t**: *nisi quasdam insidias auribus fecerint: sic*
		eloquentiae magistri, tanquam piscator, qui nisi eam imposuerit
		hamis escam **t^v**: *nisi quasdam insidias auribus fecerint. Hic*

eloquentiae magister, nisi tanquam piscator hamis escam r: <u>*nisi*</u>
<u>*quasdam*</u> <u>*insidias*</u> <u>*auribus*</u> <u>*fecerint,*</u> <u>*sic*</u> <u>*eloquentiae*</u> <u>*magister,*</u> <u>*nisi*</u>
<u>*tamquam*</u> <u>*piscator*</u> <u>*eam*</u> <u>*imposuerit*</u> <u>*hamis*</u> <u>*escam*</u>

[*LOφ]	4.2	*propellunt* r: <u>*impellunt*</u>
	4.3	*et studiosi:* <u>*ut*</u> *studiosi* r
	5.1.2	<u>*prius*</u> *more* r: *prius merae:* <u>*prius*</u> <u>*mores*</u>
	5.1.3	*polleat* r: *palleat:* <u>*poliat*</u>
	5.1.8	<u>*redemptus*</u> *histrioniae: redimitus histrioni:* <u>*redemptus*</u> <u>*histrionis*</u> r
	5.1.9	<u>*armigerae*</u> r: *crinigerae*
[*LO]	8.3	<u>*perduxit*</u> r: *produxit*
[*L]	9.4	*aucucurrit:* <u>*accucurrit*</u>: *accurrit* r
	9.10	*inquam* r: *inquit*
	10.4	*quaestionibus:* <u>*quaestibus*</u> r
	12.2	*splendida* r: <u>*splendor*</u>
	12.3	*considerare:* <u>*diligentius*</u> <u>*considerare*</u> r
	12.5	<u>*motu*</u>: *metu* r
	13.1	<u>*suturae*</u> r: *furtive*
	13.4	*quia non tantum:* <u>*non*</u> <u>*tantum*</u> <u>*quia*</u> r
	13.4	*rem reddere:* <u>*rem*</u> <u>*domino*</u> <u>*reddere*</u> r
[*LOφ]	14.2.1	*faciant:* <u>*faciunt*</u> r
	14.2.2	<u>*nulla*</u> r: *nuda*
	14.2.6	<u>*causa*</u> r: *cera*
[*LO]	17.3	<u>*inter*</u> <u>*se*</u> <u>*usque*</u> <u>*ad*</u> r: *interius in*
	17.4	*et* <u>*antecessura*</u>: *etiam a.: et antecessiora* r
	17.9	<u>*protendo*</u> <u>*igitur*</u> r: *obtendo iugiter*
	18.5	*annuissetis* r: *adimissetis:* <u>*adnuissetis*</u>
[*Lφ]	20.3	*periculosum alienis interesse secretis:* <u>*p.*</u> (<u>*esse*</u> <u>*om.*</u> r) <u>*a.*</u> *inter-* *venire* <u>*s.*</u> r
[*L]	21.1	*huic* r: <u>*hinc*</u>
	23.2	*carmen:* <u>*carmina*</u> r
	24.2	<u>*intellexeras*</u> r: *intelligis*
	24.3	<u>*meo*</u> r: *modo*
[*LO]	24.7	*manum dimisit* r: <u>*m.*</u> <u>*etiam*</u> <u>*demisit*</u>
[*LH]	27.6	*illa* r: <u>*ille*</u>
	33.8	*piperatio:* <u>*piperato*</u> r
	35.4	*sericulam:* <u>*ṣtericulam*</u>: *steriliculam: tericulam* r
	36.3	*int culis quarum: interculis* <u>*garum*</u>: <u>*utriculis*</u> *g.: intᵉculis g.* r
[*L]	79.8.5	<u>*ego*</u> <u>*sic*</u>: *ego sum sic* r
	79.9	*indormitavit:* <u>*indormivit*</u> r
[*LO]	80.9.5	<u>*mimum*</u>: *nimium* r
	81.1	*aut Scolanus: antescolanus:* <u>*antescholanus*</u>: *aut Scholanus* r
[*L]	82.1	<u>*cibis*</u> r: <u>*largioribus*</u> *c.*

[*LHφ]　43.6　*nequaquam recte faciet qui cito reddit (credit* r) r: *nunquam*
　　　　　　　　r. f. q. c. c.: numquam autem r. f. q. c. c.

　　　　44.17　*iusiurandum: ieiunium* r

[*L]　　83.1　*naturae certantia: n. veritate c.* r

　　　　83.3　*Naiada* r: *Naida*

　　　　83.5　*os* r: *ōs: omnes*

　　　　83.6　*recepi Lycurgo* r: *r. hospitem L.*

[*LOφ]　83.10.2　*auro* r: *ostro*

　　　　83.10.3　*ostro* r: *auro*

　　　　83.10.6　*desertas: disertas* r

[*L]　　85.1　*conductus: eductus* r

　　　　87.5　*vides: videris: vides* r

　　　　87.8　*tutus: tritus* r

　　　　88.2　*fecit: instituit* r

[*LOφ]　88.4　*E. quidem in cacumen excelsissimi montis conscendit: E. i. cacu-*
　　　　　　　　mine excellentissimi m. consenuit r

　　　　88.5　*aere comprehendit: ere comprehenderat* r

　　　　88.6　*avemus: audemus* r

　　　　88.7　*attigisset: invenisset* r

[*LO]　88.10　*noli* r: *nolite*

[*L]　　90.5　*recitem* r: *recitarem*

[*Lφ]　93.2.4　*Et pictis Atagen opaca pennis Atque Afrae volucres placent pa-*
　　　　　　　　lato, Quod non sunt faciles, at albus anser Plebeium sapit:
　　　　　　　　Atque aeriae volucres placent palato, Quod non sunt faciles, at
　　　　　　　　albu anser Et pictis anas renovata pennis Plebeium sapit r

[*L]　　94.8　*hemicyclo: semicincio: semicinctio: semicincios* r

[*LO]　95.8　*lictores: et coctores* r

[*L]　　98.4　*plenus continuo* r: *p. ter c.*

　　　　98.7　*mihi gratum: mitigatum* r

　　　　100.6　*et hoc inquit placuerat* r: *e. h. erat i. quod p.*

　　　　102.14　*quid tu* r: *quidni t.*

　　　　105.6　*ancillae quoque omnes* r: *a. etiam o.*

　　　　107.7　*deprecationem* r: *d. supplicis*

　　　　107.11　*mei: nostri: iiii* r

[*LO]　109.8　*capillorum* r: *in capillos suos*

[*LOφ]　111.6　*ergo* r: *vero*

　　　　111.8　*scilicet quod: s. id q.* r

　　　　111.10　*incertum habeo: [...]: [certum ab eo]: certe ab eo* r

　　　　111.12　*cinerem aut manes credis curare* r: *id c. a. m. c. sentire*

　　　　111.12　*commovere debet: commovere potest* r: *admonere d.*

　　　　112.4　*mulieris secreto: m. et. s.* r

INTERPRETATIONS

It is worth reminding ourselves that these 81 citations from **t**^{v} – **Cuiaci-anus** – are not readings rejected by the editor in the manner of **p**^{v}, had they been available for his text; nor, de Tournes cautions, does inclusion in the list imply acceptance: they are, rather, ones selected for being '*digna oculis studiosorum*' from a collation of a new manuscript provided to him after the first 112 chapters or so of his edition had gone to the printer.[185] These conditions give the interpretation of the **t**: **t**^{v} oppositions and **r**'s connection to them a special character. But one suspects that the editor did in fact avail himself of this opportunity to improve or even correct readings of **t** silently with his new manuscript, and we should take this into account when the readings of **t** are suspect. The absence of such editorial signposts as '*male*' or '*rectius*' in the *variae lectiones* is to be regretted.

Slightly more than half of the number, 44, occur in *LO and *LOφ contexts. Given the information provided on sources in the preface, we note that here a selection will have been made for the lemma of **t** between readings of an *L manuscript, represented by **Dalecampianus**, the O branch, represented by **c** and **s**, and florilegia.[186] Mathematically, we have 65 potential choices of Oφ against *L (40 O:*L, and 25 φ:*L). In these contexts, with no knowledge of **Dalecampianus** independent of use by **t**, it would be unavailing to seek to work out a **Dalecampianus**: **Cuiacianus** division on the basis of the **t**: **t**^{v} variation, though **r** may occasionally be of same help in fixing the **Memmianus** character of a reading, as against a misprint or conjecture, if it does not show up in an Oφ source.

Conversely, examination of the 37 variants cited from an *L (or *LH) context would seem of significant value for this very purpose. The number is high enough to give a fair picture of the character of the single *L manuscript available to the editor of **t** for the text up to c. 112, with its readings distinct from the manuscript ranged against it in the *varietas*. It is here that **r**'s alignment is of particular significance, whether to corrobor-ate **Benedictinus/Memmianus/Dalecampianus**: **Cuiacianus** division or to confound it. The picture may be affected modestly by misreading of his exemplar by the editor of **t**, or perhaps by printing error or emendation; but in the main I take it that here there is sufficient material to document quite reliably the **Benedictinus**: **Cuiacianus** division in *L as well as testing the broad alignment of **r** for its worth in constituting the modern text. So sustained a set of proofs will impose the best check yet undertaken on the validity of the Müllerian stemma.[187]

Analysing the reasons for the divisions represented by **t**: **t**^{v} is a microcosm of the difficulties affecting the *L-class stemma: there may be as many as a dozen of them. To be kept in view is the fact that **t^v**'s readings came from the actual medieval manuscript tradition (subject to misreading), while **t**'s are potentially capricious: the product of selection, emendation, and error. There is no mystery over why in 1.3 *sed tyrannos*, 14.2.1 *faciant*, 88.4 *excelsissimi ... conscendit*, 88.5 *aere comprehendit*, 88.6 *avemus*, 95.8 *lictores*, and perhaps the two examples at 111.12, **t**'s text goes against **t^v** and **r**: the reading of **t** was taken from **s**, a text with its roots both in **O** and in conjectural emendation. We may be able to extrapolate **O**: *L division and are interested in the relative correctness of the two branches thus represented, but cannot rule on **Benedictinus/Memmianus: Cuiacianus** division in the context of **r**'s source. On the other hand, where **r** and **t** agree against **t^v** we may be confident of **Memmianus: Cuiacianus** division; where they agree correctly we may perceive **Cuiacianus** unique in error and hence even the **Benedictinus** or *L reading behind **r**. Examples are at 2.3, 2.5, 2.7, 2.8, 3.3 *magistri*, 5.1, 8.3, 9.10, 13.1, 14.2.2, 14.2.6, 17.3, and others, for a total of about 20. **Cuiacianus** (**t^v**) recoups some of its ground with a unique correct reading against **Benedictinus**, manifested by **rt**, in the following: 12.2, 24.7, 27.6, 82.1, 83.3, 90.5, 98.4, 100.6, 102.14, 105.6, 107.7. As usual, the most reliable instances of these phenomena will be found in the unique *L context, free of even the 'silent' interference of **O**, **s**, or φ.

Sometimes the reading of **r** agrees with **t^v** against **t**, both correctly and incorrectly. The equations require careful interpretation because here there is potential evidence for consultation of **Cuiacianus** for **r**'s composition – a feature not yet fully established though firmly believed.[188] A correct **t^{v}r**: **t** reading, however, may only point up a unique error in **t**, an instance where the edition diverges from all manuscript authority, as at 3.4, 4.3, 9.4, 10.4, 23.2, 33.8, 36.3, 79.9, 43.6, 44.17, 83.1, 85.1, 87.5, 87.8, 88.2, 93.2.4, 94.8, 98.7, 112.4. These divergences are therefore due to errors by the editor of **t** (misreadings, omissions, emendations – as at 44.17 *ius-iurandum*) which **r** does not share in, not necessarily because it took from **Cuiacianus**, but perhaps because it derived the correct *L reading from a **Benedictinus**-aligned source. Some of the **t^v** readings, I suspect, are not merely new options but editorial corrections: de Tournes, as I noted above, has taken this opportunity quietly to invest the readings with proper manuscript authority.

Presumably, **t^{v}r** agreement in error against **t** would give the best evidence of **r**'s indebtedness to **Cuiacianus**. Such uniqueness is hard to come by. One example is at 80.9.5 *mimum* **t**: *nimium* **t^{v}r**. In this part of the text the other **Memmianus** scions **d** and **m** are lacking; the context is *LO, thus **t**'s reading could come either from his **Benedictinus**-aligned manuscript or from an **O** source such as **s** – where it certainly resides. In other words, *nimium* might well be the reading of ***L**, one so inept that it was readily done away with by de Tournes, Scaliger, and Pithou for their editions. Of course, unique error in **Cuiacianus**, selected by **r**, *could* be the explanation (and here the lemma of *FDG*, *nimium*, strengthens it), but the alternative exists.

t^v**r** and **l** are sometimes allied against the rest, and this might seem a hopeful prospect since **l** is a known **Cuiacianus** descendant. There is the interesting case at 79.8.5 *ego sic* **t** (also **mpl**^{margine}): *ego sum sic* **t**^{v}**lr**^{c}; perhaps the erroneous insertion did exist in **Cuiacianus**, yet **r**'s interlinear addition, though in the scribal hand, does not quite have the authority of the secured text.

Some of the most striking examples in the entire list are furnished by **t**^{v}**rl** alignments of correct readings against the rest, and these have given Müller his best evidence of **r** dependence on **Cuiacianus**; thus at 12.3 *considerare* **t** (also **dm**): *diligentius considerare* **t**^{v}**rl** (also **p**^{1}), 13.4 *quia non tantum* **t** (also **m**): *non tantum quia* **t**^{v}**rl** (also **p**^{1} and **d**), 13.4 *rem reddere* **t** (also **dmp**^{1}): *rem domino reddere* **t**^{v}**rl**. I would be more persuaded of the absence of *diligentius* in **r**'s **Benedictinus**-aligned source if it did not appear in **p**^{1}; **p**^{1} seems to show that it was in **Benedictinus** as well as **Cuiacianus**, thus we must assume either (a) (with Müller) that it was omitted in **Memmianus**, and so in **dmt**, but 'restored' by their sibling **r** from consultation with **Cuiacianus**; or (b) that it dropped out of **dmt** from three instances of independent error (not too unlikely if one notes that together with *considerare* it may seem redundant); or (c) that it indeed was lacking in **Memmianus** itself but existed somehow in the **Memmianus**-aligned *vetus Cuiacii* fragment which the compiler of **r** attests to having consulted. 13.4 *domino* lacks a presence in **p**^{1}, this time denoting **Benedictinus**: **Cuiacianus** division. Existence in **r** indicates either direct consultation of **Cuiacianus** (Müller), independent happy restoration (unlikely), or collation against a variant-carrying *vetus Cuiacii* (see below and n. 189). I favour the latter explanation. At 13.4 the word order of *quia non tantum* is within the bounds of independent copying inaccuracy: anticipation of the reason supplied. This is a not implausible alternative to use of **Cuiacianus** by **r**, since **d** and **p**^{1} share the correct reading, making presence in **Benedictinus** – thus ***L** – a virtual certainty.

THE **Cuiacianus** READINGS IN **t**^{v} SHARED BY **p**^{1v}

A few readings in **t**^{v}, not shared by **r**, are unique to known **Cuiacianus** sources save for their quiet and disconcerting existence in **p**^{1v}: 5.1.3 *palleat* ('*vet.*' $\mathbf{p^{1v}}$); 5.1.8 *redimitus* ('*vet.*' $\mathbf{p^{1v}}$); 5.1.9 *crinigerae* ('*al.*' $\mathbf{p^{1v}}$). Availability and systematic use of **Cuiacianus** for $\mathbf{p^1}$ would virtually destroy the Müllerian stemma, based heretofore on the assumption of $\mathbf{p^{1}}$'s unique use of **Benedictinus** in the sole *L passages. Fortunate it is, therefore, that the evidence is so slight, and confined to a passage reproduced in *LOφ, with its possibilities of several '*veteres.*' Seeking some explanation compatible with our present knowledge of manuscripts (that is, discounting an unfound manuscript source), one surmises that Pithou obtained these indeed genuine **Cuiacianus** readings informally and was yet to see the whole manuscript. To conclude this section, as we see from comparison with the most reliable set of **Cuiacianus** readings available, evidence for use by the compiler of **r** of **Cuiacianus** itself is far from irrefutable. The odd **Cuiacianus** reading in **r** may be due to a marginal variant in the *vetus Cuiacii* or even **Memmianus**.

r AND THE '*vetus liber Cuiacii*'

The scribe of **r** has been unusually helpful, by the day's standards, with the meticulous observation, high in the outside margin of the first folio of text (f. 7 – see Plate 11), '*Haec duo prima folia collata sunt cum fragmento veteris libri qui Cuiacii fuerat.*' This raises certain questions. Why, if true, were only the first two folios collated? Can we infer that the fragment itself concluded at approximately the page break of f. 8v, the second folio of **r**? What of the significance of the tense of *fuerat*: did the manuscript no longer belong to Cujas? What do we make of this evidence that Cujas once owned a **Memmianus**-aligned text, a 'piece of the **Memmianus**'? Finally, what does this 'collating' mean: comparison before, or after, the transcribing of **r**?

One thing is clear: termination of the fragment at the end of f. 8v (= c. 11.2) runs contrary to both the external evidence in the tradition, which has no inkling of such a text, and the evidence supplied by **r** itself: scribal marginalia with variant readings decline precipitously not after f. 8v but after f. 9v, the *third* folio.[189] Furthermore, this folio ends at c. 15.8 *foribus ridere*, only eight lines below the point where **d** leaves off (15.4 *tuberosissimae frontis*). If this coincidence and the variant activity were not enough to suggest a counting error by the copyist of **r** and connection indeed between the *vetus liber Cuiacii* and **d**, it appears to be proven conclusively by the marginal note in the scribe's hand in f. 9v, the *third* folio, keyed to a reference mark next to *frontis* (though written, as frequently, not quite opposite the word): '*non plura habebat exemplaria.*'

Thus for the production of **r** the first three folios, not two, were collated against a manuscript fragment which once had belonged to Jacques Cujas, and this manuscript reproduced exactly the same fragment as **d**, the *Schedae* written by Pierre Daniel in late 1563. The copy used by the scribe of **r** was either a sibling or the exemplar of **d** (though not **d** itself, since the text transcribed by Pierre Daniel in the back of his personal copy of Muret's edition of Cicero's *Philippics* could hardly have ever belonged to Cujas), i.e. a **Memmianus**-based text. As such, it seems to have been an independently initiated copy of that manuscript, discontinued at c. 15.4.

Implications for **d** have been raised in Chapter 4. As for **r**, we note that the impact on the text of this apparent second source (after **Memmianus**, the collating copy) should be quite modest, since its own **Memmianus** alignment ensures only a second opinion on the parent where variants occur. However, the variant in **r**^{m}, as we have seen in n. 189, frequently serves the useful function of correcting **r**'s text, though not by providing, as Müller disappointedly notes, readings consistent with the (other) manuscript of Cujas known as **Cuiacianus**. Instead, it gives a better **Memmianus reading**.

Furthermore, the association almost invariably of **r**^{m} with a **d**-type manuscript that we must relate to the *fragmentum veteris libri Cuiacii* leaves the strong conviction in me that this second source remained external to the text of **r** itself, i.e. the scribe did not so much collate his text with the fragment as annotate it.[190] Neither this manuscript, nor any other besides the exemplar, as we might reasonably infer from the supplying of this information on collation in its diligent and unique fashion, may have gone into the production of the text of **r**. As such, it may be as 'uncontaminated' as **d**, though the product clearly of a less skilled copyist.

r AND FLORILEGIA

Konrad Müller, **r**'s first evaluator, refers to certain florilegium influence in this manuscript thus: '*In marginibus codicis r nonnullae florilegii lectiones inveniuntur manu scriptae a Rogertis plane diversa; quas habeo cur a Dousa adscriptas esse suspicer.*' Müller's detection of the hand of van der Does rests largely on the assumption that the manuscript itself was written by Rogers: the second hand is taken to be van der Does' because of the demonstrated fact that Rogers lent **r** to his friend. Although this is the easier theory of authorship, as noted above, the evidence of handwriting goes directly against it: the script of **r** is very different from the confirmed epistolary hand of Rogers (cf. Plate 11 with Plate 14), and the second hand, of which we have an ample sample on f. 41v in the 16-line poem known as Fragment XXX (see Plate 12), does not have much chance of being that of van der Does: **r** appears to have been written by an *ignotus*, while the second hand, rather, is that of Rogers.[191]

None of the above has any bearing on whether florilegia were used as collating sources for **r**. We come a bit closer to this by detecting florilegium influence known to the primary hand, that of the scribe, though again in the ambiguous locale of the marginalia: at the end of 14.2.2 *potest* there is a reference mark (+), repeated in the margin next to the florilegium version of 14.2.5, *iamnunc* [*ergo* ***LO**] *iudicium.* ... Below the line is the scribe's comment: '*ita in veteri in quo cetera* [i.e. 14.2.3–4] *desunt.*' This is fully substantiated by the manner in which this poem is divided between ***L**, **O** and φ. As for the text itself, φ-readings might well agree with those of ***L** and its manuscripts because they were used, together with a 'long' manuscript (known as Λ), for ***L**'s production (see Figure 1). This complicates any investigation of florilegium dependence by **r**. It could be established only if **r** shared an error or series of errors with a particular florilegium.

C. 84.1–2 furnishes a good test, since for it several variants are shown; thus *dubie* <u>libri</u> **r**ᶜ: *dubio* **lrp**; *inimicus* <u>om</u>. **r**: <u>add</u>. **r**ᵐ; *iter vitae libri* **r**ᶜ: *iter* **r**: *vitae iter* φ; *coepit inspicere* **O**: *inspicere coepit* ***L**: *respicere coepit* φ**r**ᶜ; *diversa* Ω: *universa* **rMemmianus**; *divitias* <u>libri</u> **r**ᵐ: *diurnas* **r**; *primum* <u>libri</u> **r**ᵐ: <u>om</u>. **r**. **r**'s original effort here was extraordinarily defective. Whatever the reason for this, the deficiencies do not come from a florilegium; what the passage shows (and this may hold for the example cited above also) is that **r** has in fact 'corrected' the text, very possibly on a florilegium. This may have occurred close to the time of writing (as I believe) or considerably later, depending on one's opinion of the identity of the scribe. In any event, we do not seem to have clear evidence of use of the florilegium for **r**'s composition and can virtually rule it out as a source.

r AND **r**ᶜᵒᵐᵐ

Since the scribe of **r** copied F. Daniel's *Notae* = **r**ᶜᵒᵐᵐ into the manuscript (leaving the intervening folios 42 to 50 blank), we should consider the possibility of its influence on **r** in both text and margin.[192] Borrowing for the margin is proved conclusively by the example of *à bon escient* (see n. 189 and 191). A couple of other instances suffice to show more typical indebtedness: f. 12v, 26.5 *valgiter* **r**ᵐ, for which compare **r**ᶜᵒᵐᵐ f. 51v, *commovebat obiter labra*] <u>hoc est valgiter</u>; and f. 18, 89.1.21 *uteri* **r**ᵐ, for which compare **r**ᶜᵒᵐᵐ f. 52, *uterum notavit*] <u>imp.</u> *uteri, quod probo*. The former is a gloss, while *uteri* is an approved variant.

The textual significance of such borrowing is nil, since **r**ᶜᵒᵐᵐ's witness has not entered the text to risk contaminating it from its sources. But the

case of 83.9 *unquam* [***L**] (**r**, f. 17) is entirely more interesting. Here F.
Daniel (**r**^{comm}, f. 52) has *amor ing. neminem inquam*] *quid si legat unquam*.
Unquam is thus to Daniel's knowledge his own emendation of his manuscript, which here can only be **Cuiacianus**; indeed, *inquam* in **l** rather
confirms this. But is *inquam* an error in **Cuiacianus** or an error in ***L**?
Bücheler's apparatus has the word as in **Memmianus**; if this is correct it
is fairly safe to infer the latter. If so, whence the reading in **r** and the
printed editions **t** and **p**? Conjecture of Daniel (and not a **Benedictinus**
reading) may be the origin.[193] I would accept use of **r**^{comm} for **r** with some
reluctance, however, since the scribe to me just is not that kind of scholar.
Other options do, as usual, exist: a variant in **Memmianus** or an emendation (more or less unconscious: it is easy and natural). We may still be
quite confident of freedom from 'contamination' in **r** by an **r**^{comm} source.

CONCLUSION

Though handsomely written, with a high standard of legibility and consistency, **r** is not the work of a careful or particularly gifted scholar. The
scribe's performance came under suspicion in the last chapter, when it could
be measured against a better effort to reproduce the *Notae* of François
Daniel, and the weaknesses exhibited in **r**^{comm} have their counterpart now
in copying gaffes, such as the omissions noted above, and misreading of
the exemplar. Corrections are sometimes added carelessly; a droll illustration being at f. 19, 89.1.49 *infirmis auxiliator* **rtO**, where the correcting
hand places the emending 'u' for *infirmus* (perhaps from **s**) over the last
syllable of the second word. **r** peculiarities should not, therefore, in most
cases be imputed to the tradition – i.e. a faithful rendering of **Memmianus**
or another collated source – and an appreciation of individual error will
certainly diminish the role of contamination in the production of the text.
I believe the manuscript sustains an effort to reproduce its exemplar,
Memmianus.

8

Pierre Dupuy and **B**

Parisinus lat. 8790 A, a recent manuscript containing some passages from Petronius, is quite worthless textually, but its not unmerited obscurity to date has served to conceal both the efforts of a man not hitherto connected with French scholarship on Petronius and a source for information on **B** of potential codicological significance.[194]

The library catalogue describes the manuscript as *'olim Puteanus ... decimo septimo saeculo videtur exaratus'*; Beck identifies the author as Hendrick van der Putten, a teacher in Louvain; and Schmeling and Stuckey assign it tentatively to the 'late 16 c.'[195] One can do rather better than this, I think. The manuscript, no more than an exercise book into which favourite phrases have been copied, bears on the front flyleaf and rear pastedown at least eight specimens of the scrawled signature – *probationes pennae* – of the presumable author and owner *'Dupuy'* and *'P. Puteanus.'* This is surely the Pierre Dupuy who as Royal Librarian was to catalogue the de Thou manuscripts in 1617 (see Chapter 3). Moreover, on the front flyleaf and on page 100 appears in both Arabic and Roman figures the date 1605, which one therefore takes to be the year of the manuscript's composition.

The Petronius portion of slightly more than two octavo-sized pages consists of 19 quotations taken from the ***LO** text and one from the *Fragments*.[196] They are an assortment of improving phrases without much in common, although marginal comments in French do seem to offer suggestions for use. Each quotation is accompanied by a page reference, presumably to a printed source. Far from arousing curiosity, this feature may have led Bücheler to dismiss the manuscript as without interest.[197] This is certainly true textually, but further investigation of these references leads to a more rewarding source, also connected with Dupuy.

By 1605 the following *Satyrica* editions including the so-called **L** class were available to Dupuy for use: **t**, **p¹**, **p²**, and the editions of van der Does, Wouweren and Linocier in a number of printings.[198] The texts differ very little in pagination, yet only one fits all the citations: **p²**.[199] A swift verification was possible: of the four copies of **p²** in the Bibliothèque Nationale, one (**Rés. Z. 2472**) was clearly once owned by Dupuy, for it is neatly signed by him on the title page, and dated, below the date of publication, 1604. Finally, many of the phrases found in Dupuy's commonplace *cahier* are here underlined. It would be fair to assume, then, that in the years 1604–5 the young Dupuy had a strong interest in Petronius: demonstrably, he acquired a copy of **p²** and put it to use.

The focus of our attention now shifts from **Parisinus lat. 8790 A** to **Rés. Z. 2472**. Nearly every page of this little volume contains notes of various kinds keyed to sections of underlined text. The longer ones are *similes loci* in a score of ancient authors, and references to the published editions of a dozen contemporary scholars.[200] Cross-references in the text are numerous. There are some explanatory glosses and the occasional translation into French. Yet the feature meriting greatest interest to the textualist is the large number of variant readings cited in the margin. Over a hundred either are entered without ascription (the great majority) or are given to an individual scholar. Some 24 others are designated with a '*v.c.*' (*vetus codex*). Thus the former appear to be conjectural emendations, while the latter are assigned the authority of a manuscript.

In keeping with the present volume I shall investigate only the apparent manuscript source, making a few general remarks on the conjectures of Dupuy and his learned contemporaries. Of course, a manuscript may be lurking behind them too, but very few of the readings are confirmed by manuscript authority, and a measure of their lack of *bonitas* is that although they are known to scholarship from the great *variorum* editions and Bücheler's apparatus, Müller has in the great majority preferred the text of **p²**. It is not known what weight Dupuy would have given the conjectures if he were contemplating a Petronius edition, and how he would have cited them. Here follows a list of the variants attributed to '*v.c.*'[201]

THE READINGS OF '*v.c.*' *Puteani* AGAINST **p²**, WITH AGREEMENTS

3.4   <u>pisciculos</u>: discipulos **B** '*Autis.*' Pithoei: pisces **R** [only '*v.c.*' Puteani **B** '*Autis.*' Pithoei have this error]

4.3   mitigarentur: inrigarentur **B** '*Autis.*' Pithoei: <u>irrigarentur</u> **R** [only '*v.c.*' Puteani **B** '*Autis.*' Pithoei share this spelling]

4.5   _schedium_: _schadium_ **B** '_Autis._': _studium_ **B**^{margine} [only '_v.c._' _Puteani_ **B** share reading and marginal note]

5.1.2   _more_: _mores_ **BR**: _more_ _ceteri_ _omnes_ [only '_v.c._' _Puteani_ **BR** agree correctly]

6.1   _haec_: _hunc_ **O**

7.3   _ego_: _ergo_ **O**

7.4   _aliam_: _alteram_ **O** '_Autis._'

7.4   _lapsus_: _lassus_ **BRP**

14.2.2   _nulla_: _nuda_ **Blt**^v '_Autis._' [**BR** divide]

14.2.3   _cena_: _cera_ ***LO**: _pera_ Heinse

14.2.4   _vendere verba solent_: _verba solent emere_ **O** '_Autis._'

16.2   _dum_: _dumque_ ***LO**

16.2   _reclusaeque_: _remissaeque_ **O** '_Autis._'

17.3   _vero_: _ergo_ **O**

17.7   _timerem_: _timeam_ **BR** '_Autis._' [only '_v.c._' _Puteani_ **BR** '_Autis._' agree correctly]

17.8   _impulsi licentia_: _impulsu licentiam_ ***LO**

18.3   _providentiam_: _prudentiam_ ***LO**

18.6.3   _contemptu_: _contemptus_ ***LO**

24.6   _applicuit_: _adplicuit_ **BR**: _applicuit reliqui_ [only '_v.c._' _Puteani_ **BR** share this spelling]

24.7   <...>: _etiam_ **BRlt**^v

25.1   _devirginetur_: _devirginatur_ ***LO**

55.6.9   _tribacca_: _tibi bacca_ **RPδ**: _tibi baca_ **B** [spelling variant]: _t. bacam_

55.6.16 _linea_: _lunae libri_

80.9.2   _nobile_: _mobile_ **BRP**

It will be seen from the above that out of the known and extant manuscripts of Petronius there is a very good candidate for '_v.c._' _Puteani_, namely **B**. The agreement in all 24 readings cited is letter-perfect with the single exception of 55.6.9, where there is a spelling variant. Further, there are several instances of '_v.c._' _Puteani_ **B** dividing, either correctly or incorrectly, against all other known manuscripts. The only other surviving manuscript approaching this agreement is **R**, which however exhibits decisive differences at 3.4, 4.5 and 14.2.2.[202] 4.5 alone makes an excellent case.

It is not beyond the realm of possibility that Dupuy was using a mix of readings, both from the manuscripts then available to him and from **p**^v, since, as indicated above, most of the readings are available elsewhere. This would be stretching the meaning of the term '_v.c._,' and such a laborious editor's approach seems alien to the spirit of Dupuy's undertaking. Besides, there is a good single manuscript available, and the full slate of reading agreements with it creates the strong presumption of a single manuscript source behind '*v.c.*'

A concern lies in that Dupuy notes by no means all the differences between **p²** and the manuscript before him – if it be **B**. To cite one chapter alone, in c. 4 there are the following unexploited variants:

READINGS OF **B** AGAINST **p²**

4.2   *propellunt: impellunt*
4.2   *maius: magis*
4.3   *esset: esse*
4.4   *discit: dicit*

The possible explanations are either that '*v.c.*' *Puteani* was not **B**, or that Dupuy had no manuscript before him but a set of readings provided by someone else, or that he chose simply to record only some of the variants. The first possibility is rendered very doubtful by the agreements, and the second is not relevant because the readings would still come ultimately from **B** (although their codicological value would be diminished). It seems likely, then, that Dupuy selected only certain of **B**'s variants for entry into the margins of his copy of **p²**. He did this, I suggest, because they were the ones which he would adopt into a text or record in some other way (perhaps in a commentary), while in the other areas of disagreement he may have preferred the readings of **p²** and thus saw no reason to register the variants of his '*v.c.*' This would be consistent with contemporary practice, and it is also reassuring to observe that in his present research Dupuy does not seem to have labelled any of the conjectures (variants that lack manuscript backing) as '*v.c.*'[203]

B today is in two pieces: **Vossianus Lat. Q. 30** contains the **O** text from 3.3 to 80.9 on ff. 58 and 57, and **Bernensis 357** contains 1 to 3.3 and 109.10.2 to the end of **O** at 137.9.[204] What, then, in the above list, of the astonishing and exact occurrence of the '*v.c.*' variants within the parameters of one of the above manuscripts, the Leiden **B**? Coincidence may never fully be dismissed, but this, taken with the agreements, makes the conclusion that '*v.c.*' *Puteani* = **Vossianus Lat. Q. 30** ff. 58, 57 very hard to avoid.[205]

Pierre Dupuy thus had access to **B** only after it was already sundered, and could see very little of it. The manuscript was almost certainly intact in 1587, the year in which it is cited extensively in **p²** by Pierre Pithou, who perhaps borrowed it then from his close friend Pierre Daniel, the owner since about 1562.[206] Though Dupuy could conceivably have added the marginalia in his copy of **p²** at any time up to his death, there is something in the pains that he takes to record his acquisition of **p²** in 1604, coupled with his proven interest in taking passages from it for **Parisinus lat. 8790 A** in the following year, that promotes 1604 not just as the *terminus post quem* but as the precise date for the collation.

This was the year of Daniel's death, and upon it his manuscript collection was divided between Jacques Bongars and Paul Petau.[207] To judge from its present abode in Bern, Bongars acquired the fragments c. 1–3.3 and 109.10.2–137.9., while Petau received the portion now in Leiden, as his signature on f. 1 of **Vossianus Lat. Q. 30** could indicate.[208] It appears that Dupuy, in borrowing from Petau (not Daniel) the separated Leiden leaves of **B** and working with them in Paris in 1604–5 to annotate his copy of **p²**, fixes for us the date (1604) and the circumstance (the death of Daniel) for the dismemberment of **B**.

The subsequent history of the Petau fragment finds it passing into the hands of Alexandre after Paul's death in 1614, thence to Isaac Vos and Leiden.[209] Nothing further seems to have come of these endeavours of Dupuy: no commentary or edition followed. Yet his diligent efforts in the space of a single year yield some tantalizing evidence on the contemporary condition of **B**.

BIOGRAPHICAL NOTES ON THE PRINCIPAL SCHOLARS

The following entries were compiled largely from reference biographies and standard histories of scholarship: Michaud 1843–65, Sandys 1958, Kelley 1970, Schmeling and Stuckey 1975, Pfeiffer 1976, and Fumaroli 1980.

BONGARS (BONGARSIUS), JACQUES, 1534–1612. Orléans-born Protestant jurist, diplomat in the service of Henri IV, and scholar-collector; friend and relative of Paul Petau, intimate of Pierre Daniel, pupil of Cujas at Bourges in 1571; edited Justin in 1581, a collection of Dacian inscriptions in 1600, and a work on the French Crusades in 1611. In 1603–4 he shared, with Petau, much of the library of Daniel and bought a portion of that of Cujas. In 1612 his collection, outstanding for its holdings from Fleury, dispersed in 1562, but including Petronius **B** from Auxerre, went by bequest to Jacques Gravisset, who presented it in 1632 to Bern, native city of his wife.

CUJAS (CUIACIUS), JACQUES, 1522–1590. Born in Toulouse; inspirational teacher at Cahors, Valence, Paris, and Bourges; jurist, legal humanist, and collector. His studies led him to seeking out or acquiring manuscripts, from which he published a work of Ulpian in 1547 and later worked on the *Digest*; his corpus of editions extends to 11 folio volumes; most famous contribution is the large and erudite *Observationes et Emendationes* (1556–66). As owner of more than one Petronius manuscript, including the ***L**-class **Cuiacianus**, Cujas found himself in the position to provide the major stimulus for Petronian scholarship, in his pupils, Scaliger, the Daniels, and the Pithous, the latter acquiring most of his library and manuscripts upon his death.

DALECHAMPS (DALECAMPIUS), JACQUES, 1513–1588. Learned physician and botanist who produced a translation of Athenaeus in 1583 and edition of the elder Pliny in 1587, he is referred to obliquely by de Tournes in his preface to **t** (identity supplied by Goldast 1610) as the owner and provider of a now-lost manuscript which we thus know as **Dalecampianus**, of the ***L** class.

DANIEL, FRANÇOIS, fl. 1559–1617. A churchman much in the scholarly shadow of his brother Pierre; his claim to our notice rests on anonymous *Notae* to Petronius published in his name by Goldast 1610. After studying law he became a member of the council of Cardinal du Chatillon, then bailiff of St. Benoît-sur-Loire in 1572; but in the confusion of conscience typical of the period he had studied theology in Geneva under the influence of Calvin, and was pastor in Anjou in 1578, la Flotte in 1603, and La Rochelle in 1617.

DANIEL, PIERRE, 1530–1604. Orléans-born, of a well-connected family of Protestant leanings, he studied law at Bourges and was a pupil of Cujas. Among the treasures rescued by him from the monastery of St. Benoît in 1562 was the *Querolus* manuscript edited two years later; his other famous publication was the edition of Servius *Auctus* in 1600. Although a busy career advocate, it was as a scholarly collector and annotator in the 1560s that he attains importance for Petronian studies, evinced by possession of **B**, **Bernensis 276** and **Harleianus 2735**, and by his transcription of an *L-class fragment, **d**. Despite this interest, there was no edition; a commentary, the *Notae*, composed around 1570, is preserved in Goldast 1610 alongside the one supposedly by his brother François.

DE MESMES (MEMMIUS), HENRI, 1532–1596. Legal scholar and holder of the chair of law at Toulouse in 1548 at the age of 16; visited Italy in 1556–8 as invited magistrate at Siena; assiduous collector of manuscripts and rare editions for his renowned personal library, which he put at the disposal of his scholarly friends, notably Lambin and Turnèbe, and whence the lost *L-class Petronius **Memmianus** appears to have been borrowed and either excerpted or copied many times. A number of the manuscripts passed through his family to the Bibliothèque Nationale, Paris.

DE THOU (THUANUS), JACQUES-AUGUSTE, 1553–1617. Respected author of the massive and learned *Histoire universelle*; a modest philologist, but especial friend of Scaliger and Pierre Pithou. He formed a large library toward the end of the 1500s, having acquired some of Pithou's ancient manuscripts, including a Petronius which is probably **P**. This material may be traced via the Dupuys to the Bibliothèque Nationale, Paris.

DE TOURNES (TORNAESIUS), JEAN, 1539–1615. Printer-editor of **t**, head of the family business in Lyons from 1564–85, whereupon the religious troubles caused him to move it to Geneva.

DUPUY (PUTEANUS), PIERRE, 1582–1651. One-time student of Petronius, writer of the notebook manuscript **Parisinus lat. 8790 A**, son of the scholar Claude, who may be the author of the anonymous *Notae* in Goldast 1610 assigned to François Daniel. He made his own name as collector of manuscripts, first for himself, then for the Bibliothèque du Roy, for which as librarian he became a principal acquirer and organizer.

LAMBIN (LAMBINUS), DENYS, 1516–1572. Though Royal Reader in Greek, he became a pre-eminent Latinist of his day, celebrated for his editions of Horace in 1561 – with collations of several manuscripts found in Italy on two extended sojourns in the 1550s, rich in parallel citations from many sources, including Petronius – Lucretius in 1564, Cicero in 1566, and Nepos in 1569. A commentary on Plautus was nearing completion upon his death, said to have been hastened by the massacre of St. Bartholemew. While in Rome he collaborated with the younger Muret, an association that produced controversy over a borrowing by Muret of some of his notes on Horace. Lambin routinely used manuscripts belonging to his friend de Mesmes (himself possessing only a modest collection), and so came by the Petronius **Memmianus**.

LIPS (LIPSIUS), JOOST, 1547–1606. Dutch scholar of Latin, professor at Leiden, 1579–91, to which he had come from Louvain and the Spanish Netherlands. He had earlier spent two years in Italy (1567–9), working at Rome with Muret and collating manuscripts of Tacitus. In 1592 he was called back to Louvain as professor of History – a move requiring a return also to his native Catholicism. He produced several editions, mainly of Silver Age prose authors, among which his Tacitus (1574, 1600) is the acknowledged masterpiece. He did not work on Petronius, but shows a familiarity with him (from **p**) in correspondence.

MURET (MURETUS), MARC-ANTOINE, 1526–1585. Celebrated scholar of Latin, teacher and Ciceronian stylist, born in Limoges; in touch with many of the leading scholars of the day, he concluded an eventful career with 20 years as a professor at Rome. There placed under some restrictions, he lectured energetically on Cicero, Juvenal, Tacitus, the younger Seneca, and Aristotle and Plato, and produced editions on a host of authors, including also Catullus, Horace, Terence, Tibullus, and Propertius. His *Variae Lectiones* (1559, 1580, 1585) well demonstrate his critical range and trenchancy. Though he possessed Petroniana such as **m** and a heavily worked copy of **c**, a man whose scholarly life tended to be followed by controversy may have made sure that the connection remained informal.

PETAU (PETAVIUS), PAUL, 1568–1614. A cousin of Bongars, also born in Orléans, and another legal student and parliamentarian who found the time to indulge a love of chronology and antiquities (on which he published works in 1604 and 1610) by becoming a successful collector of classical manuscripts. He had the good fortune to share with Bongars the library of Pierre Daniel; he was a generous lender, of whose manuscripts an important number, including the Leiden **B**, which had been used by Pierre Dupuy in 1604, came via his brother Alexandre, Queen Christina, and Isaac Vos to that city.

PITHOU (PITHOEUS), FRANÇOIS, 1543–1617. By virtue of outliving his more famous brother Pierre he became guardian of the impressive manuscript collection which, not going to de Thou, was later dispersed to Troyes, Montpellier, and Rosanbo. His career followed a similar course to that of Pierre, including studies in classical literature and various branches of law (as a pupil of Cujas), conversion to Calvinism, years of restless travel, and polemics on behalf of the monarchy. As a collaborator with Pierre, and sometimes a rival, his originality is not always distinguishable; his best work is said to be a glossary to Pierre's collection of capitularies and an annotated edition of Salic law. He did not work on Petronius.

PITHOU (PITHOEUS), PIERRE, 1539–1596. Troyes-born, a key figure in humanistic scholarship on Petronius through ownership or control of several manuscripts, including **Benedictinus, P, B**, and **Cuiacianus**, and production from them of formal editions in 1577 and 1587, though this was an insignificant part of his output and did not contribute greatly to his fame. He found it in a circle of close-knit and pragmatic scholars promoting an antiquarian renaissance, at whose centre stood the godlike Cujas. Among Pithou's other mostly classical text productions were the *Pervigilium Veneris* in 1577, the Edict of Theodoric in 1579, Salvianus in 1580, Juvenal and Persius in 1585, and the *editio princeps* of Phaedrus in 1596. There is also a large simultaneous repertoire of material reflecting more nearly his contemporary concerns in a life spiced up by religious ambivalence and patriotic causes.

ROGERS, DANIEL, 1538–1591. Peripatetic English diplomatist and negotiator, amateur scholar and poet, who was friends with the relevant Continental humanists, notably Jan van der Does, to whom he lent his Petronius manuscript **r**. Though he produced no formal work on classical authors, his correspondence shows a man abreast of the scholarship of Scaliger, Lambin, Lips, and Pithou (**p¹**). He was posted to Paris in the late 1560s, and to the Low Countries in the 1570s.

SÁMBOKI (SAMBUCUS), JANOS, 1531–1584. Learned Hungarian physician, intimate of the reputed Antwerp and Leiden printer, Christophe Plantin, whom he chose for his Petronius edition of the **O** text (**s**), based on a personal copy of a better Renaissance *deterior* than the one used for the *editio princeps* (**a**; also the basis for **b** and **c**). This manuscript is identified as **Vindobonensis 3198**.

SCALIGER, JOSEPH, 1540–1609. By gifts, study, and accomplishments the most formidable philologist of his day; trained by his father, Jules-César, he mastered Latin early, then in Paris studied Greek under Turnèbe and found a patron, with whom he visited Italy (spending time with Muret), and lived in Poitou and Limousin. As a student of Roman Law under Cujas at Valence in 1570–2 not only did he form a great friendship with de Thou and a relationship of mutual respect with Pierre Pithou, but he was shown the *L-class **Cuiacianus** manuscript of Petronius, which he made the basis of his own

extant handwritten edition, l, and doubtless inspired his only formal connection – evinced in Scaliger 1572 – the editing of a number of poems from the
Satyrica and the *Fragments*. After a stay in Lausanne prompted by the religious convulsions, return to France was followed by editions of Ausonius in
1574, Festus in 1575, and Catullus, Tibullus, and Propertius in 1577. His
Manilius in 1579 is said to mark a transition from textual to chronological
studies, which he set forth in a comprehensive system in *De Emendatione Temporum* in 1583. In the relatively settled period that commenced with the filling of Lips' chair in Leiden in 1593, by brilliant deductive research he saw to
a reconstruction of the original Greek text of Eusebius' *Chronicles*, which he
printed in his *Thesaurus Temporum* in 1606.

TURNÈBE (TURNEBUS), ADRIEN, 1512–1565. Erudite Royal Reader in Greek in the
    Collège de France (Paris), teacher of Pierre Pithou and of many other leading
    humanists. He produced well-founded editions of Aeschylus and Sophocles in
    1552 and 1553, then a work on early Greek poets, including Theognis, and an
    Iliad text in 1554. Turning to philosophy, he lectured on Plato, Aristotle, and
    the Stoics, and edited Cicero *De legibus*, Philo, and Oppian; also, Varro and
    the elder Pliny were commented upon. The work of his maturity as a textual
    critic was the 30 books of *Adversaria* in 1564–5, a rich and diverse collection
    of emendations based on study of the manuscripts, including, for Petronius,
    the **Memmianus**.

VAN DER DOES (DOUSA), JAN, 1545–1604. Dutch scholar and patriot, governor of
    Leiden during the famous Spanish siege, and as curator of the University
    secured a professorship for Lips in 1579. A writer of Latin poetry – a taste
    shared with his friend Daniel Rogers, whose manuscript **r** he borrowed on
    a trip to England – his love lay also in Plautus, of whom there was an edition
    in 1587. He published a Petronius edition in 1585, which, for all its earliness,
    his acquaintance with manuscripts, and the lengthy and much-reprinted
    Praecidanea therein, was eclipsed by the textual work of Pithou, **p²**.

NOTES

INTRODUCTION

1 See Reeve 1983, pp. 298–300, and Pellegrino 1986. The indispensable modern edition is Müller and Ehlers 1983. Müller 1961 remains useful for some aspects of manuscript history, especially demonstrations, though the text has undergone changes in the most recent edition. The List of Symbols and Figures 1 and 2a contain my own stemmatic assumptions; cf. with Figure 2b, the latest stemma of Müller.

2 A case in point is the remark by Reeve 1983, p. 295 n. 2, that the identification of **Bituricus** with **P** has been disputed 'for trifling reasons.' This is treated in Chapter 3. Reeve's estimate (p. 300) of new directions for progress is worth citing in full for its striking similarity to my own long-held views, of which the present volume is an embodiment: 'What progress now? The discovery of editions used for collation by Pithou and his contemporaries [cf. Chapter 8 below]? More fruits of Daniel's example in combing glossaries and annotated manuscripts [see Chapters 4 and 5]? An identification of Scaliger's "autres traitez qui estoient avec" in Cuiacianus, which might lead even to its recovery [see my remarks below (Chapter 7, n. 182) on Pithou's library and Lanvellec, **Rosanbo 233**]? More modestly, the sixteenth-century witnesses may still have light to shed on whether the sixteenth century or the twelfth played the larger part in creating L [see Chapters 5 and 7; evidence of the integrity of **d** and **r** and of their similarity in essentials to the heavily edited texts **l**, **t**, and **p** suggest the latter].'

3 Bücheler 1862. One may infer from Pellegrino 1986, Introduction, that at least three volumes are intended; e.g. p. 27, where he promises to deal with the problems of the *Bellum Civile* in the third. But although his apparatus seeks to be the complete record of all the manuscript variants, no matter

how trivial (or so I assume), he excludes the other primary sources to be found in Bücheler, like citations from F. Daniel's *Notae* and other important early commentaries.

4 See e.g. articles on the medieval and Renaissance tradition of other authors associated in manuscripts with Petronius: Reeve and Rouse 1978, de la Mare 1976, and Schmidt 1974.

5 This in a pioneering preliminary article, still useful today, on the extrication of sixteenth-century sources, the general subject of this volume, Ullman 1930b; on **Memmianus = Benedictinus** (p. 131) see the verdict of Müller and Ehlers 1983: 'unrichtig' (p. 393 n. 10).

CHAPTER 1

6 See Müller 1961, pp. xxiii–xxvii. Ullman did not have **m** for his important 1930b article. See Sage 1936, and Fulmer 1936, p. 100. My evidence for Rose is an unpublished note (Rose 1967) to the effect that developing proof for *Fragmenta* = **m** is a 'textual task.' It will be seen, below, that I tend to discount this possibility.

7 Rini 1937, p. 65; Ruysschaert 1959, citing Rini p. 19. Rini saw **m** in 1936 and judged that it would have especial significance if its composition preceded that of **t** (1575) and **p¹** (1577) – which is certainly my conception.

8 On **d** and **r** see Müller 1961, p. xxi f.; Turnèbe 1564–73, cited also by Ullman 1930, p. 130. I treat the integrity of **d** and **r** in Chapters 5 and 7 respectively. The extent of **r**'s contamination is less than Müller believes, in my view, and not from the **O** class.

9 See Ruysschaert 1959, pp. vii–ix, and Bignami-Odier 1973, pp. 257–8. It appears that the manuscripts stayed in the possession of the Collegio Romano for some years after the books were dispersed.

10 The full library of Muret was seen by Lazeri, who published volumes of correspondence (Lazeri 1754 and 1758) of Muret with scholars of the day. De Nolhac 1883, pp. 202–38, refers to 'la liste de livres apostillés par Muret' (p. 208), shown to him by a librarian at Rome's Biblioteca Nazionale. Such a list is today apparently unavailable. De Nolhac 1883, p. 209, adds that for their own publications the Jesuit scholars at the Collegio Romano 'puiserent plusieurs fois dans leur fonds Muret,' and he notes, p. 210, that Muret's manuscripts (i.e. ancient manuscripts) have vanished. No doubt many of them are those now at the Vatican. The following **Vaticani Latini** manuscripts have been judged by Ruysschaert 1959 to have been owned by Muret, '*ut patet e perraris inscriptionis in Coll. Romano in summo f. 1 additae vestigiis*' (p. viii): **11415, 11417, 11418, 11420, 11421, 11426, 11428, 11429, 11431, 11453, 11455, 11458, 11459, 11460, 11461, 11462, 11463, 11465, 11466, 11468, 11470,**

11471, 11472, 11474, 11476, 11478, 11479, 11488, 11489, 11491, 11492, 11493,
11506, 11511, 11512, 11521, 11528, 11533, 11536, 11539, 11543, 11559, 11567,
11570, 11571, 11572, 11574, 11580, 11582, 11583, 11591, 11593, 11594, 11602,
11604. Manuscripts **11591** and **11593** are largely drafts of Muret's published
works written in his own hand. Most of the above are Renaissance manuscripts, but there is a ninth-century Cicero and Priscian (**11506**), and twelfth-
century manuscripts of Virgil (**11471**), Statius (**11472**), Priscian and Cicero
(**11474**). **11562** is a '*Catalogus Bibliothecae Mureti Ann.* 1586–1720,' on which
see next note. Prof. Paolo Renzi of the University of Siena is presently en-
gaged in editing it. I am grateful for correspondence with this scholar. A
standard biographical source for Muret is de Job 1881. A good bibliography
of the works of Muret is to be found in Delage 1905, pp. 147–80. For Muret's place as Latin stylist and educator, see Fumaroli 1980, pp. 162–75.

11 Ruysschaert 1959, pp. 308–9. One notes that this scholar is more positive
on Muret's possession of manuscripts than printed books. The list of books
in **Vaticanus Lat. 11562** (f. 66) contains two Petronius texts: '*Petronii Arbitri
Satyrae fragmentum in 4°*, Paris 1520' (= the *editio Chalderiana*, **c**, on which
see below and n. 21) and '*Idem 8°*, Antverp. 1565' (= the *editio Sambuciana*,
s). The latter entry seems to have been squeezed into the page interlinearly
in a different hand. Rome, Biblioteca Nazionale Centrale Vittorio Emanuele
II, **69.1.F.4** is a **c** with marginal annotations by Muret. It was thus owned by
him and is very likely the copy named in the catalogue.

12 Sage 1936, p. 99, evidently took these to be in some other, much later,
hand, but after studying Muret's hand with some care I am convinced that
we do in fact have a few marginal notes in **m** by Muret. Cf. Plate 10 with
Plate 9, and see discussion below.

13 The paper of **m** carries the contemporary watermark of Nicolas Lebé. Cf. the
relevance of the Briquet 1968 remark: 'Il est à noter que nous n'avons ren-
contré qu'une fois la marque de Nicolas Lebé à Troyes. Cela confirme le
vieux diction: que nul n'est prophète en son pays' (p. 47). On the watermark
see Ruysschaert 1959, p. 19.

14 **l** = **Scaligeranus 61**. For a recent discussion of it see Müller and Ehlers
1983, pp. 393–5. Still perplexing is the relation of this text in Scaliger's
hand to a 'copy' of **Cuiacianus** made by him on a visit to Cujas at Valence
in 1571. See Scaliger 1668: 'C'est le premier Petrone que nous ayons eu. Je
l'ay copié sur cet exemplaire; je l'ayme mieux qu'un imprimé.' From this imprecise language I cannot be sure whether Scaliger, in addition to the surviving **l**, which must be the Petronius of which he now says he is so fond,
made an exact copy of Cujas' manuscript. Nothing such survives, nor does
any collation of it exist in the **L** texts known to have been owned by Scaliger; see Scaliger 1609 and de Jonge 1977. Of some bearing in this question

may be the unlikelihood that **l** itself was made after 1571–2: the *Satyrica* text in it finishes at 44v; on 46–47v is transcribed the *'Vita Vergilii a Foca Grammatico Urbis Romae Versibus Edita,'* which was published (presumably afterwards) in Scaliger 1572. I believe this text was copied from **Parisinus lat. 8093** f. 37–37v, a manuscript forming a unit with **Vossianus Lat. F. 111**, which was definitely used by Scaliger (as a source for Scaliger 1572) when it was owned by Cujas in this very period. A final point is that after St. Bartholomew's Day 1572 Scaliger's life took a very different turn. On unity and possessors see de Meyier 1973, p. 255, and Munk Olsen 1985, pp. 695 and 818. For more on **l** see n. 34.

15 Sámboki too was unaware of the earlier Italian editions, deeming **c** to be based on *'unicum exemplar manuscriptum'* (cited by Rini 1937, p. 42, from Burman 1743, v. 1 p. 293). On the relation of the first three **O**-class editions see White 1933, pp. 303–9. For recent discussion of the Renaissance manuscripts see de la Mare 1976, and Richardson 1984.

16 Cujas 1562, Turnèbe 1564, and Lambin 1567, cited by Müller 1961, pp. xiv and xxi; cf. Chapter 2, n. 46.

17 Grosley 1756. This work, valuable for clues to the dispersal of Pithou's manuscripts, contains a catalogue of Pithou manuscripts given to Troyes (v. 2 pp. 275–85). Bücheler 1862, never seeing the earlier edition, is dismissive: *'Tornaesianam repetendam ... Parisiis curavit Petrus Pithoeus,'* and offers two dates, 1575 and 1577 (p. xxviii). Scruples could exert a painful influence for another two hundred years; witness the publishing history of the *Nodotianae* (see Stolz 1987, pp. 5–21), and the cancelled edition of La Porte du Theil (Omont 1917).

18 On the date of **r**, prior to 1572, see Müller 1961, pp. xxii–xxiii. Fixing it is a reference by van der Does 1583, Preface, to his borrowing it from his friend Daniel Rogers in the year in which he came to Britain. For further detail on the date of **r** see Chapters 6 and 7.

19 The all-important source for establishing these dates and facts is Muret 1562, Preface, wherein is the dedication to his French friends upon return to France after seven years; cited by de Nolhac 1883. Rome, Biblioteca Nazionale Centrale Vittorio Emanuele II, **71.3.C.20** is a copy once owned and signed (a rarity) by Muret, containing marginal notes and corrections in his hand. By what may be an extraordinary coincidence, it is into his personal copy of this edition that Pierre Daniel inscribes, in the last four blank pages, his partial rendering (to c. 15.4) of **Memmianus**, called **d**; see Chapter 4, n. 116, and Chapter 5. Coincidence or not, Daniel, as we see from the rumour described below, is our source for any connection of Muret with Petronius.

20 For example, **Leiden Lips. 4** (see Plate 10) has an original letter of Muret

to Lips on the latter's visit to Rome, written in 1569 (published in Gerlo, Nauwelaerts, and Vervliet 1978, pp. 55–6); see Ruysschaert 1947. The scholars were not on very good terms. If Pierre Pithou did not know what to make of the new obscenities in Petronius coming from the *L manuscripts, Lips shows us that he entered fully into the spirit of them. In a letter of 29 August 1576 to his friend Victor Giselin on the occasion of Giselin's upcoming wedding he cites c. 134.9 (unique *L class, obtained from Pithou's first edition, **p¹**, '*libellus quem sane in amoribus habeo*,' as an unpublished letter to Canter, 2 September 1577 [**Leiden Lips. 4**] shows): '*Adsit et ille hortorum deus, ne sis Petronii Lorum in aqua.*' See Gerlo, Nauwelaerts, and Vervliet 1978, p. 172, who however wrongly assign this quote to c. 57.8, where the phrase occurs also, but in pure **H** text unavailable to Lips. A copy of the apparently very rare Muret 1581 is Rome, Biblioteca Nazionale Centrale Vittorio Emanuele II, **71.3.D.32**, containing 106 handwritten endnotes by him, keyed numerically to the text – a fine sample of Muret's hand and mature exegesis. My thanks to Paolo Renzi for this reference, which I was able to confirm.

21 This copy of **c** (n. 11) is cited by Rini 1937, p. 38 n. 102. There seems to be one excellent emendation in it in Muret's hand, printed in Müller and Ehlers 1983 with ascription to Leo: 3.2 *nil mirum* (*nimirum* _libri_).

22 Pithou 1565 '*in meo libro, cuius ego procacitatem, petulantiam et lasciviam privato carcere ... damnavi*' (cited by Müller 1961, pp. xix–xx).

23 '*M. A. Muretus vir undecumque doctissimus, quem audio ex vetustissimo et integerrimo codice Petronii editionem absolutissimam publice parare*,' cited by Rini 1937, p. 38 n. 102, from Burman 1743, v. 2 p. 299 col. 2.

24 Burman 1743, v. 2 p. 341 col 1. Rini 1937, p. 65, says that the report of this manuscript was exploded in 1666 in *Le Journal des Sçavens* 1, 12 April 1666 (Amsterdam 1679) p. 383.

25 For example, on 1.3 *mellitos verborum globulos* we have '_Muret. Var. lect. 17 c. 15 melliti melle et saccaro conditi_' (Goldast 1610, p. 528).

26 'Il [Scaliger] passa en Italie la plus grande partie des années 1565 et 1566, recherchant avec avidité toutes les occasions de s'instruire. Le docte Muret se montra bienveillant pour lui et le mit en rapport avec une foule de savants' (Haag and Haag 1857, p. 4). Cf. Scaliger 1668, p. 234, *s.v.* 'Muret': '*Muretus me vocabat fratrem quia Pater illum vocabat filium, tam bene scripsit quam ullus veterum ... voluit Italos imitari ut multis verbis diceret pauca.*'

27 Scaliger first came to have his own Petronius five years later, as we have seen (n. 14), after 'copying' **Cuiacianus**. His comment for the year 1571 does not necessarily preclude seeing and discussing **m** earlier.

28 Haag and Haag 1857, p. 4. Composing a few Latin verses, Muret passed

them off as a fragment of an old comic poet. Scaliger pronounced them genuine. The deception revealed, Scaliger's mortification was extreme and he
never forgave Muret.

29 Here I count **l**, **m**, **r**, and **d**. Though **d** carries only 1–15.4 of the ***L** text, it
is least affected from comparison with other sources; see Chapter 5.

30 Müller 1961, pp. xxvi, xxvii (cf. his stemma, Figure 2b), accepts the higher
number: **Cuiacianus**, **Benedictinus**, β, **Dalecampianus**, **Memmianus**.
But the presence of his β rests on a **Dalecampianus**: **Memmianus** division owing to **t**: **dmr** differences for which there may be another reason.
Inasmuch as they appear largely to be palaeographic differences of opinion,
with the compiler of **t** demonstrating less ability at reading his exemplar
than the compilers of **dmr**, one need not go beyond **Dalecampianus** for
them (see my stemma, Figure 2a). Ullman 1930b arrives at three manuscripts by equating **Memmianus** with **Benedictinus**, and Rose 1967 seems
to agree because of van der Does' 1569 letter complaining of the hoarding of
a manuscript of de Mesmes by Pithou (see Chapter 2, n. 46). I favour four:
no β. Pellegrino 1986 equates **Dalecampianus** with **Benedictinus** (see n.
32), thus also perhaps favouring four. The ages of these manuscripts are
hard to establish; it is likely that the first two were twelfth-century and the
others sixteenth-century. On the age of the key ***L**-class manuscripts, their
relation to the **O** class and the character of their readings, see the important
small volume of van Thiel 1971, pp. 2–9.

31 Van Thiel 1971, pp. 19–20, went some way to recognizing this need by positing the Λ symbol in the sense in which I take it, though maintaining **L** as
the descendant composite of Λ, **O** and φ. Despite adoption of this for his
revised stemma (p. 448) Müller and Ehlers 1983 does not meet all its implications, distinguishing between 'pure L-text' ('rein') and the rest (p. 405);
nor Pellegrino 1986, p. 29 f., who uses the symbol 'λ' but continues to refer
to 'L-text,' while his stemma of this class (p. 32) oddly excludes 'L' altogether.

32 See n. 30. The identity of the owners of the two ***L**-class manuscripts used
by de Tournes for **t** was first posited by Goldast 1610 and should probably
be accepted (for the text of de Tournes' account of his '*sex exemplaria*,' from
which identity and ownership is deduced, see Chapter 2, n. 43). Pellegrino
1986, p. 15 f., however, equates **Dalecampianus** with the *vetus Pithoei*
(= **Benedictinus**). I take issue with this in the next chapter. Such disagreement shows the evanescence of establishing the readings of **Benedictinus**/
Memmianus/**Dalecampianus** and constructing a stemma on the evidence
of the variants in **dmrtp** – addressed further in Chapter 7.

33 Pellegrino 1986, p. 26: 'Si direbbe ... che il Cuiaciano non sia da porsi sullo
stesso piano del Benedettino, ma forse lo potremmo considerare un rappre-

sentante della più antica tradizione λ.' In contrast, says Pellegrino, **Benedictinus** (*vetus Pithoei*) was a recombination with elements of Λ, **O** and the florilegia. But, to judge from his earlier effort to demonstrate lacunae in **Cuiacianus** on the basis of references in **t** to the dislocation of a '*v.c.*' in the *Bellum Civile* section, some of the evidence Pellegrino uses is unreliable; see Pellegrino 1972, pp. 155–7. See my fuller treatment in the following chapter. Pellegrino 1986, p. 27, postpones his latest thoughts on this special problem until his third volume.

34 De Tournes did not necessarily commence using **Cuiacianus** at exactly page 67; see n. 37. Pellegrino 1986, p. 10, states somewhat loosely that the readings of **Cuiacianus** and **Benedictinus** were available to Scaliger, de Tournes, and Pithou. See above on how this applies to **t**. I do not believe it has been shown, with the use of either internal or external evidence, that Scaliger had for the production of **l** any other *L-class manuscript than the one he says he copied on a visit to Cujas, i.e. **Cuiacianus**. Cf. Pellegrino 1986, p. 35: 'è opportuno dedurre, sebbene abbia detto che mancano prove assolute in tal senso, che Scaligero ha potuto avvalersi di un esemplare del tipo Benedettino e in effetti, pur nei limiti della pi assoluta prudenza, un caso ci offre forse una discreta conferma in tal senso: si tratta di 111.12.' Here Scaliger inserts the word *curare* (which happens to be the reading of **Benedictinus**) in the margin of **l** with the notation '*in v.c. superinductum.*' But there are, as usual, alternative explanations for the appearance of this reading here, any of which could preclude Scaliger from having seen **Benedictinus** or a **Benedictinus** type at the time of his making of **l**: a marginal note could have been added later, even much later; see Sage 1936, p. 288: 'there is reason to believe that some of the later strata of marginalia and corrections were made after Scaliger went to Leyden in 1593.' Contemporary possibilities are a variant carrier in **Cuiacianus** or the obtaining of the reading from Pithou.

35 See Fulmer 1936, p. 100; some other readings were cited, but I have dropped them for being too weak. Differing abbreviations in the last three entries in the list make the **tm** agreements not quite exact.

36 For a convenient tabular record of the location and number of asterisks in the sources potentially deriving from *L see van Thiel 1971, pp. 68–72.

37 C. 98.1 is prior to **t**'s use of **Cuiacianus** in the text, and it is conceivable that even at 115.20, although on p. 72 of the edition, de Tournes was still using only **Dalecampianus**. The *variae lectiones ex v.c.*, in receiving their last entry on p. 67, do not prove that de Tournes received his *v.c.* here, but only *after* here, since variants are not necessarily listed for every page. In the ensuing four pages de Tournes could have found nothing in *v.c.* worthy of contrasting with **Dalecampianus**.

38 Cf. van Thiel 1971, p. 68: 'Eine Anzahl dieser Sternchen hat Pithou übernommen.'

39 Van Thiel 1971, p. 67, implies the reverse of Sage-Fulmer-Rose in his
stemma, giving the date for **m** as 1575, 'nach Erscheinen von t.'

40 *Diutius* does not show up in **t**^{v} because the editor has already obtained the
reading from elsewhere. In any case, it is unlikely that all the differences
were recorded, although de Tournes did wish to be thorough (see Chapter 2,
n. 43). In all of the *Cena* section which derives from ***L** (= **t**, pp. 18–26)
there are only three **Cuiacianus** variants listed.

41 One notes that **m**'s title is 'Petronii Arbitri Fragmenta,' a heading common to
the **L** class (*sic*). Did this play a role with Sage and Fulmer in suggesting **m**
for the '*cetera, fragmenta*' among the named sources of **t**? Fulmer 1936 implies this; but we need seek no further than **s** for the possible origin of the
title in the editions: *Petronii Arbitri Satyricon Fragmenta.*

42 Since **d** has ended at 15.4 *frontis*, only **r** remains now as a manuscript witness to **Memmianus**. Sage 1936, p. 99, quotes Lotich 1629, which has
these words following the last note in the *Coniecturae*, which occurs at 79.6:
'Cetera deerant in exemplari manuscripto, quod ex bibliotheca Petri Danielis
comparatum cum Dn. Goldasto communicavit Nobiliss. et Ampliss. Dominus
Bongarsius.' Cf. Sage 1936, p. 99: 'This raises the question of whether [**m**]
has any relation to the *coniecturae* attributed to Memmius. Since he quotes
Turnebus XIX, published in 1565, this date is a *terminus post quem*.' It could,
however, refer equally well to **B**: the manuscript was probably dismembered
by that date (see Chapter 8), and the part which can now be traced to the
library of Bongars (through its presence today in Bern) breaks off at almost
exactly the same spot as **m**, c. 80.9. Cf. Chapter 5, n. 137.

CHAPTER 2

43 **t**, known as the *Tornaesiana* after the Lyons printer Jean de Tournes, is a co-
edited work. De Tournes' collaborator and the dedicatee of his preface was
the young scholar and student of Cujas, Denis Lebey de Batilly, to whom
Müller assigns nominal responsibility for the edition (see e.g. Müller and
Ehlers 1983, pp. 395–6). But, for the sake of consistency and the familiarity
of the edition's name and symbol, I have elected to use de Tournes as editor,
without prejudice to Lebey's role, for I am unable to distinguish the respec-
tive contributions of each man. In this preface, de Tournes describes the
comparing of his readied manuscript against '*sex exemplaria ... Horum pri-
marium et vetustissimum in membranis descriptum nactus sum a* [Jacques
Cujas] *... Alterum, quod imitandum meis operis tradidi, fuit* [Jacques Dale-
champs] *... Tertium fuit Antuerpense* [= **s**] *... Quartum, editio Parisiensis* [= **c**]

... *Caetera, fragmenta fuerunt.'* The identifications of the first two were provided by Goldast 1610. De Tournes continues: '*Caeterum, prioribus huius satyrae foliis iam formis excussis, priusquam obtinuissem exemplar, cuius primo loco supra mentionem feci, gnaviter illud conferendum putavi cum iis quae iam expressa fuerant: et quae nobis praeter missa digna visa oculis studiosorum, in calce libri indicanda et adnotanda censui.'* It is worth noting that the list of *variae lectiones* is followed by this comment: '*His variis lectionibus inserui quaedam supervacua: quaedam etiam, quae non tam probo, quam quae in mea editione; sed malui hoc extremum sequi, quam eius contrarium.'* Thus **t** sets out to be a 'scientific' edition, but the mix of readings chosen is far too complex for the editor to control. On the subject of conjecture Pierre Pithou in his own *varietas* writes near the end: '*Coniecturas nec adiicere voluimus nostras, nec debuimus alienas.'* But this may only apply to the lemma in which it stands.

44 See Pellegrino 1986, particularly this conclusion, p. 32: 'la diversa natura del Cuiaciano e del Benedettino'; cf. with his earlier thoughts on this, Pellegrino 1968, pp. 79–83.

45 Bücheler 1862, pp. xiii–xv.

46 I add **Dalecampianus** as a direct **Memmianus** descendant, as defined in Chapter 1, n. 30. Among the more important textual scholars, I count Sage, Ullman, Müller, and now Pellegrino. Evidence cited by Ullman 1930b for the **Benedictinus/Memmianus** problem includes Pithou 1565 f. 3v: '*in meo libro, cuius ... copiam ... non negem, quam non ita dudum feci Errico Memmio*'; Turnèbe 1564–73, v. 2, p. 20: '*e Petronio Memmii*'; Lambin 1561 [1567] *ad Epod.*, 5. 56: '*ex v.c. Errici Memmii exemplari*'; van der Does 1569 *apud* Goldast 1610, p. 16: '*Memmianae bibliothecae exemplar, quod utinam Pithoeus nobis invidere abstineat diutius.'* This last citation is the most problematic, but it can be explained by supposing that Pithou for some reason took charge of de Mesmes' copy of his own **Benedictinus**. Ullman's confusion is due to assigning Lambin's comment to the 1561 edition, where it is notably absent.

47 See Müller 1961, p. xx: '*Dalecampianum, quem admodum recentem fuisse puto.'* For the ***L** interrelations see my stemma (Figure 2a).

48 It would be possible to reconstruct much of **Dalecampianus** for this portion by noting where the **t** readings differ from those in the other editions (barring conjectures, which must be quite few). Pellegrino 1986, pp. 15–16, cf. 1968, p. 82, believes that de Tournes received his new long manuscript, **Cuiacianus**, rather earlier: after only c. 22 had been printed. On the date of the two main sources, I infer some distinction between them from the descriptive language chosen by de Tournes (see n. 43). **Dalecampianus** is thus more recent, and of paper, although the text is older than the hand; cf. n. 47.

49 Pellegrino 1986, p. 15 f., finds 13 such variants and does not list them.
50 Pellegrino 1986, p. 15: 'Il Pithoeanus deve essere il manoscritto del dotto
   amico menzionato.'
51 Pellegrino 1986, pp. 15–16: 'abbiamo ... un sicuro elemento nel fatto che il
   Tornaesius era consapevole di avere a sua disposizione ... un discendente
   dell'esemplare del Pithou, dunque del Benedettino.'
52 The t readings at 30.1, 30.2, 30.11, 36.6 (ex silentio), 81.4 (ex silentio),
   94.15, and 106.1 are all substantiated by readings of Pithou's *vetus* in **p**ᵛ;
   that is to say, they are genuine **Benedictinus**-group readings.
53 Pithou's manuscript, from which these readings derive indirectly, was **Bituricus**, as Ullman 1930b, p. 139, first correctly concluded of the abbreviations.
   Ullman assumes an error by de Tournes in citing it as '*v.c. Br.*,' but this has
   been defended by Schmidt 1974, p. 203, as an alternative attribution, 'from
   Brittany,' the provenance prior to possession by the Duc de Berri. Ullman
   finds only seven readings. I list the nine readings given the '*Bit.*' or '*Br.*'
   ascription in **t**^margine: 55.4 *memorata* <*est*>, 95.3 *iam* [*iam*], 95.8 *soleis*
   <*ligneis*>, 96.4 *iniuria*[*m*]*que Eumolpi, advocationemque commendabam*,
   108.14.2 *heres*, 109.6 *exsonat ergo cantibus*, 109.6 *captabat*, 118.3 *inunda-
   verit*, 129.10 *frater*. Six of these readings appear, and are thus confirmed,
   among the **Bituricus**-designated variants in **p**ᵛ, though there is a discrepancy at 55.4, where Pithou points to the absence of the entire verb – plausi-
   bly seen as a typographical error or misread note carried into print. Two
   readings (96.4, 109.6 *exsonat*) do not appear in Pithou's list, while one
   (108.14.2 *heres*) seems to contradict the *heros* cited for '*Bit.*' in **p**ᵛ. This trivial difference could be accounted for, as above, by a slip of handwriting or
   typography. It seems clear that these were readings furnished by Pithou, of
   which **t**^margine has used perhaps only a selection, since **p**ᵛ cites **Bituricus**
   40 times. The real battleground is over whether or not **Bituricus** = **P**, a
   subject dealt with in the next chapter. We note for now that five **Bituricus**
   readings in **t**^margine out of the nine are exactly as occurring in **p**ᵛ under the
   citation '*Bit.*'
54 Pithou cites 60 readings from this '*Autis.*' in **p**ᵛ. Thus 4.5 *schedium* 'sic ex
   Autis. quod habet *schadium*' (i.e., Pithou corrects his manuscript; see Pellegrino 1986, pp. 16–18, for an effort to explain the correction on the basis of
   other manuscript authority); and 7.3 *inter titulos* 'sic Autis.' The full marginal
   note for the latter in t is '*v.c.* Pit. *titulos, vitulos, puellulos fortassis et titulos
   tabernarum meretriciarum.*' I interpret this differently from Bücheler 1862, p.
   10 *app.*, and editors up to Pellegrino 1986, pp. 18–19, who take *titulos, vitulos, puellulos* as the manuscript citation. I see only *titulos* as the observed
   reading: *vitulos* is offered as a conjecture for it, glossed *puellulos*, followed by
   an explanatory gloss on *titulos*, if preferred. For it is surely very difficult to

take *puellulos* palaeographically as a variant, though *vitulos* does have that capacity. If this is correct, the reading in *v.c. Pit.* and *Autis.* is one and the same. Some other glosses in **t**: 15.8 *criminantium* for *calumniantium*, 17.1 *assensionem* for *assentationem*, 28.3 *gestatoria sella* for *chiramaxio*, 29.3 *catastorum grex* for *venalitium*. Marginal notations are plentiful enough to make the distinction between emendation and gloss sometimes hard to keep: 27.5 *iubenti* for *ludenti*, 33.1 *omnino, omnium* for *omnem*, 33.3 *incubant* for *incumbunt*, etc.

55 Pithou adopts this reading in his own editions and contrasts it with the reading of his '*vetus*' in **p**ᵛ.

56 See Fulmer 1936 (her dissertation), p. 8: 'The date of [**l**] is still uncertain and its text in such confusion that the sources are not yet clearly defined and perhaps never can be.' There is some evidence, as in the present example (see also at 135.8.6, below), of consultation by Scaliger of de Tournes; but not of **t**, since post-1575 for the text of **l** seems ruled out: see above, Chapter 1, notes 14 and 34, for new evidence discountenancing a date later than 1572, though a late date is favoured by the Sage school; also by Ullman 1930b, n. 165.

57 Bücheler 1862, p. 173 *app.*, gives to Turnèbe and Pithou joint authority for *daphnona*.

58 In the stemma provided by Pellegrino 1986, p. 32, to summarize his view of the manuscript affiliations, **Dalecampianus** does not appear.

59 See n. 43. Cf. Ullman 1930b, p. 139: 'Under this head must come the florilegium which he undoubtedly used.' Ullman cites the instance of the title *de iurgio*, at 59.2 copied into **t**ᵐᵃʳᵍⁱⁿᵉ, among 15 examples.

60 Exploring the precise language of the citations is frustrating and ultimately profitless: a distinction between *legitur* and *leguntur* cannot be sustained, and the scope of *et sequent.* is always in doubt.

61 Pellegrino 1975. In the introduction to his 1986 edition he postpones consideration of this problem for the third volume, but would appear to hold fast to his early view: 'Tornaesius ci dà un rilevante numero di lezioni specifiche del Cuiaciano e notizie riguardanti lo stesso esemplare non mancano neppure per taluni versi del *Bellum* (p. 27).'

62 Pellegrino 1975, p. 10: 'testimoniato da Tornaesius che il *Bellum* tradito del Cuiaciano aveva un numero rilevante di versi in meno rispeto a quello che si lege nei codici di gruppo O, e i gruppi di versi mancanti risultano di un'estensione tanto variabile e sono posti a intervalli di tale irregolarità che è veramente arduo, per non dire impossibile, attribuirne la caduta semplicemente a un guasto mecanico dell'esemplare. Da queste premesse si deduce dunque che originariamente gli *excerpta maiora* erano cosa ben diversa del nostro gruppo L, che è il risultato della contaminazione tra gli *excerpta*

maiora originali e gli *excerpta minora* (O).' I have sought from Professor Reeve an assessment specifically of the marginal directions, since Reeve 1983 cites some of Pellegrino's data to demonstrate the character of **L**. Reeve concludes, in a generously furnished personal letter, that there is no reason to infer any more omissions than 121.119–21 and 123.213–4, and that, on the contrary, the indications imply (e.g. at 119.27 and 120.67) the presence of the very lines assumed by Pellegrino to be in lacuna.

63 The other manuscripts related to **Dalecampianus**, i.e. **Benedictinus** and **Memmianus**, seem to bear no indications of these peculiarities, however.

64 See the following chapter for an assessment of **Tholosanus** readings. To be noted also is the evidence that Pithou had first seen **Tholosanus** in 1569, when he borrowed it from Cujas, though he did not use it for his 1577 edition, perhaps because to him his **Benedictinus** was manifestly the better manuscript; on this see Chapter 7.

65 It is worth noting that **P**, a manuscript roughly contemporary with **Cuiacianus**, though of a different group, also contains senseless disturbances in word order, unrelated to those now under consideration. See Bücheler 1862, p. 154 *app.*: they are due to mechanical miscopying of the exemplar, wherein the poem was evidently confusingly set up.

CHAPTER 3

66 Six manuscripts is the count of McClure 1934, p. 430. To the four named manuscripts we may add at least florilegia, as established by Ullman 1930b, p. 145. McClure 1934 avers that 'none of these manuscripts, so far as we know, is in existence today.' On this I shall differ with her and the Sage school, below. Sources other than actual manuscripts of the author were ancient glossaries and of course the printed editions **c**, **s**, and **t**.

67 Ullman 1930b, p. 144, alludes to Pithou's 'looseness in the use of *al.* and *vetus*,' under the former of which 'he refers to printed books as well as manuscripts.' On equating *vet.* with **Benedictinus** see n. 86.

68 Pithou is on record as reluctant to use conjectures (see Chapter 2, n. 43), but the number seems to rise in $\mathbf{p^2}$, to judge from apparent suggestions in $\mathbf{p^{1v}}$ that are adopted in the later text; see the list, below. Regarding the differences between the two editions, McClure 1934, p. 430, can conclude that half have practically no significance, being due to spelling, punctuation, word order, and misprints. Both editions, she continues, bear evidence of a certain carelessness in workmanship. This factor is certainly worth keeping in mind when weighing the evidence of citations for establishing the identities of *Autis.* and *Bit.*

69 These two manuscripts, to judge from the number of recorded citations, ap-

pear to be the second-most and third-most important manuscript sources (after **Benedictinus**), in Pithou's estimation. We should assume that other readings from them have silently entered the text.

70 The form employed by Bücheler is *Altissiodurensis*, but I am keeping Pithou's method of citation, normally abbreviated by him to *Autis.*, though in **p**[v] *Aut.* is also found.

71 See Bücheler 1862, p. xviii; Sage 1916, pp. 22–3; Pellegrino 1986, pp. 37–8. In a review-article on Pellegrino 1986, Aragosti 1989, p. 152, offers a compromise: *Autis.* may be an apograph of **B**. This would not answer my objections and seems a makeshift solution.

72 See e.g. Müller and Ehlers 1983, p. 383: 'Diese Feststellung ist ... nicht unwichtig.'

73 There is another *Autis.* reading, 16.3 *sacrum*, not to be found in **B**, this time in an extant context. However, the discrepancy that this signals to Sage 1916, p. 22, followed by Pellegrino 1986, p. 37, may not exist, since the inside corner of the relevant leaf (f. 58) of **B** (here = **Vossianus Lat. Q. 30**), into which the word may have fitted, has been torn off (see Plate 1). This damage, probably sustained when **B** was dismembered in 1604 (as I argue in Chapter 8), raises a doubt about any transmissional difference here between *Autis.* and **B**. See notes 74 and 86.

74 It is true that the ultimate destinations of **Vossianus Lat. Q. 30** and **Bernensis 357**, via Paul Petau and Jacques Bongars respectively, signify these scholars' acquisition of mere fragments, but some evidence suggests that the dismemberment occurred later than 1577; see Chapter 8.

75 For the heirs see previous note; for Daniel and dismemberment see Usener 1867, p. 421, cited also by Sage 1916, p. 21, though the earlier division of the greater manuscript comprising the full Petronius **B**, **Bernenses 330** and **347**, and **Parisinus lat. 7665**, does not bear on the present question.

76 See Sage 1916, pp. 21–3, for a review of the arguments, with references. Sage was intent on proving that **B** came from Fleury and not Auxerre, and relied on his demonstration that *Autis.* (i.e. the manuscript from Auxerre, according to Pithou) is not the same as **B** to establish his case.

77 Bücheler 1862, p. xxi: '*ut exscriptum alterum ex altero credam*'; Müller and Ehlers 1983, p. 383 n.: 'Der von Scaliger und Pithou benützte, jetz verlorene *Codex Bituricus* ... war ein Nachkomme von P.'; Pellegrino 1986, p. 44: '[P] è parente del *Bituricus.*' However, Reeve 1983, p. 295, unerringly rejects the reasons for distinguishing between the two manuscripts as 'trifling'; he is equally clear on the need to accept **B** as the *Autis.* Another recent and most valuable treatment, accepting the identification, is that of Schmidt 1974, pp. 202–3; cf. Chapter 2, n. 53, for more on Schmidt and *Bit.* and *Brit.*

78 On the disturbed order of the *Bellum Civile*, and the reason for it through

miscopying the exemplar, see Bücheler 1862, p. 154. As an illustration of the haste of the copyist of **P** compare his technique with that seen in the virtually contemporary manuscript **R**: for the corrupt lines 119.9 and 119.30, rather than write nonsense, the scribe of **R** gives the first word and leaves the rest of the verses blank. In transcribing **P** I have signalled the various types of ligature with an apostrophe, e.g. *mac'losa* stands for *maculosa*.

79 On this see Chapter 2, n. 53.

80 The contents of **Parisinus lat. 8049** are: 1. *Persii Satyrae cum Glossis* (1–15v); 2. *Petronius* (17v–25); 3. *Calpurni Siculi Eclogae* (25–27); 4. *Senecae Sententiae* (28–45v). In addition, 17–17v has, anonymously, the end of a text of Cicero's *De divinatione*, the earlier part of which exists today, along with two other Cicero texts, in Berlin [East], Staatsbibliothek, **Phillipps 1794** f. 48–73: this is a sound basis for deducing the one-time unity of these manuscripts, confirmed by a table of contents (f. 3) in the same hand listing, after the three Cicero texts, '*Petronii arbitri satirarum liber unus.*' See Rose 1893, no. 201, pp. 439–41. Clark 1900, p. 41, first affirmed the identity. See also Schmidt 1974, pp. 202–4, and Rouse 1979, pp. 141–2. The combined codex seems to have been divided up and shared between Claude Dupuy, who acquired the portion which is in Berlin today (before it proceeded to the library of the Jesuit College of Clermont, Paris – see n. 85), and Pierre Pithou. Pithou of course knew the contents of Dupuy's portion, which included verses of Rivallon – establishing a Breton connection which may account for the abbreviation *Brit.* used by Pithou, together with *Bit.*, to refer to the manuscript's Petronius section; see n. 77, and Chapter 2, n. 53. For this Rivallon, twelfth-century archdeacon of Rennes, see HLF. 1868, pp. 592–4.

81 For de Thou's links to Pithou see the latter's biographer, Boivin 1715, pp. 71–3. The catalogue, of outstanding interest and at present being investigated fully by F. Laffitte at the Bibliothèque Nationale, is Lanvellec, **Rosanbo 276** f. 73v–93v, '*Index librorum manuscriptorum viri nobilissimi Jacobi Augusti Thuani qui fuerunt P. Pithoei et Nic. Fabri*'; see Genevois, Genest and Chalondon 1987, no. 1820. On f. 89 of the catalogue: no. 714. *Persius cum Glossis*; no. 715. *Petronius Arbiter*. Coincidentally or not (and the catalogue is not arranged alphabetically), these authors share the content of **Parisinus lat. 8049**. **Rosanbo 276** is a collection of catalogues assembled by François Pithou, surviving brother and heir to Pierre.

82 Dupuy's catalogue (= Paris, Bibliothèque Nationale, **Collection Dupuy 653** f. 4–58 = Paris, Bibliothèque Nationale, **Suppl. Grec. 1075** f. 37–65), '*Catalogus manuscriptorum bibliothecae illustrissimi viri Jacobi Augusti Thuani 1617 mense novembri*' is based on **Rosanbo 276**. For some reason no. 781 in **Dupuy 653** (41v–42) = no. 779 in **Suppl. Grec. 1075** (f. 58). The manuscripts

themselves remained with the Dupuy family until 1679, then entered the Cabinet de Colbert; see Quesnel 1679, t. 2 p. 462. For Dupuy's collection see Dorez 1899, 1928. The evidence for the unity of **Parisinus lat. 8049** and **Parisinus lat. 3358** is incontrovertible: the final item in de Thou 781, appearing as no. 6 in **Parisinus lat. 3358**, is the '*Ephemerides anni 1480 in quibus notantur tempora phlebotomandi et purgandi*' (f. 59–64v), this title having been added in the sixteenth century. De Thou's signature occurs at entry no. 5, eight leaves earlier. In a final confirmation of unity, the two manuscripts share a system for marking the sequence of texts or sections by an inked Roman numeral scratched onto the initial folio: 'I' commences Persius, 'II' commences Cicero, Petronius, and Calpurnius, 'III' commences Seneca (all in **Parisinus lat. 8049**; cf. n. 80), and 'IIII' commences the *Ephemerides* (in **Parisinus lat. 3358**). One may speculate that the fourth member, a late text, was torn out of its de Thou position, given a heading and rebound into the crowded, indifferent miscellany that is **Parisinus lat. 3358** under the direction of Colbert, for it leaves **Parisinus lat. 8049** with a unity of older texts of classical Latin authors. For the descriptions see BN. 1966, pp. 274–9.

83 In p^v on 136.2 *vexat cubitum ipsa stipite ardenti* Pithou writes <u>desunt haec in exemp. Io. Bit. D. non male</u>. This was in fact a deletion, perhaps an accidental one, from the archetype by the maker of the **O** class. Pithou seems not to have noticed, or not to have thought worth recording, its absence in *Autis.* also: his eyes were fixed on his *Bit.* and on the fuller text represented by **t** and **Benedictinus.**

84 On this cf. Schmidt 1974, p. 203.

85 **Phillipps 1794** (see n. 80), the part of the larger manuscript which Pithou did not acquire, came to its present abode via Thomas Phillipps, and Gerard Meerman, Dutch scholar at Leiden, who had gained possession of the manuscript collection of the Jesuit College of Claremont, Paris (see Schmidt 1974, pp. 204–5). The Jesuits may have obtained it from the Dupuy family; or else it came from Jean-Jacques de Mesmes III after the Dupuys. A catalogue of his manuscripts (= **Phillipps 1924 [Meerman 868]**), 'Catalogue des manuscrits de Monsieur le Président de Mesmes Anno 1650,' printed in 1827 but apparently not published (= Paris, Bibliothèque Nationale, **Fol. 253**; see Genevois, Genest, and Chalondon 1987, no. 1084), lists on the third of its six pages a 'Petronius Arbiter fol. sur papier.' This Petronius, so described, is unknown to me. For the life, library and generous lending habits of de Mesmes and the history of his library through his descendants see Fremy 1881, pp. 49–50, a panegyric drawing on de Mesmes' handwritten memoirs = **Parisinus fr. 729** f. 17–20.

86 On *sacrum* see n. 73. Aragosti 1989, p. 151, also seems not to appreciate

that the *Autis.* **B** 'discrepancy' signalled by Sage 1916 and followed by Pellegrino 1986 is without relevance not because inconsistency in attributing the
reading makes Pithou's testimony on *Autis.* here unreliable (as he argues)
but because of damage to **B** at 16.3 (see Plate 1). I would say that changing
the designation to the vaguer *vet.* in $\mathbf{p^{2v}}$ is consistent with the reading's de-
motion from lemma to variant. One must reject the implicit view that *vet.* is
the exclusive trademark of the '*vetus Benedictinum exemplar.*'

87 Ullman 1930b, pp. 141–4.

88 The $\mathbf{p^{2v}}$ lemma twice differs from the text: 34.5 *obīt* $\mathbf{p^2}$: *obit* $\mathbf{p^{2v}}$, 36.3 *utriculis* $\mathbf{p^2}$: *inticulis* $\mathbf{p^{2v}}$. The readings of **t**, $\mathbf{t^v}$, and Scaliger's **l** are shown. Of
the last three, $\mathbf{t^v}$ has the best chance of being **Cuiacianus** readings exclu-
sively, and one expects a high $\mathbf{t^v p^{2v}}^{'Thol.'}$ relation. With **l** a better correlation
is expected where Scaliger's choices are limited by ***L** context. **t** of course
would be expected to show no **Cuiacianus** influence (where a reading differs
with **Dalecampianus**) until after the example at 109.8, and in fact shows
none in the three readings remaining. The reading of Müller and Ehlers
1983 is underlined.

89 If **l** is not the exact copy of the **Cuiacianus** which Scaliger says he made in
1571, may we suppose that there was an actual transcript, or at least a collation, now lost? See Chapter 1, n. 14. For Müller's latest hypothesis on how
Scaliger constructed **l** from his sources see Müller and Ehlers 1983, pp.
394–5. On Scaliger's chronology and habits of composition see Grafton
1983, pp. 122–3, and p. 286 notes 129–32.

CHAPTER 4

90 Reeve and Rouse 1978, pp. 235–49. In an ensuing study Rouse 1979, p. 142
n. 58, expresses his gratitude to B. Munk Olsen 'for having alerted me to
the appearance of this hand in Berne manuscripts.' In a personal letter of 12
February 1975 Rouse informed me of finding a series of quotes from the *Satyrica* in **Bernensis 276**. The annotations date to 'the middle of the thirteenth century' (Rouse 1978, p. 235). For a standard description of
Bernensis 276 see Hagen 1885, p. 304.

91 Consult, for convenience, the **Bernensis 276** references in the Index of
Manuscripts in Reeve 1983. Authors quoted by the annotator include Calpurnius, Censorinus, Cicero (*Philippics, De oratore, De finibus, Tusculanae*),
Ae. Donatus, Cl. Donatus, Gellius, Manilius, Marcellus, Julius Paris, Petronius, Propertius, *Querolus*, the Younger Seneca, Tibullus.

92 Reeve and Rouse 1978, p. 237; cf. Rouse 1979, p. 147, for these three: 88.9
pondo (f), 119.40 *suffragia* (j), 135.8.14 *uva passa* (g).

93 **H** shares a manuscript with **A**, a *deterior* from the **O** class in the same hand.

See the stemma of Müller and Ehlers 1983, p. 448; cf. with mine (Figure 1); my *L = his L. For the use of Petronius by John of Salisbury see Martin 1979, pp. 69–76. We cannot be sure whether John consulted a *Cena* as part of or separated from the *Satyrica* archetype; see notes 125 and 126.

94 Bücheler 1862, pp. xxxviii–xxxix, and p. 105, for 88.9 *bonique*, and p. 194, for 135.8.14 *et ... racemis.*

95 See Reeve 1983, p. 298: 'The ... annotator of Berne 276 ... cites Petronius at least eight times.' For comments on Reeve's points see n. 97.

96 I have arrived at this number after two visits to the Bürgerbibliothek in Bern; it was obtained by combining my own inspections with unpublished notes generously provided by Reeve, Rouse, and Müller.

97 One concedes that the present total provides a clearer picture: seven correspondences in Daniel's *Notae.* For data set out in list form and interpretation see below. For a hint of the connection see Reeve 1983, p. 298 n. 15: 'I have failed to find in Berne 276 two passages cited by Daniel from his glossarium S. Dionysii, 2.3 *loqui debemus* and 11.2 *opertum.*' For the possible reasons for this failure see below. I do not know whether Reeve obtained the citations from Bücheler or went to the *Notae.* On Daniel's ownership (f. 2: *Ex libb Petri Danielis Aurelii 1565*') see, for example, de Meyier 1947, p. 69. On the fate of the manuscripts see de Meyier 1947, p. 61, and Chapter 8.

98 See Reeve and Rouse 1978, pp. 235–6, treated below.

99 Rouse 1979, pp. 142–5: 'Berne 276, whose copious marginalia depend on sources in Loire libraries, St Columba's of Sens, Fleury, and especially at Orléans Cathedral.'

100 This is in a kind of ex-libris on f. 2: '*iste liber papiae et sequens liber hugutionis vel hugucii sunt ad usum fratris Johannis de guidincuria pro conventu Beluacensi.*' Reeve and Rouse 1978, p. 235, and n. 3, takes this to be John of Guignecourt [*sic*], Chancellor of the University of Paris 1386–9; but Dr. Donatella Nebbiai, in a personal letter to me of 25 August 1988, is inclined to disbelieve that the two Johns of the commune of Guignencourt in the Oise near Beauvais are the same, since the man in the ex-libris seems to belong to a mendicant order, while the Chancellor 'en tant qu'universitaire, ne pouvait pas être membre d'un ordre mendiant.'

101 See Rouse 1979, p. 143: 'Surprisingly enough, Daniel seems to say that he acquired MS 276 from Fleury.' A manuscript misattributed to Fleury on grounds of possession by Daniel is **Bernensis 21**: see Nebbiai 1985, p. 187. Cf. Rouse 1976, p. 79, on conditions for supposing that Daniel-owned manuscripts emanated from the Orléanais.

102 The single word recognized and reassigned by Daniel is *pistrinum* (**Bernensis 276** f. 176v). Cf. *Querolus* I, 9: '*tu de pistrinis venis* (Peiper 1875, p. 9).' Daniel's comment, to be discussed below, is in the preface to his *Querolus*

first edition of 1564 (the year prior to his acquisition of both **Bernensis 276** and **Harleianus 2735**): '*Eiusdem [fabulae; sc. Queroli] fit mentio in vetustissimo libro glossarum quem mihi una cum hac comoedia suppeditavit amplissima fani Benedicti Floriacensis ad Ligerem bibliotheca.*'

103 This reference appears in an introductory section to his *Notae* (Goldast 1610, p. 77); the ensuing citations that go with it are repeated in the body of the commentary; see entries (c) and (g), below.

104 It was Müller 1965, p. 405 n. 29, who identified **Harleianus 2735** as the manuscript source of Daniel's quote in the *Notae* (Goldast 1610, pp. 77 and 84). For a description and title see Loewe 1894, p. xxv: '*glosae antiquorum auctoritate roboratae et studio eorundem collectae feliciter*'; on possessors and acquisition by the British Library see Wright 1972.

105 For Daniel's ownership of **Harleianus 2735** (f. 1: '*Ex libb Petri Danielis Aureliani 1565*') see, for example, de Meyier 1947, pp. 61 and 69.

106 That is, seven citations directly ascribed to Petronius by the **Bernensis 276** annotator are used by Daniel for his commentary; four others either he had no use for or he missed. The *Notae* show further evidence of use of the manuscript: on occasion words treated by Papias himself, as opposed to the annotator, are picked up by Daniel for use in his commentary if he sees them in Petronius. Conversely, other useful Papias entries, like f. 276 *Satyricon*, are ignored. Both categories are of course not given an ascription to Petronius in the manuscript; see (l) and (m).

107 See page 75 for a full comparison of the manuscript's methods of attribution with those of Daniel.

108 One may compare the citation practices of Pierre Pithou for his two editions (dealt with in the previous chapter). In Daniel's case his terms may not always be random; for possible patterns of consistency see below.

109 See n. 102 for the text of Daniel's comment on the provenance of his *Querolus* citation.

110 *Plaut. In aulularia. 'Lar./QRL, Apagesis homo ineptissime: hic nullum est prestigium; desiste nisi excipere mavis trina pariter vulnera.'* = *Querolus I*, 2 (Peiper 1875, p. 9). It is very faded, in light brown ink, possibly added above the column by the scribe himself, or possibly it is a little later. It is unclear whether Rouse 1983, p. 330 n. 3, himself referring to the presence of 'extracts from the *Querolus*, quite probably by Heiric ... added in the margins' of **Harleianus 2735**, has seen attributions to the *Querolus* by name or the above and other similar material. In either case he may well have reconsidered his earlier finding for **Bernensis 276**.

111 Perhaps with good reason: a high proportion of the odder words do not appear in Lodge 1924; other '*exempla de Plauto*' are quite banal, like f. 5v '*aedem*' [*aedium Aul.* 438]. Another play expressly identified by Daniel in the margin of **Harleianus 2735** is at f. 25 '*eruca*': '*Plautus, in Cistellar.*'

112 Nebbiai 1985, p. 92.

113 Nebbiai 1985, pp. 125–6.

114 See, among many accounts, de Meyier 1947, pp. 58–9.

115 Nebbiai 1985, pp. 137, 187, 227. Of St. Denis manuscripts, Daniel is
known to have possessed **Bernensis 21** and **Vaticanus Ottob. Lat. 259**.

116 Daniel's interest in Petronius is very well established. In October 1563 he
had acquired a Muret 1562; see Chapter 1, n. 19. A short time later (probably before 1565, the date of **s**) he copied into the back of it a fragment of an
*L manuscript representing the first 15 chapters of the *Satyrica*. This text,
known as **d**, is reproduced in its entirety in Plates 5 to 8; see the next chapter for transcription and account. The first independent mention of **Bernensis 276** is in van der Does 1585, v. 3 p. 17: '*Istud Petronii Arbitri in libros
distributum ac dispartitum fuisse, satis magno argumento est nobis veteris Glossarii fiducia, quod apud literatissimum antiquae fidei custodem Petrum Danielem
nostrum in publicos potius, quam privatos usus adservari intelligo.*' Van der
Does also picks up *satis constaret ... Neapolitanam* (a). It would be interesting
to know if he had been shown the *glossarium* itself or had obtained his information from Daniel's notes, 25 years prior to their first publication.

117 See page 66 and n. 108.

118 For a recent review of the value of the evidence pertaining to book numbers
see Müller and Ehlers 1983, pp. 407–13. It seems impossible to get away
from the thesis that our text is drawn in some way from Books 14–16 of the
original *Satyrica*, according to the evidence.

119 Wehle 1861, p. 61 n. 1: '*Suspicor pro "in I Satyrarum" reponendum esse "in
I̅" – id est in libro – "Satyrarum"*'; quoted by Bücheler 1862; see p. 69 (c).
Reeve 1983, p. 299 n. 25, accepts the references as they stand, relating
them, however, not to *Satyrica* books but to the annotator's use of the first
of two manuscripts. I would be readier to concur in this hypothesis had there
been an indication of the second.

120 It is worth looking ahead to my conclusion that the annotator's manuscript
was of the medieval **O** type, akin to **P**, and that this tradition is entirely
innocent of any reference to book numbering (cf. Müller and Ehlers 1983, p.
410: 'Buchzahlen kennt die O-Überlieferung nicht – auch der L-Überliefer-
ung und den Florilegien sind sie unbekannt').

121 The age of **O** receives a *terminus ante quem* with the date of **B** (latter half of
the ninth century, according to Chatelain 1894–1900 and Billanovich 1956,
cited by Müller and Ehlers 1983, p. 382 n. 2). The age of the ***L** hyparchetype may not be known with exactitude, but its apparent corruptions put it
on a level with **P**.

122 **R** seems to show no influence on the Italian manuscripts or on the sixteenth-century sources, and we should take it to have been unknown to the
French scholars. It may have been in Italy in the fourteenth century, accord-

ing to de la Mare 1976, p. 220. There is strong evidence for accepting **B** as
Pithou's **Autissiodurensis** (see previous chapter); likewise the connection
between **P** and **Bituricus** used by Pithou and Scaliger may eliminate the latter as a separate entity.

123 These manuscripts revert to ***L**, the contaminated remnant of a tradition – Λ
– which may have contained everything of the ninth-century archetype. See
Müller and Ehlers 1983, pp. 423–4, and refer to van Thiel 1971, p. 7 n. 2,
for the possible date of ***L** and its relation to the **O** class.

124 See Reeve 1983, p. 298: 'The first set of citations [i.e. those qualified by '*in
<libro> primo Satyrarum*'] he must have taken from a source close to P,
the only manuscript that garbles *Satiricon* [cites the title as *Satyrae?*] in this
way (and he also cites Calpurnius).' But Reeve strains his point by slightly
misrepresenting the annotator's attributions as 'often from "*<primo> libro
satirarum*".' In fact this spelling is not used and the formula is more often
something else (see p. 75). Of course **P**'s existence, age, provenance, and
shared content do make it, of the manuscripts surviving, the most plausible
relative of any Petronius manuscript consulted by the annotator. For the link
between the glosses and the **P** incipit see, originally, Wehle 1861, p. 61.
Wehle did not know the source of Daniel's glosses, and he took them
(wrongly) to have '*insignia ... antiquioris memoriae vestigia.*' They and **P** led
Wehle to prefer *Satyrae* for the title of the work.

125 The best evidence for the availability of the rare *Cena* text close to this period is the use of it, as we have seen (n. 93), by John of Salisbury and by
the maker of φ (see Figure 1). If the annotator had seen such a manuscript
it is worth asking why he did not use it more, for it is rich in philological
interest.

126 We recall also that the *Cena* hyparchetype was in all likelihood furnished
with references to book division that the annotator would probably have used
had he seen them: see Müller and Ehlers 1983, p. 407. The manuscripts
usually contain incipits and explicits giving the title of the work.

127 So Müller and Ehlers 1983, p. 447: 'Es gab also noch im dritten Viertel des
13. Jahrhunderts in der Gegend von Orléans (vermutlich in Fleury) eine Pe-
tronhandschrift (Λ), die von den Satyrica noch einiges mehr enthielt als das,
was L aus Λ übernommen hat'; cf. Reeve 1983, p. 129: 'In the neighbour-
hood of Orléans, therefore, it was still possible in s. xiii 3/4 to consult not
only a manuscript like P but also one that contained passages of Satyrica absent from L.'

128 This was an entry that Reeve 1983, p. 298 n. 15, failed to find in the *glossarium* (see above, n. 97), perhaps because he was looking in the margins for
it as an annotation complete with the Petronius ascription. Occurring in the
Papias text, it qualifies equally well in Daniel's eyes (see n. 106) as a citation from the *glossarium*.

129 Daniel may have wished to highlight his lemma, *opertam*. This rarer variant
    was likely picked up from **d**, which Daniel owned (see n. 116). Occurring
    also in **m**, it was almost certainly the reading of **Memmianus**, a sixteenth-
    century apograph of a **Benedictinus** text.

130 This is the other entry (cf. notes 97 and 128) that Reeve had failed to find
    in the *glossarium*. Having failed also, I propose below that it truly is absent:
    a misattribution.

CHAPTER 5

131 The recent critical edition of Pellegrino 1986 takes up this challenge, in
    some respects unsuccessfully, as I hope to demonstrate.

132 For **d**, its relations and readings, Müller 1961, pp. xxiii, xxvi–xxvii, is still so
    far the only reliable source. However, Müller and Ehlers 1983, p. 400, be-
    lieves that **d** was controlled on an **O** text – possibly **c** – because of certain
    readings (1.3 *ego*, 4.2 *quoque suas*) omitted by **r** together with, allegedly,
    Memmianus. Independent editing by the source for the **Memmianus** read-
    ings is also a possibility. The Pellegrino collation, while fuller, contains inac-
    curacies and cannot be used without verification. The shelfmark cited for **d**
    by Müller and successors was met with incomprehension when I visited the
    Stadt- und Universitätsbibliothek in Bern to inspect it in 1988. It was re-
    trieved under **Bong. IV. 665 (10)** (= Plates 5 to 8).

133 Unless the **d** variant is due to **Benedictinus**: **Cuiacianus** division when
    Cuiacianus and **O** happen to agree.

134 This equation is defined by Pellegrino 1986, p. 66, typically as 'sed tyran-
    nos: Ls m p¹ s t [**lmp¹st**], et tyrann. *ceteri cum Cuiaciano teste Tornaesio*,'
    which misleadingly implies a preponderance of ***L**-class support, i.e. a manu-
    script validity, for the correct reading. In reality, this reading came from a
    conjecture in **s**, and none of the so-called **L** texts here cited communicates
    the actual ***L** variant. Hence the unsatisfactory nature of such an apparatus
    and, more broadly, the need to be able to distinguish between ***L** and **L**
    readings and to reflect more accurately their links to the entire record of
    cited variants. Müller 1961's solution for showing the paths of indebtedness,
    while not fully consistent (in that it gives incidence of *et tyrannos* without
    distinguishing origin), provides a more accurate picture: 'sed tyrannos *s* [**s**]
    → *lmt* [**lmt**]: et tyrannos *tᵛdrpO** [**tᵛdrpO**].'

135 See Müller 1961, pp. xxii–xxiii and xxv–xxvii, and Müller and Ehlers 1983,
    pp. 398–400, for an account of **dmr** and the evidence for their **Memmianus**
    alignment. Müller (p. xxii) takes **r** to have been written by the purported
    first owner, Daniel Rogers (ex-libris on flyleaf; see Chapter 7, n. 173), but a
    signed example of his correspondence in **BPL 885** (see Plate 14), written at
    Frankfurt in 1577, shows a very different hand, to me bearing a decisive re-

semblance to some of the marginal notes, e.g. at f. 1, '*vide Taciti locum fo. 504-505 ubi plane hunc* [i.e. Petronius] *notat'* (which in turn Müller believes to be the hand of van der Does), and – a fine test – to the hand transcribing the 16-line poem, *Somnia quae mentes*, which we know as Fragment XXX, copied on 41v at the end of **r** under the heading '*Ex Cod. v[etere]. m[anuscripto]. et hoc petron[ii]. desumptum'* (see Plate 12). Drs. Obbema and Heesakkers in Leiden firmly exclude van der Does on the basis of good examples from that scholar in **BPL 742**, copies of which they have kindly provided; and I concur. The manuscript source for this poem is **Vossianus Lat. F. 111** f. 38v (then in the possession of Cujas); but Rogers' heading is misleading, since variants tie **r** 41v not to the manuscript but to Scaliger's *Catalecta*, i.e. to his edition of the poem published in Scaliger 1572, v. 2 p. 256 (4 *languent* Scaliger **r**: *urguet* cod.; 6 *saevit in urbes* Scaliger **r**: *eruit urbes* cod.; *pavido* Scaliger **r**: *pavidi* cod.); and there is even better correlation with **p** (the above, plus 8 *perfuso* **pr**: *profuso* Scaliger cod.). For further remarks on the two sixteenth-century hands see Chapters 6 and 7. The textual links between **d** and **r** appear to be strengthened by the inclusion in **r** 51–52v of a commentary by François Daniel, brother of Pierre, the owner of **d**; see Chapter 6, n. 148. For a recent commentary on Fragment XXX see Courtney 1991.

136 This was first noted by Müller 1961, p. xxiii.

137 The termination of **m** at 80.9 suggests a second incomplete **Memmianus**-based exemplar. A hint of the existence of just such a copy is furnished by the cessation at 79.6 of lemmata taken from a manuscript by an *incertus auctor* of conjectures, now to be found in Goldast 1610. Lotich 1629 attributes these to de Mesmes himself; see Bücheler 1862, p. xxxix, and Chapter 1, n. 42.

138 There are in fact **dr** peculiarities, putatively **Memmianus**-derived but not present in **m** because it corrected them with **s**. **m** was greatly given to this, to the point that **Memmianus** witness based on **dmr** is virtually non-existent, although **mr** agreement against **ltp** (**m** failing to 'correct') does occur, infrequently, after **d** leaves off; see Müller 1961, pp. xxvi–xxvii.

139 The scribe of **r** saw two **Memmianus**-text manuscripts, one complete, the other the fragment witnessed by **d**. Both **r** and **d** must have been written in Paris. Daniel Rogers, diplomat of scholarly tastes and '*protestantissimus*,' was in Paris between 1566 and 1570 in the employ of the British ambassador, Sir Henry Norris (DNB. 1897); see also Wood 1813–20, v. 1 p. 246: Rogers was 'a good Latin poet.' It is likely that **r** was acquired by him during this time. By all accounts it was this decade that saw the appearance of the new 'long' manuscripts (the ***L** class), their copying, study, and sharing of readings, all in central France.

140 There is indication of this in the margins of **m**, for example, where readings
are ascribed to Turnèbe five times – though these may have come from Turnèbe 1564 (see Chapter 1). **d**'s evidence, however, goes in the opposite direction: certain gaps (that might easily have been closed by a conjectural
variant of some other provenance) are left deliberately, signifying both difficulty with the exemplar and Daniel's responsible approach to copying.

141 Müller 1961, p. xxvi; see n. 138.

142 Whether directly or indirectly remains to emerge from the discussion of this
manuscript in the next two chapters. For **dm**: **r** and the **Cuiacianus** 'contamination' alleged see Müller 1961, p. xxvi, and Chapter 7. However, in
regard to 1–15.4 Müller's disappointed verdict is that **r** '*ne unam quidem ex
eo codice [Cuiaciano] lectionem adscripsit* (p. xxii).' One should like to know
how he made this determination. The contamination which Müller signals
could not have entered from the printed **L** editions or **l**, since **r** was written
prior to 1572, but only from **Cuiacianus** or readings communicated informally. My judgment is of virtually no **Cuiacianus** influence.

143 For the alleged uncertainty over **B** see Chapter 3. On **E** (**Codex Messa-
niensis deperditus**) see Bücheler 1862, p. xx, and Richardson 1984, pp.
95–8. The principal victim and unlucky champion of Jahn was Beck 1863,
pp. 1 and 30–1.

144 See Pellegrino 1986, pp. 36–8, and the assessment in Chapter 3. The number of **d**: **d** according to Pellegrino examples might swell if the correct readings were logged.

145 Influence of the **O** text **c** (printed 1520) is still a possibility, but I have not
detected it; see n. 132. See Chapter 1 on the seductions of **s** for the editors.

146 In the collation below I have not used the **d** symbol unless there is an ambiguity. Selected readings of Müller are accompanied by their source.

147 See Chapter 1, notes 31 and 33; agreements between ***L** and certain **O** readings from the inferior **O** manuscripts restrict our ability to acquire genuine Λ
readings in these instances. We should recall that **Cuiacianus**, **Benedictinus** and **P** are likely to have been contemporaries; on this see van Thiel
1971, p. 7 n. 2.

CHAPTER 6

148 '*Franc. Danielis Aurelii IC Notae. In Petronii Arbitri Satyricon*,' in Goldast
1610, pp. 57–67. Much of the material is to be found in Bücheler 1862 *app.*,
cited under the name of '*Puteanus*'; see p. xxxix: '*Francisci Danielis notas ex
bibliotheca Bongarsiana quas Lotichius Claudio Puteano adsignat*'; cf. Ullman
1930b, p. 153: 'Goldast prints some notes which he attributes to F. Daniel,
but Lotich, on the authority of Bongars, assigns them to Puteanus (Cl. Du-

puy) and dates them 1570'; and n. 2: 'The identification may be correct, but it is worth remarking that there are four references to Puteanus in the notes of P. Daniel and one in Tornaesius, and not one of them is found in the Puteanus notes'; cf. n. 168. Goldast's attribution of these anonymous *Notae* to François Daniel may be due to the reference in *FDG* at 20.4 *duas institas protulit e sinu]* '*Vide Papiam & Fratris* [sc. *Petri*] *notas*'; see n. 155 and Chapter 4. On the date of composition, which seems to square well with the other external evidence and that of the readings, see below. Müller 1961, p. xix, establishes the connection with **Cuiacianus**: '*Aut ipso Cuiaciano aut exemplari aliquo ex eo descripto usum esse Franciscum Danielem manifesto apparet ex eius Notis in Petronium quae a Goldasto editae sunt anno 1610. Itaque cum Cuiaciani memoria plerumque utamur tam ambigua ut vel tenuissimi eius rivuli diligenter colligendi sint, lectiones a Daniele exscriptas quatenus res afferebat adnotavi.*' '*Res afferebat*' eleven times in Müller's apparatus: seven to establish **Cuiacianus** and four to trace to Daniel the source of a conjecture in the margin of other ***L** editions; see Chapter 7, n. 193. Pellegrino 1986 recognizes for the *Notae* a limited role: 'Esse non ci sono, è vero, di grande aiuto' (p. 13 n. 7). On this role see n. 167.

149 Goldast 1610 keys Daniel's commentary to page and line of his own Petronius text, though the lemmata are not necessarily the same. I have adapted these references to the modern system of chapter, paragraph, and verse. I saw little point in reproducing the entire set of lemmata with variants, not wishing to detract from the data of special importance to investigation of Daniel's sources, as defined in the lists on pp. 106–17, and other material selected, below.

150 Rose 1967 had intended to use the '*vetus F. Danielis*' extensively, but there is the sense of it being made to refer to the same manuscript each time. Rose believed that a *codex Mureti* (either **m** or its exemplar) was in some way connected to this *vetus*, but this is surely wrong since Daniel uses ***L** text long after **m** terminates. The generic character of the term is to my mind the same as our 'MS'. Not even with the *vetus* [*Pithoei*] in Pithou's editions can we assume consistent, exclusive reference to **Benedictinus** (see Chapter 3, notes 67 and 86), though it would certainly qualify for the *vetus* tag, and at least Pithou cites another manuscript source by name: **Bituricus**.

151 See James and Jenkins 1939, pp. 796–7. **r** appears on f. 7–41; f. 42–50 are blank; **r**[comm] takes up f. 51–52v in the same hand. This version of the *Notae* was known to Müller, who had examined **r** for his 1961 edition, but he dismisses it without an inspection as a kind of excerpt: '*notulas foliorum 51–52 Rogers ex Francisci Danielis Notis excerpsit.*' This is not true in the sense of an even and systematic abbreviation, since the writer of **r**[comm] set out to reproduce the commentary faithfully and omits lemmata and variants only accidentally, as we shall see below.

152 I am thinking particularly of whether we really need to accept a manuscript
called β, which is predicated on discrepancies between readings in **t** and
Memmianus-derived sources **dmr**; see Chapter 1, n. 30. It is likely that **t**'s
source, **Dalecampianus**, is a sibling of **dmr**; see Chapter 2.

153 A thing which r^{comm} possesses and *FDG* does not is page breaks, signalled by
a '*Pag.*' in the centre of its own line. These occur after 5.1.5, 7.3, 11.1, 14.3,
17.4, 28.1, 31.3, 55.6.13, 79.6, 81.3, 44.17, 83.9, and then discontinue,
though we are only halfway through the commentary. One assumes they refer to folio changes in Daniel's text, but they do not seem regularly spaced.

154 A good example of this is the elimination, in the lengthy note on *Sicel* at
14.3, of a five-line biblical gloss.

155 I include a selection of representative errors. Out of sequence: at 29.3 *venali-*
cium] part of the note was missed and has been entered in a large space after
31.3; the order at 118.5 *extra corpus orationis*] and *sed in texto vestibus*] has
been reversed. Lemma/note confusion: 2.1 [*primum*] *in culina*], 4.4 [*rectius*]
quisquis]. Note at wrong lemma: 95.5 *tot hospitum potionibus liber*] with the
note on the next lemma, 95.7 *scordalo*] (lemma omitted). Omission of a
note: at 6.1 *motus incedo*]. Omission of entire lemma with note: 20.4 *duas*
institas protulit e sinu] (here a typesetting error in *FDG* also signals a problem
with Daniel's note: the entry is not set up as a lemma with its page and line
reference, but occurs in the body of the note to the previous lemma). Given
the interest of this entry (see n. 148), its omission in r^{comm} is unfortunate.
A paraphrase at 97.3: '*Ceterum quod hic verus fuerit mos furti perquirendi, qui*
a Petronio describitur, indicant hi Plauti versus' (*FDG*): '*Ceterum ut quibusdam*
locis Plauti apparet ita solutum perquiri furtum' (r^{comm}). In return for all this
r^{comm} shows one lemma (without note) that is missing in *FDG*: at 55.6.9
Tribacca indica]; are we entitled to take this to be a unique glimpse of Daniel's intended Petronius edition?

156 In this and subsequent lists a closing square bracket indicates that the entry
is a lemma; otherwise it is a variant taken from the notes. In this list, r^{comm}
shows the superior text.

157 Herein lies r^{comm}'s truly original contribution of new **Cuiacianus** material.
The more than 60 other **Cuiacianus** readings which I adduce in the *Notae*
corroborate and are corroborated by readings in other known **Cuiacianus**-
aligned texts.

158 Müller's symbols for the earliest **O** editions are *med.*, *ven.*, and *par.* I use
those of Sage. On the absence of **a** and **b** see White 1933, p. 305: '[a and b]
have played very little part in the history of the text, since [they seem] to
have been unknown until the latter part of the eighteenth century.'

159 Rogers' time in Paris was from 1566 to 1570; see Chapter 5, n. 139. The
convergence of Bongars' testimony (see n. 148) and this evidence is perfect.

160 In this list and the two following I employ for convenience the reading of

FDG, giving that of **r**^{comm} if it differs. There is no implication of a difference from that of Daniel's own reading. The order of citation in the list is *FDG***c: s**, etc.

161 See the list on p. 115 and the subsequent remarks on the apparent acceptance by Daniel of **c**'s text for his lemmata.

162 In this and the later lists the reading of the *Notae* is supplied by the best authority of *FDG* and **r**^{comm}, i.e. the commentaries are adjusted against each other for error. The comments in underlined italics are in all cases those of Daniel.

163 The exception which spoils the perfect record is at 79.3, where a '*vet. lib.*' is adduced for the variant *scriptos*. This reading is attested in no other Petronius ***L** source, and I am wondering whether the reference is not to a manuscript of Gellius.

164 That conjectural emendation is one of the duties of the scholar of the day is well illustrated by a remark of Daniel at 2.5 which we may take as programmatic: '*aut certe corruptus est locus. Unusquisque pro ingenio emendabit, aut supplebit, aut interpretabitur.*'

165 **p²** had **Benedictinus**; **r**, **Memmianus**; and **t**, **Dalecampianus**. As for **l**, though no manuscript source seems indicated, I need merely quote Ullman 1930b, p. 146: 'Internal evidence tends to indicate that L [i.e. **l**] is not the copy of the Cuiacianus of which Scaliger makes mention, but an edition based on various sources. It indicates further that L was not written in 1571 but after the publication of the Tornaesius edition in 1575 and possibly even after that of Pithou in 1577. I cannot solve here this most knotty of all Petronian textual problems.' But see my evidence in Chapter 1, n. 14 that **l** could not have been written after 1572.

166 I provide the full list of these variants, together with their collations, in Chapter 7, p. 122. A list with discussion of **Tholosanus** variants in **p²ᵛ** appears in Chapter 3, p. 61.

167 For the *furtivè* given by Daniel as his conjecture, Pellegrino 1986, p. 13 n. 7, oddly prints *furtivae*, which of course hides the exact correlation of Daniel's implied conjecture with **t**ᵛ, associating it instead with **l**^{margine'*Cuiac.*'}. Here Pellegrino agrees with Müller 1961, p. 12 *app.*, that *furtivae* is the conjecture of Cujas, and so do I, but it need not have been carried as a variant in **Cuiacianus**: it could have passed to Scaliger in some other way. It is perhaps relevant that Scaliger rather heavily scratches out *furtivae* in his margin, replacing it with *futura, sectura/ l. suturae*; see Plate 15.

168 Hamacher 1975, *s.v.* 'Petronius,' pp. 122–37, sees *siris* in three florilegia, p a e (his symbols; his p = my **par**), and *sircis* in another, v. He reads *Sirtis* in the text (p. 137). This is essentially in accord with Ullman 1930a, p. 16, except that Ullman does not have v and gives *sirtis* to n (**Parisinus lat.**

17903) and to **par**^{margine} in the hand which he assigns to Pierre Daniel (Ullman 1930b, pp. 151–2: 'There are a number of marginal readings in p by a sixteenth-century hand. Among them is an attribution of *Afrae* (93.2.2) to Puteanus. Now Daniel in his note on this passage also credits Puteanus with this. Is it not likely that Daniel himself wrote the attribution of Puteanus in p and that he is responsible for all the other late readings in p?'). See n. 148.

169 Ullman 1930b, p. 147, believes differently, that *sitis* entered Scaliger's l as a correction to *Siris* in p a e, 'proving' Scaliger's use of one of these florilegia.

170 It must be admitted, however, that *cinnamomum* and *cinnamum* of **par** and **par**^{margine} respectively (Ullman 1930a, p. 16) is rather a coincidence, but if this be Daniel's source why does he not cite a *vetus*? – possibly because he received these variants at second hand. In that case '*legitur*' would be a perfect lead-in.

171 Ullman, who, as we have seen (n. 148), is familiar with the *Notae*, does not address the question of florilegium influence in them, so we must presume *ex silentio* that he also discounted it.

CHAPTER 7

172 See Müller 1961, pp. xxi–xxiii, xxvi–xxvii; cf. Müller and Ehlers 1983, p. 398, and his stemma, Figure 2b.

173 The identity of the scribe has not so much a bearing on the exact date of **r** as on the date and character of its marginalia (those in the scribe's hand) and their relations with **r**^{comm} and other texts. On the flyleaf there is the ex-libris Κτῆμα Δανιῆλος Ῥωγηρίον.' The Greek characters prevent comparison with the text's hand; the pen and style are not dissimilar. On Rogers and the scribe see Chapter 1, n. 18; Chapter 5, notes 135 and 139; Chapter 6, n. 142; and Chapter 7, n. 177. See the discussion of the marginalia, below.

174 For proven use of the Petronius **Memmianus** by contemporaries such as Turnèbe, Lambin, Pithou, and others see Ullman 1930b, p. 131, citing Lambin 1561 [1567]: '*descripsi autem nuper ex v.c. Errici Memmii exemplari, cum id esset Petro Ronsardo, Antonio Baifio, Remigio Bellaqueo, poetis nostris Galliae clarissimis, et mihi commodatum*'; van der Does 1569: '*Ad Petronium ... Gallicanum Memmianae bibliothecae exemplar, quod utinam Pithoeus nobis invidere abstineat diutius.*' On this, and how Pithou had a manuscript of de Mesmes and what its connection may have been with his own **Benedictinus**, see Chapter 2, n. 46. Scaliger knew in 1568 of Pithou's possession of a Petronius manuscript, but I do not presume, with Ullman 1930b, in whom find the reference, his p. 131 n. 5, that it was the same one; and Turnèbe 1564, who,

however, refers to attempts to limit the manuscript's influence: '*Haec ego e Petronio Memmii v.c. descripsi, quem domi sub sera et claustro habet, ne quem foris obscoenus et lascivus scriptor impura sua petulantia contaminet.*'

175 Actually, I should discount this in favour of **B** (here = **Bernensis 357**) since no **Memmianus** alignment is evinced. The only point of similarity is termination at c. 80, and for this **B** qualifies too, as well as being on hand in the library of Bongars. See Chapter 1, n. 42.

176 See also Chapter 5 for the relation of this fragment to **d** on the basis of its evident length and readings, insofar as we can judge them from the **Memmianus** orthodoxy even of the specially collated section (1–15.4) now referred to by the scribe of **r**.

177 As recounted (see references in n. 173), Müller 1961 proposes Rogers and van der Does, while I prefer an anonymous copyist and Rogers, respectively. The reader may compare Plate 14, the known hand of Rogers, with Plates 11 and 12. For the hand of van der Does see Chapter 5, n. 135.

178 **r**, in fact, has not been annotated very heavily or frequently. The look is of a manuscript worked on intensively at around the time of production, with a limited number of marginal sallies in a second hand during Rogers' lifetime. The dots and underlines are of course harder to place. See below on comparison of **r** with **r^comm** and the strong impression that these texts were written in rapid order.

179 See Chapter 1, n. 14, and Chapter 3, n. 89. Müller and Ehlers 1983, pp. 394–5, offers a scheme of composition for **l**.

180 One may develop some evidence (see Chapter 3, n. 89, and Chapter 6, n. 165) to postulate that the text of **l** was not constructed without the aid of **t**, that is, in 1575 or shortly thereafter. This would supply **l** with a second *L source, **Benedictinus**-aligned. Other evidence (see Chapter 1, n. 14) goes, typically, in the opposite direction. See Chapter 1, n. 34 for my debate with Pellegrino on the *L sources for **l**.

181 So Müller 1961, pp. xxvi–xxvii, interprets **r** agreements with known potential **Cuiacianus** sources like **l** and **t^v**, without offering any explanation for the occurrence and scope of this phenomenon other than '*contaminatio.*'

182 See Chapter 1, n. 14, for Scaliger's narrative. For fixing 1574 see Omont 1885, p. 233–7. No. 21 is a '*Petronius Arbiter.*' This *enumeratio librorum* was compiled that year in an exercise book (= **Parisinus lat. 4552**, f. 288–294) by a pupil of Cujas, Jean de Limoges. In the inventory of materials made in 1590 after Cujas' death and prior to sale (= Lanvellec, **Rosanbo 276** f. 38–72; cf. Chapter 3, notes 81 and 82), despite a large increase in holdings a Petronius is no longer present (see Omont 1888, pp. 3–12). However, Pierre Pithou had access to **Cuiacianus** in 1587, as **Tholosanus**. It is attractive to take this to be the '*Petronius Arbiter*' seen in Cujas' inventory in 1574 but

not in 1590. Shortly before his death in 1596 Pithou compiled a catalogue
of his books and manuscripts which he wanted 'kept' (i.e. in the family) =
Lanvellec, **Rosanbo 233**, upon f. 32 of which is listed a Petronius, in the
company of Lucan, Cicero's *Tusculanae* 3–5, *De amicitia* and *De senectute*,
and the pseudo-Alexander *Collatio*. This mix is unparalleled in other known
Pithou-owned material; thus the Petronius appears to be not the **Bituricus**
= **P**, say (for whose codicology see Chapter 3, notes 80 and 81), but a non-
extant manuscript, very possibly **Cuiacianus**. **Rosanbo 233** is an extraordinary document, and the Petronius in the list of manuscripts on f. 27–39v is
our best clue in the continuing search for a surviving medieval manuscript of
the ***L** class. A photocopy of a microfilm of it may be seen, with special permission, in the Codicology Section of the Institut de Recherche et d'Histoire
des Textes, Paris. A mid-seventeenth-century copy of **Rosanbo 233** f.
27–39v exists: it is Leuven, Katholieke Universiteitsbibliotheek, **A 251** f.
2–9v, owned formerly by Omont.

183 See Chapter 1 for a fuller depiction of Muret's life and its possible bearing
on his scholarship: a certain prudent self-censorship coupled with a mask of
disapproval is evinced in the years prior to the appearance of **t** in 1575; cf.
the remarks of Turnèbe, n. 174, which are capable of being read ironically in
view of scholars' irritation with *bibliotaphes* like the Pithous and de Mesmes
himself; see Ullman 1930b, pp. 131–2.

184 For an account of **s** and its influence upon the sixteenth-century editors, especially the maker of **m**, see Chapter 1.

185 See Chapter 1 (especially n. 34) for other discussion of the relative use of
Dalecampianus and **Cuiacianus** in **t**.

186 For the text of the preface relating to the '*sex exemplaria*' see Chapter 2,
n. 43.

187 I am referring to the putting of the proper interpretation on a considerable
number of **t**'s unique readings. Differentiated readings in **r** and their relation to the other, particularly manuscript, texts help to build a case for non-
transmitted **t** idiosyncrasy. See my comments on the number of ***L**-manu-
scripts available to the sixteenth-century scholars: Chapter 1, n. 32, and
Chapter 2.

188 See the view of Müller 1961, pp. xxvi–xxvii.

189 Thus on f. 7v there is, in red ink, 3.3 and 4.3 *nihil* **r^m d**: *nil* **r**, 4.4 *quisque*
(red) **r^m d**: *quisquis* **r**, 5.1.8 *histrioni* **r^m d**: *histrionis* **r**, 5.1.9 *sed* **r^m d**, with the
comment, in red, '*ita videtur scriptum et in alio manuscripto v.*': <u>om.</u> **r**; on f. 8
there is, in red, 5.1.13 *et* **r^m d**: *e* **r**, 5.1.14 *liber ... arma 'v.'* **r^m**: <u>om.</u> **rd**, 6.1
doctorum (red) **r^m d**: *dīctor [perpere pro dictorum]* **r**, 6.1 *fugam* (red) **r^m d**: <u>om.</u>
r, 6.1 *suasionem* (red) **r^m d**: *suasoriam* **r**, 7.4 *tandem* (red) **r^m d**: *tarde* **r**; on f.
8v: 9.3 *et* (red) **r^m d**: <u>om.</u> **r**, 9.4 *velle* (red) **r^m d**: <u>om.</u> **r**, 10.1 *ergo* **r^m d**: *ego* **r**,

in L only

11.1 'à bon escient' r^m, an evident French translation of *bona fide*, made by F. Daniel in his *Notae* and copied from r^{comm}, f. 51; on f. 9: 11.2 *cellam* $r^m d$: *cellulam* r, 12.4 *examinatus* $r^m d$: *exanimatus* r, 13.2 *querebar* $r^m d$: *querebatur* r, 14.2.2 ac r^m: *aut* rd, 14.2.5 *iam nunc* ..., with the comment *'ita in veteri in quo cetera desunt'* r^m: *ergo* rd; on f. 9v: 14.1 *ambiguam* $r^m d$: *antiquam* r, 14.3 *dipondium* $r^m d$: *disponendum* r, 14.5 *tenete* r^m: *tenere* rd, 14.7 *panuciam* (red) r^m: *pannuciam* rd, 15.2 *uti* $r^m d$: *ut* r, and, in r^m, referring to a '/' after 15.4 *frontis* in r: *'non plura habebat exemplaria'*. After this the margins get almost no further use, with only two entries, one from an r^{comm} (f. 51v) gloss, 26.5 *valgiter* r^m: *obiter* r, in the next six folios. We note how very high is the $r^m d$ correlation, much like what one would get if the scribe of r checked his new text on a manuscript (= *vetus Cuiacii?*) closely related to d, or even d itself. I have little doubt, therefore, that the scribe miscounted the folios depending on this other source, perhaps by inadvertently turning over two folios at once.

190 The Müller 1961, p. xxii, verdict on the fragment's affiliation: *'sed quod speraveram fore ut particulam saltem codicis Cuiaciani accuratius inde cognoscerem, ea spes me fefellit: nam ille ne unam quidem ex eo codice lectionem adscripsit.'* The r: $r^m d$ divisions bear the marks of instances of faulty copying of **Memmianus** (omissions, etc.) by the scribe of r, followed by his marginal correction or supplement from the *fragmentum Cuiacii*, which may have been less difficult to read. I take it, therefore, that the latter manuscript was not availed of until after the scribe produced r from **Memmianus**. Müller's latest stemma (see Figure 2b) should be modified in the **Memmianus** range (cf. my stemma, Figure 2a) to show d's dependence on the intermediary that could very well have been this *fragmentum*.

191 See Chapter 5, notes 135 and 139; Chapter 6, n. 148. A further, though perhaps subtle, argument against the hand of Rogers is in the choice of marginalia selected from r^{comm}. I refer particularly to 'à bon escient.' (f. 8v – see n. 189), a French translation of 11.1 *bona fide*, which may have held more interest for a native copyist. This marginal note had bothered Rose 1967.

192 The reverse (and this may be significant for understanding how this scribe made r), that r influenced r^{comm}, may be ruled out very effectively by comparison of r^{comm} with *FDG* (see Chapter 7). The scribe diverged from his exemplar deliberately only as a practical expedient, not for scholarly reasons. In the citations which follow, the scribe of r^{comm} makes no distinction of format (as I do) between variant and note.

193 The conjectures of Daniel, to be found in the commentary portion and not in the lemmata of *FDG* and r^{comm}, were considerable and much valued by his contemporaries (cf. Chapter 6, and notes 148 and 164). Evidence of their

popularity may be developed from Müller 1961, p. 84 *app.* *ad* 79.3 *prudens enim [prudens]* '*lr vetus Fr. Danielis*; *del. l^c, secl. Bücheler:* pridie *mr^mtp* (*omnes ut opinor ex coniectura Fr. Danielis)*'; p. 85 *app.* *ad* 79.4 *creta quae* '*m^mr^mt^m* (*item ex coniectura eiusdem Fr. Danielis)*'; *app.* *ad* 79. 6 *intervenisset* '*l^mp^2, coniecerat Fr. Daniel*'; p. 94 *app.* *ad* 87.6 *ususque* '*r^mt^mp* (*omnes, puto, ex emendatione Fr. Danielis)*'; cf. others, not noted by Müller, as 83.5 *Hylan* **l^margine:** *Hylam* **pt^margine** (both conjectures of F. Daniel): *hilari* **lr** *veteres Pithoei Danielisque.*

CHAPTER 8

194 This chapter is a lightly adapted version of Richardson 1986. My thanks to the Director of Publications of the Centre National de la Recherche Scientifique (Paris) for permission.

195 BN. 1744, p. 494; Beck 1863, p. 11; Schmeling and Stuckey 1975, p. 41. The manuscript contains excerpts from Salvianus, Sallust, Petronius, Agathias, *Historia Augusta*, Quintilian, Tacitus, Optatus Milevitanus, Ctesias, Apuleius, Ovid, St. Bernard, St. Augustine.

196 Text quoted is that of Müller and Ehlers 1983. The passages selected by Dupuy, with occasional small changes, are: 17.4 *nemo* (*neque codd.*) ... *aspexit*, 17.6 *ac ... mea*, 83.8 *ego ... solet*, 84.4 *bonae ... paupertas*, 88.6 *at ... discimus*, 106.4 *nec ... sit*, 107.8 *vultum ... parat*, 107.13 *quod ... est*, 113.8 *nec ... rescinderet*, 114.14 *procurrere ... auxilium*, 119.45–50 *pellitur ... praeda*, 120.64 *Iulus ... Romam*, 122.163–4 *sanguine ... exul*, 122.167–172 *at ... vici*, 122.176 *inter ... vinci*, 123.183–4 *fortior ... Caesar*, 126.4 *sive ... debeam*, 140.15 *sicut ... morderent*, 141.1 *itaque ... suam*, Frg. XXXII (Bücheler 1862) *vilis ... casam.*

197 Bücheler 1862, p. xv.

198 These correspond to entries 13 to 34 in Schmeling and Stuckey 1975.

199 The placement of Fragment XXXII (**p^2**, p. 113) was decisive.

200 Commonly cited authors are Ausonius, Catullus, Cicero, Curtius, Gellius, Horace, Lucian, Martial, Ovid, Pliny, Probus, Sallust, Sidonius, Tacitus. Editors quoted frequently are Bongars, Casaubon, Cujas, van der Does, Lambin, Scaliger, Turnèbe, Wouweren.

201 The *v.c.* variant is cited against the **p^2** reading, with a brief apparatus in brackets and comment in square brackets. The readings of Müller and Ehlers 1983 are underlined: somewhat over half are those of '*v.c.*' *Puteani* **B**.

202 The 'other' manuscript with which the readings of '*v.c.*' *Puteani* agree is the *Autis. Pithoei*, in all eight instances where the readings of these two can be made to coincide (note especially at 3.4). This may be taken as further support, if it were needed, for *Autis.* = **B** (see Chapter 3).

203 A practice not unknown among contemporaries, according to Sage 1936, p. 269: 'It may be taken as certain that some manuscripts quoted never existed.'

204 The unity of the two fragments was apparently discovered by Mommsen, in time to be noted by Bücheler 1862 (p. xviii). For a facsimile of f. 58v see Plate 1. Another portion of **O** text, extending from 81.1 to 109.10.1, is still missing; see Chapter 3.

205 It is still arguable that Dupuy's fragment was longer and that he by chance had no use for variants that occurred outside the range; but this argument from silence is not a serious obstacle.

206 See Usener 1867, and Sage 1916, p. 21. Pithou cited **B** under '*Autis.*' in **p¹**. I cannot properly say whether he kept it, borrowed it again, or relied on notes and collations for **p²**.

207 But see de Meyier 1947, p. 60, on Daniel's personally dividing a Fleury manuscript, giving part to Pithou and keeping part for himself (**Bernensis 172**). One cannot be sure that Petau and Bongars acquired the whole Daniel collection between them; on this see Vidier 1965, p. 33.

208 Naturally this depends on whether the Plautus (f. 1–56) and Petronius (58, 57) were bound together at the time of signing. See de Meyier 1947, pp. 25 and 126.

209 For accounts of Vos' dealings as librarian for Queen Christina of Sweden see Blok 1974, pp. 20–34, and Callmer 1977.

INDEX TO THE *SATYRICA* AND *FRAGMENTS*

Boldface denotes areas of special comment or assessment. More than one occurrence of the same reference on any single page is not noted.

INDEX OF MANUSCRIPTS

This is an index of manuscript names and symbols, and of shelf-marked early editions, in the main body of the text and the notes. It was not practical to include the symbols appearing in lists and citations, or in affinities of **dlmr**.

INDEX OF NAMES AND SUBJECTS

This index presents a selection. For a register of scholars employed in the notes see Works Cited.

PHOENIX SUPPLEMENTARY VOLUMES

Phoenix Supplementary Volumes